AF650112

ADVANCE PRAISE

In eight chapters, Sreeradha Datta covers old ground with new eyes with a sharp focus on the economic concerns of the region especially those concerning border economies and international trade. She cautions that for the much-propagated Act East Policy (which often appears to people from the region as an 'Acting' East Policy) to have local resonance and commitment, ground realities need to match the pace of the top-down approach. Dutta warns against the mantra of connectivity as a panacea and reflects on the growth of local elites at the cost of the population. She is concerned about rushing into developmental activities that can play havoc in a environmentally fragile, socially sensitive region which is ill equipped to handle such a burst of activities. The book, built on years of grounded research, sensibly does not ignore the political and social anchors of the economic aspects, while deftly handling the touchy issue of the National Register of Citizens.

Sanjoy Hazarika, International Director
Commonwealth Human Rights Initiative (CHRI)

An extremely readable book that puts government's initiatives in proper perspective. Unlike many other books of its genre, it does not call for any generic policy for India's Northeast, but takes a nuanced view and argues for one that will remain sensitive to local conditions, local resources, even to local knowledge systems, not as deterrents but as enabling factors. The book, thus, helps dispel the stigma long attached to the region as a stumbling block to development.

Prof Samir Das, Calcutta University,
Formerly Vice-Chancellor of the University of North Bengal

An important contribution to the literature on the Act East Policy, this book examines multiple aspects of this policy through contemporary lens from the Northeastern region. It reflects upon the possibilities without losing sight of the ground realities and is cautious and pragmatic about the possible outcomes of the development process underway. Datta is able to weave the Act East policy with the region's domestic conditions rather adroitly and offers a view that is different from the common narrative so far.

Prof TB Subba, North-Eastern Hill University, Shillong,
Formerly Vice Chancellor, Sikkim University.

ACT EAST POLICY *and* NORTHEAST INDIA

Sreeradha Datta

Vitasta

Published by
Renu Kaul Verma
Vitasta Publishing Pvt Ltd
2/15, Ansari Road, Daryaganj
New Delhi-110 002
info@vitastapublishing.com

ISBN 978-81-948200-5-5
© Vivekananda International Foundation
First Edition 2021

MRP ₹850

All Rights Reserved.
No part of this publication may be reproduced, stored in a retrieval system, or transmitted in any form, or by any means—electronic, mechanical, photocopying, recording or otherwise—without the prior permission of the publisher. Opinions expressed in this book are the author's own. The publisher is in no way responsible for these.

Edited by Manjula Lal
Cover by Somesh Kumar Mishra
Layout by Vits Press
Printed by Chaman Enterprises, New Delhi

To Dishari Dutt, who has inspired our direction

CONTENTS

Acknowledgements	*ix*
Preface	*xv*
Introduction	*xix*
Potential of NER Economy	1
Transport Connectivity within NER	51
Energy Potential	112
Tenuous Political Stability	141
Growing Cross-Border Linkages	177
Transforming the Border Economy	237
Postscript	*281*
Abbreviations	*293*
Bibliography	*299*
Annexure 1 CAA	*309*
Annexure 2 MoU	*312*
Index	*315*

ACKNOWLEDGEMENTS

The Northeast region has been a continuum in my research interests. I went back to it with greater expanse and depth thanks to the opportunity provided by Maulana Azad Centre for Northeast Studies during the 2011-2017 period. This work sits in the cusp of my interest in domestic politics and its interplay with the foreign policies that India hopes to further through its Northeast region. Apart from the Azad Centre, Universities and Institutes in the region offered me new insights into the region. I am grateful to many of the Vice Chancellors and also to the Asian Confluence in particular for such opportunities.

While Maulana Azad Institute of Asian Studies (MAKAIAS) gave me the opportunity to travel and absorb the region at close quarters (and of course a whole lot more in terms of knowledge and experience), the Vivekananda International Foundation (VIF) provided the atmosphere where I could go back to my writing and reading that did not involve green sheets of papers and government circulars. The two worlds are a contrast at best. And also, a perfect blend that any researcher would value.

My research journey is filled with numerous amazing people I have come across over the years in institutions like IDSA,

MAKAIAS and VIF and with all those whose paths crossed mine in India and outside; those who opened up their world for me to soak in. Journeys are never without some glitches and each only contributed to my growing resilience and gave me deeper appreciation for many of my friends and mentors who helped me stay the course.

Several seniors, Professors OP Mishra, Tanka Subba, Raja Mohan, Amitabh Mattoo, Ranjan Chakraborty, Partha Ghosh, Amarjyoti Choudhury, Mihir Choudhuri and Sujit Datta as also Tarun Basu have all been a continued source of strength and support over the years. Dr S Narayan and I worked on a project together recently, and I know I can count on his sage counsel always.

Then there are friends who ensured I escaped unscathed from some nasty surprises—the names of Shakti Sinha, Alok Bansal, Arvind Kumar, Manish, Pratim Ranjan Bose, Parama and Amitendu Palit come to mind immediately. Friends like Meena Singh Roy and Ajey Lele have always been just a phone call away. Ajay Behera, Ravi Prasad Narayan, Alok Mukhopadhya and Kshitij Prabha remain connected despite all of us having moved on from our earlier avatars. My colleague at IDSA Lt Gen Harinder Singh's meticulous planning made my exhaustive field trip to the Northeast region not only possible but ensured it was seamlessly executed. I also am grateful for the support extended by Brigadier Atul Kumar and Col Amarinder Singh who ensured my safety, security and hospitality during that journey.

The MAKAIAS years were exhilarating. The kindness of Ambassador Krishnan Srinivasan and support of many of my colleagues including Sri Jawahar Sircar, Professors Uma Dasgupta, Asish Roy, Mushirul Hasan and Suranjan Das enriched the experience considerably. There are many others, but I would specially like to acknowledge Sri Pankaj Rag's and Dr Arun Chakravarti's support.

The reconnect with Jadavpur University and specially with Professors Anindya Jyoti Majumdar, Shibasish Chatterjee, Sucheta Ghosh, Sanjukta Bhattacharya, Rabindra Sen and Purushottam Bhattacharya not only brought a strong sense of *deja vu* but was also fulfilling in many ways. The re-igniting of the bond with my Modern High School friends and going back to school as a Chief Guest and deliver their annual lecture, are memories of a lifetime. The Kolkata years were precious; the time spent with my extended family of Mamu, Mini, Mashis and the cousins gang made the six-plus years unforgettable.

Apart from being our one-stop medical SOS, the hangouts and addas with sister-in-law and her family—Mitali and Ramesh, Rishabh and Anoushka—were another bonus of the Kolkata days. But the period was also filled with deep losses. Losing Mashima, who called me every day and cooked me the most amazing pakoras every time I dropped by unannounced, left a void that nothing and no-one can replace. She was an anchoring rock even before I became their *bahu*. So was Bapi (my late father-in-law) whose interest in my work is unmatched by anyone in my family.

Although I don't see Ambassador Deb Mukharji and Matiur Rahman, Editor Prothom Alo as much as I would like to, they remain my greatest source of inspiration. Mati Bhai is my family away from home just like few of other friends, Professors Amena Mohsin, Debapriya Bhattacharya, Mustafizzurr Rahman, Rashed Titumir as well as Major Shamsul Arefin.

The time spent at German Institute of Global Affairs (GIGA), Hamburg, was precious. I deeply cherish my association with Dr Sandra Destradi, Dr Johannes Plagemann and Dr Christian Wirth as also with Dr Patrick Kollner. Another colleague at GIGA, Sangeeta Mahapatra, filled my Hamburg days with loads of fun. I am grateful to all of them for their friendship.

Whatever I write–whether he even reads it or not–will have his imprint on it, Professor Kumaraswamy got me hooked onto writing and gave me the gift of a lifetime. Thank you, Kumar.

I am grateful to Dr Arvind Gupta for the opportunity at VIF as well as his and Ms Anuttama Ganguly and General Ravi Sawhney's support during one of my toughest periods, soon after joining the VIF. Their kindness will stay with me always. Thank you Alakh Ranjan for your research acumen and Samriddhi for helping with the bibliography.

This book was conceived during · very difficult phase of my life, when Baba (Prodyot Kumar Datta) was unwell and his composure and grace during his brief but intense medical struggle was a lesson in living for all of us. His ability to live on his own terms, never wavering from his principles, remains our guiding light. The endless outpouring of tribute from friends, relatives and all those who were touched by him is a small testimony to his strength, his character and his ability to make a difference.

Ma (Krishna Datta) will always be the love of our lives; her ability to put us before anything else has spoilt us rotten but given us the strength to reach for the sky. Her *joie de vivre* is infectious, to say the least, for all who know her. The two girls, Dishari and Tanishi, both a handful, bring zing to our family and Dada-Prasenjit and Ishita remain my safe happy corner.

The book got completed during the worst phase in many of our lives. The Covid-19 pandemic brought forth deep uncertainties and painful truths, like the loss of dear friend Professor Hari Vasudevan, who not only handed over the baton at MAKAIAS but stayed close, guiding the 'madam director' while sharing many moments of laughter, all through my six years at the Institute.

I dedicate this book to my daughter, Dishari Dutt, who we always knew was a champ but did not fully understand her strength till she showed us how to manage and reorganise oneself during the extended lockdown phase. Her reinventing of self has been one of my greatest learning experiences. Arup's influence on her resonates strongly—doffing my hat to both.

PREFACE

Assam, Meghalaya and Tripura were the three states to record the highest number of Covid-19 cases in the Northeastern region, although significantly lower than the Indian average. Anxiety in the region has been high. Health services here are not exactly exemplary and they remain largely dependent on Central Government funds. The way ahead seems fraught with problems. Effective management from the early days kept the virus from spreading, but overcrowded urban pockets will have to tread with trepidation until there is some certainty about the virus, its medication and vaccine.

Although too early to predict the mutating nature of the virus, the region hopefully will be able to tide over the crisis by the onset of 2022 but will have felt the impact in many ways, adversely affecting daily lives and livelihood patterns. While the impact will be nationwide, the Northeastern region will feel the ill effects more intensely. Apart from the direct health and medical factors, the economic impact of the nationwide lockdown is bound to be significant and long lasting. The densely populated urban pockets with few local industry and manufacturing units will face severe disruption due to lack of flow of funds, inability to access the market, transportation disruption and low demand--all of which would contribute to near paralysis of the economy.

This region's economy has never been very strong. The nationwide lockdown effectively paused most commercial activity, causing a cyclic decreased consumption due to low earning and unemployment. Low purchasing power resulted in further under-consumption and inability to produce. Nothwithstanding the governmental schemes, the consequences of the lengthy lockdown on market access and limited availability of financial and other services are having numerous spinoffs with a devastating effect on the people of the region. And in all likelihood, Central Government financial assistance will be compromised.

The region is also feeling the impact because large numbers of people from the region are employed in different parts of India. Migrant outflows from the region were mainly of two types. One, of educated youths in the organised sector and the other, unskilled workers in the organised as well unorganised sectors. English-speaking educated urban youth have found employment in the medical profession, hospitality and retail businesses as well. A certain section of skilled labour also found employment in the manufacturing units spread over India, like the plywood business.

Although data and statistics are not fully available, the shutdown has direct implications for majority of them. The huge infrastructure construction that was ongoing in the region has witnessed an inevitable slowing down and while the government reallocates to more immediate and essential sectors, it will be a while before momentum picks up for various infrastructure projects. For those in the unorganised sector, their return and possibilities of gainful employment will depend on a variety of factors. Thus, the uncertainties ahead are aplenty.

In the post-Covid months, agro-based and small-scale industries will be able to pick up sooner while the large-scale industries will take some time to recover. Strong pharmaceutical presence is also seen in this region. This sector would see a jump too as many countries will increasingly look at India for future requirements and this region will be able to consolidate their pharma sector. Public health services ought to see improvement in the days ahead and with greater capacity-building initiatives, the large workforce of educated youths of the region would find greater scope for engagement. Given the fears of physical contact associated with Covid-19, e-commerce will have higher potential and will open up a new range of activities. The digital spectrum will widen too as will public health sector investments. As tourists will tread cautiously for reasons of safety, the states of Assam, Meghalaya and Sikkim will feel the pinch greatly.

Notwithstanding these setbacks, the early days of the Covid-19 outbreak revealed the ways in which states in the region could work together. Unlike in the earlier practice of being competitive, the states coordinated their moves, including imposition of similar alcohol tax. The pandemic also opened up areas in which the region could be self-sufficient, like supply of fish as well as some vegetables, but the pandemic caused many more disruptions that will take the region a while to overcome.

INTRODUCTION

For most part of the past seven decades, India's eight Northeastern states, known collectively as the Northeast (NE), have drawn attention of the Central Government only for security-related concerns, remaining peripheral to the development pattern that the rest of India embarked upon. Indeed, until the advent of the British, Northeast did not exist as a concept. The geo-political contour of a 'North East Frontier' first emerged by the turn of the last century, during the eastward sweep of the British leading to the subjugation of the territories between Bengal and Burma (now Myanmar).

The construction of a region called the Northeast is a post-1947 development. The Partition of India aggravated its geo-political isolation as the region is linked with the rest of the country by a narrow land corridor, nicknamed 'Chicken's Neck', and is surrounded by international borders. Earlier, various tribal regions had closer ties with the adjoining areas of Bengal and Burma than with each other but Partition almost physically separated the Northeast from the Indian heartland. This, and the Chinese takeover of Tibet, replaced the earlier soft territorial frontier.

In other words, an area of more than a quarter of a million square kilometres bordering China, Bhutan, Myanmar and Bangladesh (erstwhile east Pakistan) now only has a tenuous land connection with the rest of the country by the 21-km wide Siliguri corridor. Less than one per cent of the external boundaries of the region are contiguous with the rest of India and the remaining ninety-nine per cent adjoin international borders.

While for sake of brevity all the eight states are referred to under the broad NE framework, it is important to remember for purposes of this study that each state (Assam, Arunachal Pradesh, Manipur, Nagaland, Meghalaya, Mizoram, Tripura and Sikkim) has a distinctiveness that not only accords it a uniqueness but also brings forth different sets of issues, opportunities as well as challenges. The states greatly differ from one another in size, location and environment, not only due to vivid socio-cultural traditions but also livelihood patterns. Their aims and aspirations are at variance too.

Arguably, the geographical distance between the Northeast and the rest of India has hampered trade and economic opportunities. The unique and complex nature of the region, its prolonged socio-political isolation from the rest of the country and its geographic vulnerability required special measures from the Centre. Since Independence, the region has attracted considerable attention in the form of political accommodation, economic largesse and administrative concessions.

Gradually, over the years, the geo-political environment changed and the Centre adopted a number of economic measures for the development of the region and its integration with the Union. The incremental internal stability being nurtured within the region has led to a spurt of new ideas and options for tapping its vast unexplored natural resources, including an emergent tourism circuit. There appears a tangible effort towards closing the gap between mainland India and this critical region. For long, governments in the states and the Centre seemed disconnected and rarely in sync. Not only has that situation changed in recent times, but the state governments have seen greater *raison d'être* to work closely with the Central governments. Apart from domestic factors, Northeastern leaders have a key role in Government of India's outreach to the neigbourhood.

Northeast's geographical position has assumed greater salience in contemporary times on account of three broad underlying foreign policy issues. Firstly, India's keenness to deepen its engagement with its neighbours, both with the South Asian and the South East Asian economies; and its new-found interest in making regionalism and sub-regionalism become effective in and around its neighbourhood. But more importantly, with recent global developments, especially in the Indo-Pacific region, India staking its rightful claim in the extended littorals is also impinging upon how it manages Northeast and how that region can dovetail with its larger leadership role in the Bay of Bengal and Indian Ocean too.

Policies Unveiled

In the aftermath of Partition of the sub-continent, states like Assam and Meghalaya found some relevance in central India policies given their traditional trade and commerce activities.

For the most part, the states of Arunachal Pradesh and Mizoram were seen as too remote; Manipur and Nagaland were seen as problem states that needed to be 'managed'. Undoubtedly, issues of governance dominated the political narrative. The issue of unresolved international borders added to the neglect as well as ignorance.

For New Delhi, the NE was a domain for the security establishment to engage with. The North Eastern Council that was set up way back in the early 1970s did not do much to change the popular narrative of a region that was troubled and isolated. It was only when the 'Look East Policy' (LEP) got initiated in the early 1990s, coinciding with the liberalising of the economy, that the view of NE altered, at least at the level of discussions and some brainstorming that ensued amongst the stakeholders. Subsequently, the region received greater attention with a relatively new ministry dubbed Development of North East Region (DoNER), that focussed on the ground potential, examined ways and means to encourage economic development of the region and supported the other ongoing initiatives involving the region.

While the LEP did actually lead to establishing substantial terms of engagement with economies of the East and South East Asian Nations, the rise of trade and commerce bypassed the Northeast region. This gap was then attempted to be closed through the newly minted 'Act East Policy' (AEP) under the Narendra Modi Government in the post-2014 period. It was essentially meant to include the Northeast Region (NER) in India's outreach with the immediate and extended neighbourhood.

Towards actualising the AEP, Prime Minister Narendra Modi unveiled a strong developmental plan including building a network of roads and highways, organising investment fairs, encouraging tourism and building high-level educational institutions for not only establishing a connectivity within the region and with the rest of India but also with its immediate neighbourhood, especially those in the East. This dovetails into the government's 'Neighbourhood First Policy' which has been able to reach some clarity in its bilateral ties with Bangladesh, Myanmar, both immediate eastern neighbours, as well as Nepal and Bhutan, its Himalayan neighbours. Thus, cross-border infrastructure development, including improving physical connectivity between the neighbours and the building of an energy grid has seen a new momentum in recent years.

Moving Towards Regionalism

The Northeast assumes a criticality in India's attempt to make regionalism work in this region. Unable to move the South Asian Association for Regional Cooperation (SAARC) forward, India began exploring other options of sub-regionalism. At present, India is pursuing few other regional initiatives in its neighbourhood. The sub-grouping of Bangladesh, Bhutan, India and Nepal (BBIN) would introduce seamless cross-border trade and transportation through signing of the Motor Vehicle Act. However, this is yet to be fully implemented.

This is certainly not the first of the sub-regional attempts in this region. Bangladesh, China, India and Myanmar Economic Corridor (BCIM EC) was one such grouping that also fell through over political differences between India and

China. There were a few more similar attempts, but none achieved any significant gains. India is keen to infuse energy to the twenty-two-year-old Bay of Bengal initiative for Multi-Sectoral Technical and Economic Cooperation (BIMSTEC). This sub-group comprises five South Asian states--Bangladesh, Bhutan, India, Nepal and Sri Lanka--and two South East Asian immediate neighbours in the region--Myanmar and Thailand. Although it has recorded slow progress in some sectors in recent times, India is keen to make this organisation functional as it is suitably poised to complement Indian national efforts to tap the potential of the Northeast region as well as its bilateral efforts to engage with the adjacent neighbourhood.

A functional BIMSTEC organisation will not only be the precursor to establishing trade and connectivity and creating cross-border value chains with member states but will also generate an economic momentum that will vitalise land and sea route connections to mainland India via the Northeast.

The government has not only positioned the Northeast as the gateway to South-east Asia and beyond but through its multi-pronged efforts of a sustained engagement, developing physical connectivity and encouraging greater investment flows, has given rise to a distinct upbeat mood about the region. Currently, this region has assumed an unprecedented prominence for both domestic and foreign policy factors as never seen before. New projects and policies involving the NER is a serious attempt to change past narratives into a positive story in the journey of making of a new India. Hopefully this time round, the time is ripe for the drawing board plans to be finally translated into reality, thereby changing substantially the scope and ethos of the NER.

It is possible to attribute a few reasons for the lack of development and growth in the NER.

First, the security establishment in India had for long dominated the policy in this region and there was no political will to change course. Several developments in the neighbourhood had finally led to the recognition of the hollowness of the policy to keeping the region insulated to safeguard against confrontations from across the border with China. It took several incidents to appreciate that while the Indo-China border dispute was not going to be resolved soon, physical connectivity and upgradation of defence infrastructure in the borderland region was going to be a vital component for India's preparedness' for any aggression. Continuing to struggle with the spectre of threat emanating from China, India belatedly understood the criticality of improving its border zones and has commissioned a large number of highways and other infrastructure development plans in Arunachal Pradesh, Nagaland and Manipur. Indeed, the construction of the four-lane Dimapur-Kohima highway was a reflection of that political will, till then invisible.

Second, the thrust on border and infrastructure development was necessary to implement the sub-regionalism that was necessitated in the sub-continent in the wake of ineffective SAARC regionalism. Increasing India's influence in the region would be ineffectual without carrying the neighbours with it. With the exception of Bangladesh, much of the bilateral 'neighbours first' policy has lost much of its sheen. As it stands now, Nepal is yet to signal its forgiveness for the closure of the borders, engagement with Sri Lanka has been 'business as usual' without any significant breakthrough. Bhutan, a most valued partner, cannot be taken for granted. In the absence of significant bilateral partnership, the sub-regional initiative seemed a preferred alternative to engage with the neighbours. Although the Motor Vehicle Agreement amongst the four members--Bhutan, Bangladesh, India and Nepal (BBIN MVA)--has encountered problems due to Bhutan's environment concerns, India is hoping the BIMSTEC regional grouping will provide an alternative for the states to collectively move ahead on infrastructure, trade and investments. Also, befriending states in the neighbourhood is invaluable in the face of the strong partnership that China has already built in and around India's neighbourhood.

Third, the present government is keen to expand its political footprint in the Northeast states. Having formed governments in Assam, Manipur, Tripura and Arunachal Pradesh, the BJP is part of the ruling coalition in Nagaland and Meghalaya too. Electoral gains in the region are considered critical in sending a strong message to its detractors as well as in implementing some of its national and foreign policy promises. Towards this end, the Nagaland peace talks and subsequently, a comprehensive agreement seem critical to its plan for the region. The various Naga factions that remain outside the peace talks must be co-opted. The planned transport projects and economic corridors have large gestation periods and it is unlikely that any significant changes are likely to be recorded in the immediate period towards transforming the economy and making NER a stakeholder in the AEP or similar government policies. The NER has inherent difficulties and to overcome them necessitates sustainable developmental programmes.[1]

Sharp Focus

The scope of this book is limited. It essentially argues that the new communication corridors through the NE will enable growth of associated economic activities along the path with an emergent new momentum for employment and greater opportunities. It also seeks to understand how these polices will engage the region with the AEP. The new infrastructure development will make NE the bridge between the two immediate neighbours, Bangladesh and Myanmar as well as joining the two regions of South Asia and Southeast Asia.

The Northeast economy is largely agrarian and dependent on mainland states for essential consumables. As yet, no significant scope for exports to the neighbouring region is discernible. Some noteworthy studies from 1970s have identified the tremendous scope and potential that exists in NER. However, as the subsequent chapters underline, the actualisation of this potential has been limited. Often, ground conditions are not factored in adequately and therefore not fully realised. This is not to argue that the states have not developed and moved towards greater prosperity but their scope to engage and contribute to the economic corridors emerging through their region seems limited in the immediate period.

---

1 This is a modified and expanded version of author's publication in *India Review Analysis* 2018.*

It has also often been argued that land corridors do not necessarily support the economy of the states they pass through, the Land customs Station (LCS) at West Bengal being a case in point. The Integrated Check Post (ICP) at the border crossing between West Bengal's Petrapole and Bangladesh's Benapole records the highest land border trade between the two neighbours but the West Bengal component of that trade is rather minimal. This certainly has never been a cause for concern for India, nor for West Bengal, but the ground situation in the Northeast is not comparable. The implementation of corridors through NER will take shape over a period of a decade or more. In that time, the small economies of NE need to become an integral partner with India's Act East outreach to the neighbouring states. Ground conditions of the NER are different. The states, after prolonged period of conflict and political tension, have stabilised to a certain extent. But the fragility persists. And the fault lines remain.

There seems little understanding about how the new project is likely to bring the people of the Northeast region dividends. They understand that the better physical infrastructure network will lead to better movement and greater access to markets but that is not enough. The large unused cold storages and much of the infrastructure, including border trade points, is testimony to these incomplete plans. The large volume of unemployed and underemployed population and burgeoning number of youths are waiting for opportunities to come their way. How will the AEP impact upon their lives?

Apart from the hardware development, there is very little attention being paid to capacity-building processes and other related software issues essential for operationalising trade and commerce that actually involve the local population in the NER.

The book essentially examines the following:

The first chapter gives an overall view of the NER economy, how the agrarian states too can support local industry, and how the transport infrastructure is likely to benefit the border economy. The next chapter assesses the status of transport corridors in NER, domestic road, railway and air networks that are built, used and proposed. Then follows a chapter on the energy potential of the region, which essentially examines the possibilities ahead. The region is far off from being self-reliant. Also while there have been several estimates about the huge potential of hydro energy specially, actualising them has been fraught with challenges. The region, however, will provide a great space for cross-border regional energy trade.

In a democracy, much hinges on political stability. A separate chapter is devoted to the fact that despite grandiose plans and projects planned and implemented, NER has not enjoyed political stability. Political developments in the region will essentially also impact many of its plans, especially those that relate to foreign policies.

Then we come to the crux of this book. How is the Act East Policy panning out for the NER? The thrust on new infrastructure and creating multimodal transport systems will connect not only inter-region, but also the region with the rest of India, as well with the neighborhood by revival of the earlier physical connections that this region had enjoyed. But importantly, there are tremendous possibilities at the borders to tap the ground potential as well as transform the local, social and economic situation. Thus, issues beyond the developmental paradigm are discussed, and the implications for the region at large. Also, can some of the states that have marginal presence in the entire new developmental plan hope for transformation on the ground?

The last chapter sums up the research findings of the previous chapters, including an assessment of the economy, state of industry as well as the prevailing political situation.

Put together, the research material in this book points towards the potential and possibilities of the Northeast region, which is on the cusp between the two regions of South Asia and South East Asia, exhorting them to come together experience the dividends of cross-border development and growth of regionalism.

Potential of NER Economy

Development is the only way ahead. We will carry forward the good work done by Atal ji for the Northeast.

—Narendra Modi, 2014

THE NOMENCLATURE 'Northeast' for the seven states of the region entered the popular lexicon only in the 1970s.[1] After Sikkim joined the Indian Union, it became the eighth Northeastern state. While this region has often been referred to as a single entity, it needs to be reiterated that the Northeast (NE) is not a homogenous area nor can it constitute a single indivisible geographical whole. People living in these Himalayan states do not have a common history, nor did they inherit interlinked developmental problems.

1 The Constituent Assembly founded in 1950 had made special provisions for the administration of the erstwhile North East Frontier Tracts. In 1954, these areas were put in the Sixth Schedule under the North East Frontier Agency (NEFA) and included Arunachal Pradesh.

The NE states together cover 7.9 per cent of the total area of India (2,62,179 sq km of 32,87,263 sq km) and 3.76 per cent of the country's population (4.55 crore out of 131 crore).[2] To put these figures in context, it is less than half the population of West Bengal and about two-thirds the population of Gujarat. The region is sparsely populated. The average population density of the eight states is less than half the average for the country. Of course, simple density figures should be interpreted with caution as large parts of the region are hilly or mountainous and significant portions are covered by forests.

The region's contribution to the national economy, as indicated by the combined Gross State Domestic Product (GSDP) of the states, is less than 3 per cent. This can be primarily attributed to the low population. The GSDP per capita, however, is about three-fourths of the national average, hinting at the overall economic backwardness of the region.

In terms of area, the NE states fall in roughly three groups:

Arunachal Pradesh and Assam, the two largest states, are of comparable size and by far much larger than the other six states. The two smallest states, Sikkim and Tripura, also of comparable size, make up the 'small' group. The 'middle' group consisting of Manipur, Meghalaya, Mizoram and Nagaland, of

2 As per Census 2011, (DoNER Ministry at https://mdoner.gov.in/about-north-east), Arunchal Pradesh area is 83,743 sq km, population 13,82,611; Assam 78,438 sq km, population 31,169,272 , Manipur 22,327 sq km, population 27,21,756; Meghlaya , 22,429 sq km, population 29,64,001; Mizoram 21,081 sq km, population 10,91,014; Tripura 10,486 sq km, population 36,71,032, Nagaland 16,579 sq km, population 19,80,602, Sikkim 7,096 sq km, population 6,07,688.

approximately similar size. And in terms of population, the distribution is extremely skewed—one single state, Assam, comprises of close to 70 per cent of the total population of the region. Arunachal, the largest state of the area, larger than Assam, is home to barely 3 per cent of the total NE population. Sikkim and Mizoram are still less populous.

The slow growth of the NER economy and its tendency to lag behind states similarly endowed with natural resources has been a subject of serious cogitation for both analysts and policy makers. It has often been cited as the cause for many of the socio-political problems that are peculiar to the region while others argued the economy has been left behind because of some of the prevailing issues that the region grappled with for long. Much of the past ethnic tension and conflict was reduced to manageable limits through negotiated political settlements and India found a new role for the region.

For the Northeast to be the bridgehead between South Asia and South East Asia, a focus on its economy is imperative. This region, as well documented, has been isolated and neglected for long. Partition, which cut off the existing transport and communication facilities, dealt a severe blow to the economic prospects of the region. The region's access to the sea through the plains of what is today Bangladesh was severed and one of the vital links for commerce, trade and industry disconnected. This single historical event continues to handicap economic development till the present. The sole connectivity to the rest of India is through the so-called 'Chicken's Neck' 21 Kilometre long corridor in northern Bengal. The terrain for most part is mountainous and the road links within the region were underdeveloped for most part of the past seventy years.

NER, though endowed with an abundance of natural resources, has continued to remain backward. Natural resources such as oil, tropical forests, tea, coal, timber, silk and jute are found in the region; the rivers have abundant potention to generate electricity. Some of these resources have been explored while others remain under-utilised. High rates of population growth, a restricted range of resources, labour immobility, restricted land market, volatile and uncertain political and social environment and largely subsistence economies are the defining characteristics of the region. Sluggish economic growth, poor infrastructure, lack of market accessibility and underutilisation of the natural resources of the region have plagued the economies of its states. All these factors together increase transportation costs, adding to the cost of doing business, and engender a sense of isolation in the minds of those not familiar with the region—and, more importantly, the investors.[3]

When industrialisation did come to the region, it was mainly concentrated in Assam. The lack of local or regional markets did not lead to large-scale growth of modern industry. One of the reasons for economic stagnation was the resistance of people to socio-economic changes and the structural rigidity of the traditional society. Ethnic tensions and resentment over the influx of outsiders did not provide any enabling atmosphere for investments, of which the region had a dire need. One of several studies on the subject pointed to the limited market size, transport bottlenecks, lack of infrastructural facilities,

3 Sreeradha Datta 'What Ails The Northeast: An enquiry into the economic factors', *Strategic Analysis*, 25:1, 2001,73-87

poor technology, lack of reliable skilled labour as factors contributing to the lack of development in the region. Growth was hindered by lack of manufacturing and industrialisation, which in turn crippled employment opportunities in the region. The problem was further aggravated by high population growth. The agro-based economy was limited, with recurring insurgency and violence. Lack of markets did not invite much entrepreneurship.[4]

The report identified export-oriented industrial development as a way of reducing the dependence on forest resources and creating employment and income. The opening up of the economy to external markets would attract investments, establish export-oriented industries, create employment opportunities, offer transfer of technology, help in earning foreign exchange and facilitate development of the region as a whole.[5]

While writing about the economic potential of the region and other similar issues in 2001, it was evident that despite the governmental efforts at policy formulation to cater to the developmental needs of the NE states, no significant development had occurred during that phase. In fact, the steady flow of central funds into the hands of the local elite has indirectly discouraged local initiatives, which could have been otherwise harnessed to raise the financial resources of the different states in the region.[6] In 2020, what has changed? In

---

4 All India Shippers Council, 'Study Report on Building External Market Linkages for Entrepreneurs in the N.E', Planning Commission Report, Oct 2001, New Delhi at planningcommission.nic.in/reports/ser... - All India Shippers Council, New Delhi . Accessed on 2 Dec 2014

5 Ibid

6 Sreeradha Datta, North-East Complexities and Its Determinants, IDSA-Shipra, New Delhi, 2004

the present state of development and economic growth, how will NER be a stakeholder in the AEP? While there is a new thrust by the government to develop physical infrastructure and other corresponding facilities, efforts by the private sector remain limited and the investment environment does not look promising. For the NER economy to grow and develop at greater rates than recorded in the past decades, the efforts need to be go beyond the government sector.

But for that to happen, certain ground conditions and preparedness are essential. At present, it remains a work in progress and we are yet to see any significant growth unfolding in any of the sectors. Also, most of the data available and that which is being relied upon is within the organised sector domain. Exclusion of data from the unorganised sector makes the task of understanding the impact that much more difficult and complex.

At the present juncture, it is important to understand how the NER economy can actively engage with the AEP. There has been plenty of contemporary writing about the existing potential and how it can transform the region. Presently, barring Assam, which has been able to develop at a greater pace due to its historical and locational advantage, all other NE states are dependent on central funds and lack sufficient food and other essential commodities. Some states like Mizoram and Sikkim have recorded progress in term of economic growth and development in some sectors. However, to engage with AEP, their levels of productivity and involvement with the process of trade needs to be at higher levels. They also need to dovetail with AEP projects and policies and the envisaged growth corridors.

In short, geographical limitations, lack of comprehensive economic development and with the growth of major industry remaining at low levels, the states' inherent capacity to be a partner to the growth corridor seems limited. Interestingly, there have been suggestions for the NE states to replace their planning departments with an 'SDG (sustainable development goals) monitoring unit'. According to NITI Aayog Vice Chairman Rajiv Kumar, with an SDG monitoring unit, 'We will have competitive federalism.'[7] This would undoubtedly contribute to greater clarity about the status of the state of economy and other indicators in the region, but also provide greater understanding about the comparative levels and how these states are exactly located individually but also with reference to regional and mainland parity.

Status of the Economy

The economic development of the Northeastern region is characterised both by trends prevailing in the country as a whole as well as some distinct features, which are unique to this region. In colonial times, NER was an exporter of primary raw materials. The post-colonial mode of development also seemed to endorse such a policy. This is evident in the way transportation and communication linkages developed in the region, which remain concentrated in the upper Brahmaputra valley. The sprawling rural hinterlands continued with traditional agriculture, while the revenue from tea and oil sustained the urban centres.

7 'Niti Aayog Vice Chairman Rajiv Kumar calls on North-East States to set up SDG monitoring units', *BusinessLine*, 25 Feb 2020, at https://www.thehindubusinessline.com/news/national/niti-aayog-vice-chairman-rajiv-kumar-calls-on-north-east-states-to-set-up-sdg-monitoring-units/article30910305.ece#

The natural fallout was disparity in various sectors of the economy and various sub-regions. Economic development of the region followed a specific pattern.[8] Economic activities got concentrated in select pockets and for a variety of reasons economic development did not take place uniformly. Apart from incremental growth—that too in specific areas—the economy in NER did not witness the changes that were happening in other parts of India.

With the exception of three to four districts in lower Assam, most of this region was known to produce one crop a year—mostly rice, using techniques and implements that haven't changed much over the last century. The yield per hectare in the Northeast is amongst the lowest in the region and contributes only 1.5 per cent of country's food grain production, making it dependent on supplies from the rest of the country.[9] NER continues to be one of India's low level economically developed regions, contributing only 3 per cent of the country's gross domestic product. As per the report, the productivity of agro horticulture crops in NER is significantly lower than the prevailing national standards. It remains highly dependent on other regions for most of its essential consumables. The absence of adequate institutional and physical infrastructure, both national and international, has slowed down the NER's growth process.[10] Less than forty per cent of the geographical area is under cultivation. The prospects for modern industries

8 Sreeradha Datta, 'What Ails The Northeast', op cit

9 Pratim Ranjan Bose, 'Connectivity is no Panacea for Unprepared North-East, *Strategic Analysis*, 43:4, 335-41 Aug 2019

10 Prabir De, 'Assessing Economic Impacts of Connectivity Corridors,' RIS Report, 2018. New Delhi

have not been very promising, and the lack of local or regional markets has not facilitated that process. The growth of transport corridors should be able to address this gap in the economy. But this is unlikely to happen overnight.

Various Central Governments have assisted NE states with subsidies, grants and special development package, much more in comparison to other states. However, investments in infrastructure and industries were negligible. The backwardness of the region and insurgency are inter-linked: lack of economic development has fostered discontent and violence, and this in turn has impeded development. The lack of infrastructure has been responsible for the sluggish growth of industries in the region despite abundance of natural resources and endless planning to modernise the economy. Development and modernisation of the Northeast has been the victim of a vicious circle. Arguably, the lack of infrastructure has hampered industrialisation and industrialisation has not materialised because of the poor infrastructure.[11] It has been further suggested that 'the NER has the potential to grow faster than its current pace by improving connectivity, logistics and trade facilitation, more particularly with Bangladesh, Myanmar and other South East and East Asian countries'. Development of (transport) corridors, which connect the NER with the other states of India and the neighbouring countries, can enhance both trade and connectivity.[12]

---

11 BG Verghese, *India's North-East Resurgent Governance Development* (2nd edition 1996) Konark Publishers, New Delhi, p336

12 Prabir De, Sunetra Ghatak et al. 'Assessing Economic Impacts of Connectivity Corridors in North East India: An Empirical Investigation', *Economic and Political Weekly*, Vol. 54, Issue 11, 16 Mar 2019

For long, the blame for low levels of infrastructural development and lack of industry was often ascribed to insurgent movements. There is no doubt that insurgency, political instability and ethnic conflict are inimical to economic development. Widespread and prolonged socio-political conflict results in economic destruction and social disorganisation. This is, however, only one aspect. It has been further argued that often national economic development is not the only or principal concern of the government and the political elite. More often than not, economic considerations and goals of development are sacrificed to other politically valued gains.[13] It is possible to suggest that one of the important reasons for the economic stagnation of the region was the socio-economic resistance of the people to change and the structural rigidity of a traditional society. The resentment of, and movements against, outsiders have robbed the region of investments, which could have given a fillip to economic development.

Over the years, economic development of NER has been planned and implemented by a multiplicity of specific organisations and departments, besides the Central and state governments. In 1972, the North Eastern Council was mandated as the nodal agency for economic and social development[14] and since 2001, the Ministry of Development of North East Region

13 Sreeradha Datta, 'Northeast turmoil: Vital determinants', *Strategic Analysis*, 23:12, 2000

14 In June 2018, PM approved the proposal of Ministry of Development of North Eastern Region (DoNER) for the nomination of the Union Home Minister as ex-officio Chairman of North Eastern Council (NEC), a statutory body with Governors and Chief Ministers of all the eight North Eastern States as its Member. The Cabinet also approved that Minister of State (Independent Charge), Ministry of DoNER would serve as Vice Chairman of the Council.

(DoNER) assumed the same role. The main thrust of the Central schemes has been to support the development of the economy through the establishment of industries and expansion of transport and communication facilities. With expansion of transport network, many other related organisations have been engaged with growth and expansion.

Agrarian Economy

Except for 3-4 districts in lower Assam, most of NER was known to produce rice using techniques and implements that haven't changed much over the last century. The land available for cultivation is limited. Compared to an all-India average of 64 per cent, arable land under use in Assam, Meghalaya and Nagaland is 40-50 per cent. Champai district is known to be the rice bowl of Mizoram but does not contribute much to Mizoram's internal consumption.

Only a small portion of the agricultural land has irrigation facilities. Thus, the yield per hectare is amongst the lowest in the country and contributes only 1.5 per cent of the country's food grain production, productivity being significantly lower than the prevailing national standards. Not unexpectedly, their dependency on supplies from the rest of the country is high for most of its essential consumables.[15] It also adds to the cost of many of these essential goods.

There are several causes for such low agricultural productivity.

- Agricultural land including fallow is 22.20 per cent (varying between 37.43 per cent in Assam and 4.40 per

15 Pratim Ranjan Bose, 'Connectivity is no Panacea for Unprepared North-East', *Strategic Analysis*, 43:4, pp335-41, Aug 2019

cent in Arunachal) as against 54.47 per cent in India.[16]

- Irrigated cropping is practised in about 30 per cent of the plain areas, though the Angami Nagas have beautifully terraced fields, as do the Apatanis in Arunachal Pradesh's Ziro valley. Terracing is also found in Sikkim. The Brahmaputra and Barak valleys in Assam have an abundance of water, but recurring floods and limited agrarian reforms have made for agricultural instability. The groundwater development is low too.[17]
- The practise of *Jhum* cultivation and subsistence farming is leading to deterioration of available resources.
- The land tenure system does not facilitate productivity. Essentially two types of land tenure systems are prevalent:
  - i) Government-administered revenue system operates in the plains and valleys of Assam, Tripura, Manipur and in the hilly state of Sikkim
  - (ii) Village-level customary land tenure system operates in the hilly states of Arunachal Pradesh, Meghalaya, Mizoram and Nagaland and in the hilly parts of Assam, Manipur and Tripura. The land records system is outdated and farmers' access to it is time-consuming and expensive. Only in Assam is

---

16 Amrit Patel, Harnessing Agricultural Potential in North Eastern Region of India, *India Microfinance*, 25 March 2013 at https://indiamicrofinance.com/agricultural-in-north-east-india.html

17 Report 'Development and Growth in the North-East,' Strategy Report 36397 IN, World Bank, June 2007, p41

the land records system being computerised.[18]

- Proper resource management is lacking.[19]
- NER is endowed with 33 per cent of the country's water resources. However, the rate of harnessing and utilising irrigation potential has been low. Only 11 per cent of net cultivable land is irrigated.
- The numbers working in the fields is low. The cultivators (41.61 per cent) and agricultural labourers (13.07 per cent) together constitute the majority of the workforce as against 31.65 per cent and 26.55 per cent respectively in India.[20]
- The absence of adequate institutional and physical infrastructure, both national and international, has slowed down NER's growth process.[21]

These apart, one needs to be cognisant of issues about increasing production. Given the experience in the region where the population is sensitive to being exploited, a World Bank Report cautions that local investments and interstate cooperation need to go hand in hand if benefits are to be maximised. Also, development in the region needs to ensure benefits are created at local levels. 'This type of activity would focus, for instance, on community-based forest management, built on local traditions; creation of access to local markets

---

18 Amrit Patel, op cit

19 NEC Draft North Eastern Council Regional Plan (2017-18 to 2019-20) http://necouncil.gov.in/sites/default/files/about-us/Final per cent20Regional per cent20Plan per cent20NEC per cent2025_04_2017.pdf

20 Amrit Patel, op cit

21 Prabir De, 'Assessing Economic Impacts of Connectivity Corridors,' RIS Report, 2018. New Delhi

for produce; enhancement of local inland water transport options; watershed management and local erosion control; local adaptation to floods; and management of *beels* (seasonally flooded wetlands).'[22]

Limited Engagement

It needs to be underlined that the region's trade with the outside is limited. As per a FICCI study, the share of the North-East in trade with the neighbours has been consistently hovering in the range of 1-2 per cent.[23] This report also points out that there has not been much growth in large-scale industries and the industrial sector in the region primarily consists of small and medium enterprises. Most of the large industries are based in Assam and are in sectors such as refining, cement, chemical and fertilisers, paper and paper products.[24] While food processing has been identified as one of the fastest growing segments in the region, many of the previous investments in this sector in Tripura and Meghalaya have not been successful and the units remain closed.

To understand how the Act East Policy is likely to change and impact upon the NE states, a brief summary of the NE states' level of development would be useful.

As per a Tripura government report, there are about 181 large and medium-scale industries in the region, over 70 per cent of which are in Assam. Most of the units are based on resources such as oil, gas and wood. Tea plays a vital role in

---

22 Report, Development and Growth in the North-East, Strategy Report 36397 IN , World Bank, June 2007.p vii

23 Report, 'Gateway to ASEAN: India's North-East Frontier', FICCI-PWC, 27 Nov.2019.

24 Ibid.

Assam's economy. Also the scope of downstream industries petroleum and gas cracker project needs to be explored. The significant deposits of limestone in Meghalaya and Arunachal Pradesh can be used for setting up medium-sized cement industries by using the deposits of natural gas in the region. The enormous hydroelectric potential of the region could be exploited to augment the available power supply, as regular and quality power supply can be an important incentive for setting up manufacturing units. Regular power supply is also essential for cold storage infrastructure. In the initial years, the increase in power generation may not be absorbed entirely and states would be able to generate financial resources by selling power to the national grid (as in the case of Sikkim). Over time, the absorptive capacity of the region for power consumption would increase and a significant portion of the power generated would be used for expanding economic activities.[25]

Assam

Assam accounts for about for about 54.11 per cent of the total geographical area of the state and including persons dependent on plantation, more than 80 per cent of the total population of Assam is dependent on agriculture. The socio-economic condition of Assam largely depends on its agricultural production. Thereby, the Assam department of agriculture has decided to take up various development measures to ensure growth in crop production.[26] It also has the largest

25 Report 'Tripura—Act East Policy'. Govt of Tripura at https://planning.tripura.gov.in/sites/default/files/Tripura_Act per cent20East per cent20Policy per cent20 per cent28Modified per cent29.pdf Accessed 30 July 2018

26 Status of Environment and Related Issues, ENVIS Centre, Assam , 30 Dec 2015 at http://asmenvis.nic.in/Database/Agriculture_839.aspx Accessed 30 July 2018

concentration of industries, which is roughly 70 per cent of the total industry in the region. There is hardly any large or medium private industry outside Assam. Most are located in three districts of Kamrup, Tinsukhia and Dibrugarh. Gross output per employee as well as fixed capital per employee is less in the region compared to the all-India average. This indicates either low fixed capital or over-employment. The region contributes a little over 1 per cent to the value of output of the manufacturing sector of India.

Tripura

The second most populous State in NER after Assam, Tripura shares over 856 km with neighbour Bangladesh. It is largely dependent on imports of essential commodities like rice, vegetables, clothes, building material and even milk (often in the form of powder).[27] NER imports milk (usually milk powder) worth around Rs 18,000 crore each year, with Tripura accounting for Rs 1,100 crore).[28]

It holds a strong tea plantation base in India, with 58 tea gardens covering an area of around over 7,000 hectares. Due to large availability of land along with appropriate climatic conditions, a gradual boost to the tea production in the state has been witnessed. In 2019 tea production in the state stood at 10 million kg. It is rich in natural resources such as natural gas,

---

27 RN Bhaskar, 'Tripura likely to see a business boom but challenges remain', *Money Control*, 28 Feb 2019 at https://www.moneycontrol.com/news/business/economy/tripura-likely-to-see-a-business-boom-but-challenges-remain-3593901.html Accessed 30 July 2019

28 Economic Review of Tripura 2017-18, Directorate of Economics & Statistics Planning (Statistics) Department Government of Tripura, Agartala 2019 at https://tripura.gov.in/sites/default/files/Economic_Review_2017-18.pdf

rubber, tea and medicinal plants. The state is also known for its vibrant food processing, bamboo and sericulture industries. The state is the second largest natural rubber producer in the country after Kerala and has unrealised potential. But its contribution remains unknown and the private sector is also to be blamed.[29] However, the state has been making various attempts including organising a 'Run for Tea' march in early 2020 to revive this industry. It is also weighing various options to export tea to Bangladesh. Interestingly Tripura has recorded increase in its trade with Bangladesh from a low of Rs 4.12 crore during 1995–96 to over Rs. 536 crore during 2018-19. Both sides are hoping to increase this number.[30]

Many of the unexplored sectors such as organic spices, bio-fuel and eco-tourism are now being discussed for future development. The Central Government wants to tap the Bangladeshi medical tourist. Tripura hopes to capture some of that revenue by building hospitals in Agartala affiliated to the largest hospital chains in India.[31] Its tourism sector has been growing every passing year. Revenue of Rs 203.85 lakh was earned from tourism during the year 2013–14, which rose to Rs 345.66 lakh during the year 2017–18, showing an increase of about 70 per cent in five years.[32] With greater physical connectivity since 2008, Tripura has now broad gauge railway

---

29 'Bangladesh withdraws import restrictions on nine items from Tripura', *BusinessLine*, 14 Dec 2019 at https://www.thehindubusinessline.com/economy/policy/bangladesh-withdraws-import-restrictions-on-nine-items-from-tripura/article30305243.ece

30 Economic Review of Tripura 2017-18 Directorate of Economics & Statistics Planning (Statistics) Department Government of Tripura, Agartala 2019 at https://tripura.gov.in/sites/default/files/Economic_Review_2017-18.pdf

31 RN Bhaskar, op cit

32 Economic Review of Tripura 2017-18, op cit

track connecting it with Delhi since 2016 and also South India from January 2018. These will bring a growth momentum in the days ahead.

Manipur

Manipur is a single crop economy presently, with only 6.74 per cent of land under agriculture of the total geographical area, but providing for livelihood of more than 52 per cent of the total population of the state. Rice, being the staple food crop, accounts for about 95 per cent of the total food grains productions and covers about 72 per cent of the total cropped area of the state.[33]

Manipur is one of India's largest bamboo-producing states and a major contributor to the country's bamboo industry. Handlooms are the largest cottage industry in Manipur and the state ranks among the top five in terms of the number of looms in the country. While, the state has made tremendous progress in production of horticultural crops, the low productivity is due to many limitation viz., prevalence of shifting cultivation, hilly terrain, unpredictable climate changes, low levels of infrastructure. [34] Manipur and its political instability has been a major roadblock for many of the issues. Despite 'Investment India' road shows, there has not been much response from any neighbour nor Indian private capital.

A proposed Integrated Infrastructural Development Project (IID) project at Moreh with a total project cost of $1.19

33 Manipur Y, Santosh Singh and BK Bera, Present Scenario of Agricultural Sector of Manipur, *Economic Affairs*, Vol. 62, No. 2, pp225-32, June 2017

34 Ibid at http://ndpublisher.in/admin/issues/EAv62no2d.pdf Accessed 30 July 2018

million is underway. Substantial investments are underway under the Bharatmala project. The trilateral highway, apart from the proposed 111-km Jiribam-Tupul-Imhal rail lines, has tremendous prospects. Nearly 1,000 medical tourists visited Imphal hospitals since 8 August 2018, when passenger movement was allowed.[35] Much is unfolding but as author Sudeep Chakravorti suggests, 'the economy of conflict has remained more seductive than the economy of peace. This must be reversed'.[36]

Nagaland

Nagaland, a state with prevailing poor infrastructure and a fragile peace, has never experienced a strong economy. But according to a 2015 survey, in comparison to the nine other states, Nagaland outranks the richer, best-performing states of Kerala and Goa in four of the 20 indicators analysed, featuring among the top five in fourteen.[37] The Niti Ayog Report notes that agriculture is the major economic activity in Nagaland with more than 70 per cent of the population employed in agriculture. There is high potential for boosting agriculture production to a commercial level but there are inherent limitations of hilly terrain and topography of the state.[38]

---

35 Pratim Ranjan Bose, 'Is Manipur Ready to face the wave of infra change', *BusinessLine*, 4 November 2018 at https://www.thehindubusinessline.com/news/is-manipur-ready-to-face-the-wave-of-infra-change/article25498346.ece Accessed 30 July 2019

36 Sudeep Chakravarti, 'Manipur: Reverse the economy of conflict', *Live Mint*, 16 Feb 2017

37 Alison Saldanha & Angel Mohan, 'Nagaland outranks rich states in health, gender equity, but jobs a concern', *Business Standard*, 27 February 2018 at https://www.business-standard.com/article/economy-policy/nagaland-outranks-rich-states-in-health-gender-equity-but-jobs-a-concern-118022700141_1.html Accessed 30 July 2019

38 Report of the Task Force, Nagaland, Niti Ayog, 2018

While agriculture is a major source of income for rural masses constituting 70 per cent of Nagaland's population, it is a major contributor to the state's economy. However, there has been an ever-increasing trend in cost of production of all crops but stagnation in prices for farm produce. There is a high level of post-harvest losses and an uncertainty of market price due to market glut.[39] A Niti Ayog report highlights that Nagaland, being constrained by geographical isolation and socio-political instability, has experienced low rate of growth in comparison to other parts of the country, but has identified sericulture as having great potential to create more employment opportunities and uplift the rural economy. The Naga Peace Process hopefully will usher in stability and development.

Mizoram

Sharing borders with Myanmar and Bangladesh offers Mizoram the opportunity to be a gateway for engaging in international trade with South-east Asian countries. But in reality, the roads and border crossings are inaccessible and as yet remain remote and underdeveloped. The state has the potential to harness 4,500 mw of hydro power. As of April 2019, Mizoram had an installed capacity to produce 97.94 mw of hydro power. The state has a large forest area and contributes 14 per cent of the country's bamboo production. The climatic conditions in the state provide a breeding ground for commercial exploitation of all kinds of silkworm. Zoram Industrial Development Corporation (ZIDCO) is responsible for the overall development of industrial infrastructure in the

---

39 Ibid

state. Mizoram has eight industrial estates, of which five are operational and the remaining are yet to be developed.[40] At the 'Magnetic Mizoram Investors Summit', the state signed a letter of intent worth Rs 600 crore in solar energy and Rs 1,500 crore in hospitality sectors with private investors.[41] According the Central Government's investment portal, Mizoram recorded over $1 million worth of exports in 2017-18, registering more than 30 per cent growth over the previous year.

Sikkim

The state of Sikkim is an exception, according to the Department for Promotion of Industry and Internal Trade (DPIIT). FDI inflows totalled $5.43 billion between April 2000 and March 2019. Merchandise exports from Sikkim have increased from $3.91 million in 2014-15 to $13.96 million in 2017-18. During 2018-19, the exports from the state stood at $7.91 million. The Sikkim government had announced a technical collaboration with floriculturists from the Netherlands and Thailand to develop the state's potential in floriculture and market cut flowers from the state globally.

Arunachal Pradesh

Prime Minister Narendra Modi announced three key project in 2018 and has also recorded a total revenue generation of

40 Report, 'Industrial and Economic Growth in Manipur', IBEF at https://www.ibef.org/archives/state/maniupr-reports/industrial-dev-economic-growth-july-2019. Accessed 30 July 2019

41 'Mizoram one of highest growing state economies: CM', *Business Standard,* 15 August 2018 at https://www.business-standard.com/article/news-ians/mizoram-one-of-highest-growing-state-economies-cm-118081500555_1.html. Accessed 30 July 2019

Rs 1,598.49 crore in 2017-18.[42] It will also witness a growth of a wide network of transport systems. But none of these above indices or development portends to any intense economic activity that will lead to substantial contribution to the economy or lead to any immediate transformation in the next few years. Arunachal is largely an agrarian economy with very limited industries. Indeed, there are only a few medium and small scale industries. Despite some attempts to tap the horticulture and agro sector, the entrepreneurship development policy is yet to be translated into any tangible progress.

Horticulture

As is well known, horticulture forms a major component of Indian exports of agricultural commodities. Within the horticulture sector in the NE Region, fruit crops occupy 40.14 per cent, vegetables 51.83 per cent and spices 8.03 per cent area. From the production point of view, fruit crops contributed 37.75 per cent, vegetables 57.60 per cent and spices 4.65 per cent. Contrary to popular belief, the productivity of different horticultural crops in NER is quite low as compared to national productivity. The scope for horticulture is well documented; however, its potential is yet unfulfilled. The area is a vibrant source of varied horticultural crops, constituting 2.34 per cent of the total horticulture area in the country. From the

42 'Arunachal touches record high Revenue Generation', *Economic Times*, 28 Dec 2019 at economictimes.indiatimes.com/articleshow/67284462.cms?from=mdr&utm_source=contentofinterest&utm_medium=text&utm_campaign=cppst. Accessed 30 Dec 2019

production point of view, NER region produces about 314.67 thousand million tonnes (mt) of horticulture products.[43] However, despite these distinct advantages, NE horticulture has not grown at par with the rest of the country. The National Horticulture Mission (NHM) is one of the sub-schemes of Mission for Integrated Development of Horticulture (MIDH) which is being implemented by State Horticulture Missions (SHM) in selected districts of eighteen states and four Union Territories. It has had some success stories in states like Tripura and Meghalaya in pineapple, *musambi* (a citrus fruit) and exotic flowers. But the level of production is not enough to even cater to the domestic market, leave alone to export.

Nearly a decade ago, in January 2000, an Export Development Fund (EDF), was set up for promoting exports from the Northeast. Forty-seven projects have been sanctioned under the EDF so far. The proposals for funding through the EDF that have been approved include passion fruit in Mizoram and Nagaland, *safed musli* (a herb used in Ayurveda medicine) in Assam, ginger in Manipur and Nagaland, cluster development of farms for organic farming in Nagaland and Tripura. Additionally, agro export zones (AEZs) have been set up for the region at Tripura for pineapple, Sikkim for floriculture, orchids, ginger and cherry and Assam for fresh and processed ginger.

43 'From the production point of view, NER region produces about 7,815 thousand million tonnes (mt) of horticulture produce', *Economic Times*, 30 January 2019 at https://economictimes.indiatimes.com/news/economy/agriculture/production-of-horticulture-crops-seen-at-record-314-67-million-tonnes-in-2018-19/articleshow/67759160.cms?from=mdr

An NEC report of 2017 notes that the region is still not at par with the rest of the country in agricultural productivity, cropping intensity, irrigation coverage, application of fertiliser and pesticides, credit flow, organised marketing facilities, construction of adequate number of godowns and warehouses, crop insurance and production of large quantities of value-added products.[44] Even though the horticulture industry is not doing that well in NER, there are examples where value addition of horticultural crops has clearly shown a contribution to income generation and poverty alleviation. For example, ginger is grown in almost whole of NER, and is one of the most important cash crops of this region. Other than ginger, other crops of NER also have a demand in the market. Fruits like banana, pineapple and orange cover about 60 per cent of the area and account for 66 per cent of the production. Other important crops include litchi in Tripura and Assam, apple in Arunachal Pradesh, passion fruit in Nagaland, Mizoram and Manipur, cashew nut in Assam and Tripura and coconut in Assam, Tripura and Nagaland. Despite surplus production, there has been not been much processing of these fruits.[45] It has also been pointed out that while exports of horticulture produce from the region have occurred through land custom stations with Bangladesh, Myanmar and China but the quantity

44 Draft North Eastern Council Regional Plan 2017-18 to 2019-20, NEC , 24 April 2017 at http://necouncil.gov.in/sites/default/files/about-us/Final per cent20Regional per cent20Plan per cent20NEC per cent2025_04_2017.pdf Accessed 30 July 2018

45 Mohammad Rais, Shatroopa Acharya, and Gary W. Vanloon, 'Food Processing Industry: Opportunities in North East Region of India', *The NEHU Journal*, Vol XII, No. 1, Jan-June 2014, pp37-51 https://www.nehu.ac.in/public/assets/files/journals/NEHUJournalJan_June2014_Art3.pdf Accessed 30 July 2018

of export is 'dismal'.[46] In the same vein, journalist Pratim Bose notes:

> Interestingly, much of the North-East India continues to be 'organic' with limited use of chemical inputs, and farmers practice traditional methods of farming. A variety of organic crops are grown, including tea, Joha rice and lemon in Assam, large cardamom and ginger in Sikkim, king chillis in Manipur, sugarcane, cowpea and paddy in Mizoram, passion fruit in Meghalaya and pineapple in Tripura. While some Indian corporates such as Chamong Tee Exports recognised the export potential for commodities such as organic tea from Assam as early as 1990s, the export of other organic food products from the region continues to be low.[47] Although some vegetables were exported during the last winter, potatoes were taken by Maharashtra and Karnataka mushrooms went to Bhutan. While farmers in NER do not use much chemical fertiliser, their seasonal farm is small or scattered in pockets.[48]

Studies have shown that the export potential of agro-based, forest-based products, mineral products including coal, limestone and stone boulders as well as tea, textiles

---

46 Sriparna Pathak Raimedhi, 'Foreign trade and North-East India', ORF commentary, 20 July 2015, at https://www.orfonline.org/research/foreign-trade-and-North-East-india/. Accessed 30 July 2018

47 Arpita Mukherjee, 'Organic food from North-East States The Untapped Potential, *The Pioneer*, 22 October 2017, at https://www.dailypioneer.com/2017/sunday-edition/organic-food-from-north-east-states--the-untapped-potential.html Accessed 30 July 2018

48 Pratim Ranjan Bose, 'Fruit of Assam's efforts—Agri-exports from N-E Up', Business Line, 8 Mar 2019 https://www.thehindubusinessline.com/economy/agri-business/fruit-of-assams-efforts-agri-exports-from-n-eno-are-theyno-up/article26474651.ece Accessed 30 July 2019

and handicrafts, are negligible, and the majority of them are exported through Assam. Other Northeastern states hardly generate substantial domestic goods. While the lack of demand is the prime cause for low cargo generation, one cannot refute the region's poor infrastructural facilities as a major hurdle.[49] As pointed out, economic dividends to the state or region, the lack of growth of any medium-scale industry capable of bringing in greater manufacturing is hardly 2 per cent of the GDP in most NE states. Industrial investment is yet to pick up due to lack of conditions for large investments and other necessary factors.[50]

Even though Assam boasts of better facilities, the non-availability of authorised packing services in Guwahati and low availability of refrigerated containers has led to exporters routing exports through Mumbai, invariably making the costs rise and hitting profitability. As pointed out by one exporter, 'Infrastructure inadequacies make exports from Guwahati costly, and it will take two-three years of effort for things to improve'.[51]

Sriparna Pathak Raimedhi also points to inherent weaknesses in the growth of this agro allied sector, that include:

- Poor marketing linkages
- Lack of infrastructure and awareness
- The markets in these eight states being largely unorganised and controlled by small private traders
- Facilities such as storage, warehousing and transportation are largely missing which affect the mobilisation of the goods

49 Sreeradha Datta , 'What Ails The Northeast…':op cit

50 SS Sangwa, Developmental Setbacks in North-East India: The Role of Bank Credit, *Social Change* 46 (1) 1–21 p16

51 Pratim Bose, Fruits of Assam efforts...' op cit

- The development of the processing industry has been negligible in the region, which adversely affects the goods produced[52]
- Fruits and vegetables being a perishable commodity and marketing costs high, market glut, price fluctuations and other similar problems are associated with this commodity. Lack of technology has been a recurring problem that is associated with this crop. It still lacks adequate supply chain management.

The state government has taken a few initiatives to address the gap in the agro allied industry.

Industry Growth

According to a 2016 report, the share of the industrial sector for all eight states has increased while the share of agriculture and allied activities has declined.[53] Amongst many other schemes, the government has initiated the Pradhan Mantri Kisan Sampada Yojana (PMKSY) for promotion and development of food processing industries in NER, including;

(i) Mega Food Parks; (ii) Integrated Cold Chain and Value Addition Infrastructure; (iii) Creation /Expansion of Food Processing & Preservation Capacities; (iv) Infrastructure for Agro-processing Clusters; (v) Creation of Backward and

---

52 Sriparna Pathak Raimedhi, 'Foreign trade and North-East India', ORF commentary 20 Jul 2015, at https://www.orfonline.org/research/foreign-trade-and-North-East-india/. Accessed 30 July 2018

53 Pranchi Salve, Sanjana Pandit: India's fastest-growing state: Meghalaya (and other North-East surprises) *Business Standard*, 1 Feb 2016 at https://www.business-standard.com/article/specials/india-s-fastest-growing-state-meghalaya-and-other-north-east-surprises-116020100274_1.html

Forward Linkages; (vi) Food Safety and Quality Assurance Infrastructure and (vii) Human Resources and Institutions.[54]

But clearly much more needs to be done to tap the potential that exists. The government had sanctioned Mega Food Parks for all the Northeastern states except Meghalaya and Sikkim in 2019. In December the same year, three-day North East Food Show was held in Shillong for support to building an industry that would help create employment.[55] Earlier only one mega food park in Nalbari (Assam) has materialised because entrepreneurs remain sceptical of building parks in remote areas without supporting infrastructure such as road access, cold storages, trade routes and air network.[56] A few state governments have taken lead to develop fruit drinks. The success of the kiwi drink from Arunachal Pradesh has led to the possibility of others following the same as well as make fruit wines.[57]

Weaving of textiles has always been a thriving cottage industry in NER. However, it suffers from lack of markets outside the region, the high cost of handlooms and weaves compared to factory products, dwindling expertise and in general limited awareness about the uniqueness of these traditional designs and textures compound the issue. Slowly, it has faded into an

---

54 Lok Sabha Questions, Unstarred questions 1056, 24July 2018 at http://loksabhaph.nic.in/Questions/QResult15.aspx?qref=69717&lsno=16 Accessed 30 July 2018

55 News on Air, 'Meghalaya: 3-day-long North East Food Show begins', All India Radio, 4 Dec 2019 at http://newsonair.nic.in/News?title=Meghalaya%3A-3-day-long-North-East-Food-Show-begins&id=375601

56 Akshay Mathur, 'A Winning Strategy for the North-East', Gateway House Research Paper No. 1, July 2011 p36 https://www.gatewayhouse.in/wp-content/uploads/2011/07/1.-North-East-Paper-PDF_no-crops.pdf. Accessed 30 July 2018

57 'Fruit Wine Can Boost Arunachal Economy: Experts', *Shillong Times*, May 11, 2015 http://theshillongtimes.com/2015/05/11/fruit-wine-can-boost-arunachal-economy-experts/

unprofitable business. The Central Government is trying to support and revive the handloom industry. Attempts are being made to provide marketing platform to the handloom agencies and weavers to sell their handloom textile products directly to the consumers.[58] Under the North Eastern Region Textile Promotion Scheme, an amount of Rs 286 crore has been spent during the last two years.[59] It will take serious investments and designing issues to keep the indigenous textile sector alive in the region. Their ability to develop its true potential and make it cost effective for larger markets will not happen overnight.

Bamboo grows in abundance in the region. In 2019, the Cane and Bamboo Technology Park was established with the objective of providing training to craftsperson as also access to improved technology and standardisation. This was expected to generate income and to create employment opportunities among the unemployed youth of the state.[60] Earlier, 35 per cent of total bamboo production in India came from the North East, but it was not utilised due to obsolete laws. Bamboo has now been exempted from the Forest Act and it can be utilised for commercial use and to boost handicrafts.[61] The allocation of Rs 1,290 crore from a restructured National Bamboo Mission has raised hopes for a range of bamboo-based industries, from

---

58 SS Sangwa, op cit

59 PIB, Ministry for Development of North-East Region Industrial Development in North-Eastern Region at https://pib.gov.in/newsite/mberel.aspx?relid=147899. Accessed 30 July 2018

60 DoNER Min Inaugurates Cane & Bamboo Technology Park, 25 Sept 2019. Accessed 30 July 2018 http://theshillongtimes.com/2019/09/25/doner-min-inaugurates-cane-bamboo-technology-park/

61 PIB, Dr Jitendra Singh presides over as Chief Guest at the Curtain Raiser event for the North East Expo 2019 15 October 2019 at https://pib.gov.in/newsite/PrintRelease.aspx?relid=193822. Accessed 30 July 2018

food processing and construction.[62] This has been a core and versatile industry in the region and has seen successes like few other agro-based industries available. With the National Bamboo Mission, this industry has prospects of growth and also becoming a successful export commodity. Bamboo forests cover a large extent of area in Mizoram, Assam and Tripura and there is much scope for making this a successful initiative.

The region has a considerable variety of medicinal plants. The pharmaceutical sector has received some investments, and Sikkim garnered over $400 million investment from twenty-two major pharma companies in the last three years. Five of Indian well-known pharmaceutical firms are spread over Arunachal Pradesh, Assam, Meghalaya, Mizoram, Nagaland, Tripura and Sikkim. The Department of Biotechnology established a dedicated North Eastern Region Biotechnology Programme Management Cell (NER-BPMC), with an annual investment of Rs 180 crore to evolve, implement and foster biotechnology research in NE states.

It has launched a programme with three major objectives: [63]

(i) Captive cultivation of selected medicinal plants, which are in great demand, to ensure supply of authentic and quality botanical raw material to the user industries in the country.
(ii) Development of technology packages for production of GMP grade medicinal plant extracts for export markets.

62 Rahul Karmakar, Budget Brings Hope to Bamboo-rich North-East, 1 Feb 2018, *The Hindu* at https://www.thehindu.com/news/national/budget-brings-hope-to-bamboo-rich-North-East/article22623985.ece

63 PIB,' Attaining New Heights in Biotechnology', 20 Sept 2017 https://pib.gov.in/newsite/PrintRelease.aspx?relid=170969

(iii) Production of safe and efficacious phytopharmaceuticals from medicinal plants of NER for unmet medical needs using modern scientific tools and following global standards.

Indeed, NER's healthcare system is much below the national average. The Government of India, in its Annual Report 2015-16, had identified issues plaguing the health sector in NE states. While Northeastern medical staff, especially nurses, are very coveted in premier Indian hospitals, the region's hospitals, their complementary structures, as well as technologies and skills, are very low. 'Skill shortage is a biggest barrier to the promotion of medical tourism in North-East India. Except Assam, Manipur and Meghalaya (post graduate institute), the rest of the North-East states do not have a single credible medical college'. While Manipur seems to be attracting some medical tourism from across the border, much more needs to be done.[64]

Additionally, the education sector has received a boost. Institutions of higher learning and excellence have also opened up in NER, mainly Assam and Meghalaya. With the opening of the Indian Institute of Technology (IIT), Indian Institute of Management (IIM), All India Institute of Medical Sciences (AIIMS) and other institutes, Guwahati is fast emerging as an education hub.[65] The Union Government laid the foundation

---

64 'North-East: Prospects & Constraints in Healthcare Sector', North-East Window, 31 July 2018 at http://www.theNorth-eastwindow.com/2018/07/North-East-prospects-constraints-healthcare-sector/

65 Ram Madhav, 'North East India: The Centre of Gravity in 'Act East' Policy', *Open Magazine*, 20 Jul 2018 https://openthemagazine.com/columns/guest-column/north-east-india-the-centre-of-gravity-in-act-east-policy/. Accessed 30 July 2018

stone of Film and Television Institute in early 2019.[66] A Sports University, presently the only central university in India that focuses on sports education, was inaugurated in 2019 in Manipur.

The financial sector is vital to supporting the policies undertaken by the Centre. The initiative of North East Small Finance Bank, the first small finance bank from the region, with three bank branches in Tripura, one in Meghalaya, Sikkim and Arunachal Pradesh and the rest in Assam, is one move in the right direction. So far, agriculture and allied sector has been allotted the highest percentage of loans at 39.40 per cent followed by petty trade (32.91 per cent).[67]

Support to Develop Industry

To increase the number and types of industry and production level, the government has initiated several schemes. One is tax breaks to new industrial units in the region, by way of reimbursement of the goods and services tax (GST) for a period of five years from the date of commencement of production. There is also a transport incentive of 20 per cent of the cost of transportation using railways and inland waterways, and 33 per cent in the case of air freight for perishable items. The North-East Industrial Development Scheme, announced on 21 March 2018, with an outlay of Rs 3,000 crore, and broadly aimed at encouraging development of micro, small and medium

66 Three years after it was decided to build this.

67 'Tata Launches North-East's First Small Finance Bank', *Shillong Times*, 17 June 2018 at http://theshillongtimes.com/2018/06/17/tata-launches-North-easts-first-small-finance-bank/ Accessed 30 July 2019

enterprises (MSMEs) capped at Rs 200 crore per unit..[68]

Slight improvements can already be seen. For instance, the share of industrial activity has risen in all eight states in the region, with Meghalaya, Tripura, and Arunachal Pradesh recording the highest growth.[69] Most development indices also show a positive performance in the region when compared to other states in India. To attract investors in the region, in February 2018, the summit 'Destination Assam' was held in Guwahati to explore business collaboration between India and its neighbouring nations. Assam, as mentioned earlier, has the maximum workforce and industrial capital (73 and 76 per cent shares respectively) in the formal sector and leads even the informal sector in size and workforce, followed by Manipur and Tripura.

Small industries dominate the industrial scenario in NER, so special efforts are required for their expansion and growth. As the recent NEC report noted, capacity development is an imperative for all private public and government institutions. Most of the economic activities in the region are pushed and supported by the government and substantial resources are made available by the Centre. Thus, capacity building occupies a strategic position for the overall development of the region for which the NEC extends support to the NE states.[70]

---

68 Rema Nair, 'Scheme for industrial development in North East India approved by Cabinet', *Live Mint*, 22 Mar 2018, https://www.livemint.com/Politics/ArGuDzUJXgdFSsgxrn81rJ/Scheme-for-industrial-development-in-North-East-Inda-approv.html. Accessed 30 July 2018

69 Pranchi Salve, Sanjana Pandit, 'India's fastest-growing state: Meghalaya (and other North-East surprises)', *Business Standard*, 1 Feb 2016 at https://www.business-standard.com/article/specials/india-s-fastest-growing-state-meghalaya-and-other-north-east-surprises-116020100274_1.html

70 'Industries' NEC, 12 March 2020, at http://necouncil.gov.in/nec-project-sector/industries. Accessed 30 March 2020

The important sectors in the region identified included: agro-based industry, tea, food processing, crude oil, natural gas, petrochemicals, IT/ITeS, forest and mineral-based industries, engineering industry, chemicals, handicrafts, textiles, tourism, hospitality and horticulture.[71]

There is also a lopsided growth of industry in the region. Assam, as the Economic Census data suggests, has 64 manufacturing units with more than 500 workers and 3,420 units with 10-plus workers concentrated in one state.[72] Pepsico expressed plans in February 2020 to invest Rs 400 crore; the state had previously invited 27 firms with Rs 4,781 crore capital. The earlier 'North East India Industrial Policy' of 1997 with an allocation of Rs 15 crore failed due to connectivity issues and lack of linkages to market linkages. It was not able to promote balanced growth in the region. Assam and Meghalaya accounted for 94 per cent of the investments, while Manipur and Mizoram hardly attracted any investor.[73]

Similarly a report a few years later identifies 181 large and medium-scale industries in the region, over 70 per cent of which are in Assam.[74] Most of the units are based on natural resources such as oil, gas and wood. Tea plays a vital role in Assam's economy.

---

71 'Investing in North-East India: Incentives for Industries', IBIEF, 9 May 2018, at https://www.india-briefing.com/news/investment-north-east-india-incentives-industries-16790.html/ Accessed 30 July 2018

72 Report, Industrial and Investment Policy of Assam, Ministry of MSME, 2014 at http://www.dcmsme.gov.in/Policies/National per cent20 per cent20Policies/9. per cent20Assam.pdf Accessed 30 July 2018

73 Padmaparna Ghosh 'Revamp Really?' *Down To Earth*, 4 July 2015 https://www.downtoearth.org.in/news/revamp-really-9845

74 Deepak K Mishra, Vandana Upadhyay, *Rethinking Economic Development In North-East India*, Taylor & Francis New Delhi, 2017

Scope of downstream industries on petroleum and gas cracker project has also been identified. Significant deposits of limestone in Meghalaya and Arunachal Pradesh can be used for setting up medium-sized cement industries by using the deposits of natural gas in the region.[75]

Energy would be a core requirement too for industries to function fully. So to augment production by exploiting the enormous hydroelectric potential of the region, as regular and quality power supply can be an important incentive for setting up manufacturing units. Regular power supply is also an important necessity for cold storage infrastructure too. While in the initial years the increase in power generation may not be absorbed entirely and states would be able to generate financial resources by selling power to the national grid (as in the case of Sikkim), over time the absorptive capacity of the region for power consumption would increase and a significant portion of the power generated would be used for expanding economic activities.[76]

Historically, the discovery of tea and oil in Assam led to building a metre gauge rail link between Digboi and Chittagong during the British period in India as well as the steamer link connected Dibrugarh with Bengal. The Partition and subsequent developments changed the trade momentum. While there was sustained development across India, it would not be gross exaggeration to assert that NER was completely

---

75 Report, North-East Vison 2020, NEC, May 2008

76 Report, Act East Policy Tripura , Government of Tripura at https://planning.tripura.gov.in/sites/default/files/Tripura_Act per cent20East per cent20Policy per cent20 per cent28Modified per cent29.pdf Accessed 30 July 2018

bypassed in terms of infrastructure or economic opportunity.

Several studies have identified the huge potential that NER holds. A 2013 study reiterates, 'All the eight states have different developmental prospects and resources to support their efforts in contributing to the regional as well as national economy'.[77]

In a related issue, there have been suggestions that this region should have a different working timeline to make effective use of the early sunrise. The working hours could start earlier, which could in the long term give greater time span to interact with neighbours in the east. Clearly, despite potential, growth and progress is still below expectation. The region's capacity to actively contribute to the Act East Policy remains remote, at this level of development.

It is not only about developing export potential, it is also about skill development. As per this report, there will be 17 million people in 2021-22, leading to an excess of 14 million job-seekers in the region. Assam is the only state capable of offering employment to some extent. According to a study, the eight NE states—Arunachal Pradesh, Assam, Manipur, Meghalaya, Mizoram, Nagaland, Sikkim (added in 2002) and Tripura—are educating their people at a rate much faster than the rest of India, reducing their dependence on agriculture, and generally prospering, but the growth is not creating enough jobs and livelihood opportunities.[78]

The manufacturing sector has seen growth in Sikkim, where it has increased from 3.86 per cent in 2004 to 37.59 per

77 Report, 'India's North-East Diversifying Growth Opportunities', ICC &PWC, New Delhi 2013 at https://www.pwc.in/assets/pdfs/publications/2013/north-east_summit-2013.pdf Accessed 30 July 2018

78 Pranchi Salve, Sanjana Pandit, 'India's fastest-growing state…' op cit

cent in 2015. Sikkim has emerged as an industrial hub in the region. The increase in the contribution has been witnessed in states like Meghalaya, Tripura and Manipur also. However, the region's average share, except for Sikkim, is presently below 10 per cent of the state GDP, and in some states such as Arunachal Pradesh, Mizoram and Nagaland, it has moved 1-2 per cent of the state GDP only.[79]

For long, tourism has been flagged as an important sector. It certainly has much potential but the numbers do not add up to any substantial amount. In March 2018, DoNER Ministry signed four MoUs for promotion of tourism in NER. The region's demographic diversity offers huge variety of cultural tourism, war tourism and other opportunities. It was hoped that tourists arrivals would double in the next three years for which higher fund allocations were sought.[80] For a variety of reasons, NE barring Assam has not become a major tourist destination, despite its rich cultural heritage and scenic beauty. According to a recent study, the NE hosts less than one per cent of tourists and Assam hosts 70 per cent of that number.[81]

New hotels are opening within the region itself and young entrepreneurs are taking the lead. Indeed, Northeast is fast

---

79 Prabir De, Sunetra Ghatak & Durairaj Kumarasamy, 'Assessing Economic Impacts of Connectivity Corridors: An Empirical Investigation', RIS, 2018, New Delhi at http://aic.ris.org.in/sites/default/files/Publication per cent20File/Assessing per cent20Economic per cent20Impacts per cent20of per cent20Connectivity per cent20Corridors_Report-5 per cent20July-min.pdf Accessed 30 July 2018

80 'Government-initiatives-in-north-eastern-region-during-2018', PIB https://pibindia.wordpress.com/2018/12/19/government-initiatives-in-north-eastern-region-during-2018/ Accessed 30 July 2018

81 Report, 'Connectivity led Development of North-East India through the BBIN Corridor', ATKearney- FICCI 2016

emerging as the new startup destination for youngsters from all over India.[82] Startups have also come forward and opted to work in the handloom and textile sector.[83] This indeed has potential to not only provide employment but also revive an indigenous industry that can bring the region on the world's textile, fabric and fashion map.

This apart, there have been attempts to energise NER's trade and economy, including launching of 'Make in North-East' initiative as a follow-up to the 'Make in India' initiative in February 2018. The idea was to develop a unique product with an exclusive identity of its own in each of the eight states.[84] In the overall regional context, while India's trade with Thailand and Vietnam has grown from Rs 81,385 crore in 2009-10 to Rs 184,687 crore in 2013-14 at a rate of 23 per cent, the share of NE in this trade has been 1-2 per cent.[85]

Identifying the Gaps

In the context of the issue of economic development in the region, there have been several discussions and debates. It has been argued that the perception that the region's people are 'backward' and in need of 'modernising' led to the centralised approach of the Indian Government to drive the development

---

82 Some of the starups in the region are: IamContenting, Mind Zones, Jump Up High Digital Marketing & Communications, Medilane Healthcare

83 PIB, North-East emerging as new 'StartUp' destination: Dr Jitendra Singh , 16-October-2017 https://pib.gov.in/newsite/PrintRelease.aspx?relid=171739 Accessed 30 July 2018

84 'Government-initiatives-in-north-eastern-region-during-2018', PIB https://pibindia.wordpress.com/2018/12/19/government-initiatives-in-north-eastern-region-during-2018/ Accessed 30 July 2018

85 Report, 'Gateway to the ASEAN India's North East Frontier', FICCI & PWC Nov 2017.p.10

agenda and at the same time ensure that national security imperatives are met.[86] Past experience looms constantly. Duncan McDuie raises the question whether the Northeast is poor because of conflict, or there is conflict because the Northeast is poor? He suggests the solution is therefore to either stop the conflicts that are leading to underdevelopment or address the underdevelopment that leads to conflict, which is comparatively easier. Consequently, development in the North-East is a national security project.[87]

Has the lack of *laissez* faire been the bane of NE? The role of the Centre, the geographical distance, lack of specialised industry have all contributed to the lack of significant development. The lack of industry growth has been attributed to 'limited access to raw materials, fuel and demand centres, land acquisition concerns, difficulty in obtaining forest and environmental clearance and lack of banking infrastructure.[88]

Thus, Gulshan Sachdeva suggests the Centre has a role to help the NER but in a market economy, the Central Government can only play the role of a facilitator rather than a promoter of development.[89] Gurudas Das suggests, 'Even if state-sponsored peripheral growth efforts succeed to create better infrastructure, they cannot reduce the geographical

86 Duncan McDuie, 'Between National Security and Ethno-nationalism: The Regional Politics of Development in North-East India', *Journal of South Asian Development* 3:2 (2008): 185–210

87 Duncan McDuie, ibid, p186.

88 Sujan Ghosh, 'Is the Indian Government Impeding Infrastructre Development in the North-East', *EPW*, Vol. 54, Issue No. 17, 27 Apr 2019

89 Gulshan Sachdeva , *Economy of the North-East, Policy Present Conditions and Future Possibilities*, Konark Publishers, Delhi 2000. p11

distance of the peripheries from the main centres of trade and commerce.[90]

According to Sumarbin Umdor, 'Given the lack of job creation in other formal sectors, most of the employment outside agriculture is therefore in the low productivity informal sector, particularly in informal construction, retail trade and transportation'.[91] While the need to enable job creation where majority of population remain employed in government is imperative, such developmental projects that are being planned have their drawbacks too. A World Bank report also cautions about the problems of job creation in NER. 'Job creation ensures that the general benefits of broad-based growth will eventually percolate through the economy. But some enclave industries either have small multipliers or low poverty elasticity, implying that few of the benefits flow through the economy. This is true of those developments that are (a) capital intensive and employ few people; and (b) create large and concentrated rents for those who control resources.[92]

To attract private investment and capital, some fundamental changes are necessary at several levels, both when looking at the big picture as well as the low immediate contexts. Ease of doing business seems to have been in focus but how relevant is that on the ground in the rural remote, not fully connected peripheries of NER? There seem many reasons to be cautious about the desirable spurt in NER development.

---

90 Gurudas Das, *Security and Development in India's North-East*, Oxford, New Delhi, 2013, p145.

91 Pranchi Salve, Sanjana Pandit, op cit

92 Report. 'Development and Growth in the North-East', Strategy Report 36397 IN , World Bank, June 2007 pp18-19

As pointed out by Rakhee Bhattacharya:

> The new industrial opportunities are expected to transform the region with more economic vibrancy to break the perpetual low equilibrium trap but care should be taken to avoid further intraregional disparities. It needs to be remembered that in this ethnoecological sensitive region, industrial transformation, which depletes the non-replenishable natural resources may harm the ecology irreparably without generating sufficient sustainable employment. The 'start-up' ventures at this hour need to create scope in the small states of the North-East with activities to promote entrepreneurship towards a green growth model and with an anchor with small and medium enterprises, which is also the major objective of this year's World Bank report on Doing Business. With a gradual increase in demand for traditional activities of the North-East, MSMEs need more support for modernisation, technical expertise and investments, which have the potential to revive local markets and can also attract global players in the long run. Current industrial endeavours like the NEIIP and NEIDS need careful implementation with appropriate thrust on the economic activities of the smaller states to sustain the local economy of the North-East; add to India's business index and reduce the prolonged industrial disparity within the region and beyond it.[93]

To address the slow pace of development in the NER, a

---

93 Rakhee Bhattacharya, Small industries of North-East towards a much-needed revival, *The Statesman*, 12 Nov 2018 at https://www.thestatesman.com/supplements/north/small-industries-of-north-east-towards-a-much-needed-revival-1502707213.html Accessed 30 July 2019

report suggests using different lenses to bring about socio-economic development. According to this report, the economic policy for the region has to be conceived differently taking into account its geo-economic and geo-political predisposition. Economic policy should not be merely a matter of 'quantum variation in monetary allocation.[94] After an analysis of the state of economies in the region and the constraints hampering their growth, the report argues in favour of free border trade with Bangladesh, Myanmar and the Tibet region of China. The report suggests a common economic zone including Bangladesh as the 'ultimate solution' to the economic woes of the North-East.[95]

In similar vein, former Union Tourism Secretary MP Bezbaruah, opined, 'Opening up of border trade will not help much in employment generation in a region which has a high literacy rate and low job openings, unless production of various commodities based on resources available in the region goes up.'[96] Without any doubt it is important to ensure that the people of the region develop a major stake in trade development.

Pertinently advising caution about the hype about connectivity being the panacea for the Northeast, Pratim Ranjan Bose highlights the consequences of the linkages that

94 North Eastern Congress (I) Co-ordination Committee, A Scheme for the Economic Development of North- East, extract from the Report of General Secretaries to the Eighth General Conference (Special) of the North Eastern Congress (I) Co-ordination Committee, Dimapur, June 1993

95 North Eastern Congress (I) Co-ordination Committee, Ibid, See PS Datta, Ed. *North- East and the Indian State: Paradoxes of a Periphery,* Vikas Publishing House, New Delhi, 1995, Chapter 9.

96 *The Assam Tribune*, 24 August 1999

are growing without the region actually being prepared for them. It may not be able to handle the volume that may come in from outside and may not be an internal growth story.[97]

> However, connectivity might pave the way for cheaper imports from South-East Asia. Considering the North-Eastern region's thin population, difficult terrain, fragile ecology and volatile political environment, it was never seen as a natural destination for investment. It is a market with marginal production opportunities. Indeed, there is a risk that better connectivity may wipe out whatever production opportunity is left in the North-East. West Bengal, Bangladesh or Myanmar may gain as natural investment destinations to cater to the regional market. The trends are already visible.

That NER may not be equipped to handle the effects of infrastructure growth also needs to be understood in the context of the border trade facilities that are still inadequate to support the rising trade volume. In other words, to make full use of the unfolding region's NER needs drastic improvement in border infrastructure, particularly dealing trade with Bangladesh and Myanmar. Success of connectivity corridors will happen only when border infrastructure is upgraded to facilitate trade and investment at the border.[98]

---

97 Pratim Ranjan Bose, 'Connectivity May Not Put NE on the Industry Map', *BusinessLine*, 17 May 2019 https://www.thehindubusinessline.com/news/national/connectivity-may-not-put-north-east-on-industry-map/article27164934.ece#

98 Prabir De, *et al*, op cit

The World Bank Report (although dated) has pointed to the risks involved in the spurt of development that is taking place within the region. The cost of developmental activities that can create havoc in a region that is not only environmentally fragile but socially sensitive and locally ill-equipped to handle such sudden activities.

> It requires attention to other elements of well-being such as economic opportunities, education and health. This implies that it is not only desirable to protect the poor and the vulnerable from adverse shocks that they suffer as the country seeks to build its infrastructure, but to ensure that they too are able to reap the benefits from such infrastructure development. Second, to sustain an economically efficient development trajectory, it is necessary to address the economic, social, and environmental externalities created by large development projects and other economic activities. These impose costs on the economy that can impede growth and constrain development. development. For instance, deforestation, overgrazing pastures, polluting rivers, mining fertile soils, and depleting groundwater will generate immediate gains but will also reduce the productivity of economically valuable natural assets. Addressing these environmental issues may be costly. However, these costs need to be compared to the benefits of prudent and sustainable management of natural assets.[99]

One would also have to factor in the ground situation,

99 Report, 'Development and Growth in the North-East', Strategy Report 36397 IN , World Bank, June 2007 p18-19

which would face a sudden disruption once the projects are fully implemented. There are various vested pressure groups that run and dominate many of the transport and other commercial systems in operation. It is unlikely that these groups will easily give way to other processes and a level playing field will be made available. Their ability to create disruptions will need to be factored in too.

Interestingly, as a CUTS study points out, seamless transport corridors that is being planned under the Motor Vehicle Agreement under the aegis of BBIN will actually result in loss of economic activity in the initial stages. Those involved in loading and off-loading at the borders will be redundant once the cross-border seamless transport system is effective.[100]

Prabir De and Kavita Iyengar are more upbeat about the possibilities ahead. In their words, 'A transport corridor in a geographic space is enhanced with improved infrastructure and logistics, and grows as an economic corridor. The economic corridor approach emphasises the integration of infrastructure improvement with economic opportunities such as trade and investment, and it includes efforts to address the social and other outcomes of increased connectivity'.[101] Thus, states which are closer to or passing through the transport corridors incur less trade costs compare to the states which are relatively far away from the corridors. Therefore, the price of the goods consumed in different states would vary, depending on how

---

100 A bridge across forever, CUTS Policy Brief on Connectivity, 20 March 2019, Jaipur.

101 Prabir De and Kavita Iyengar, 'Making the Case for Economic Corridors in South Asia' in Prabir De and Kavita Iyengar Ed. *Developing Economic Corridors in South Asia*, ADB, Manila, 2018

close or far away from the production.[102]

The study illustrates how an increase in economy activity in terms of growth of GDP would positively influence the growth of freight movement. In addition, infrastructure development, better connectivity, vehicle speed, political and cultural factors also influence the growth of freight movement. As the study shows, an increase in economy activity in terms of growth of GDP would positively influence the growth of freight movement, *ceteris paribus*. In addition, infrastructure development, better connectivity, vehicle speed, political and cultural factors also influence the growth of freight movement. Further, De and Iyengar argue, 'Economic corridors play a key role in integrating economies across regions. Some of their environmental effects notwithstanding, well-functioning and efficient economic corridors are essential for the development of a region'.

This is the compelling idea for NER: that it will not only provide the bridge head to South East Asian economies but also develop its economy alongside. Indeed under Bharatmala Pariyojana (BMP), 3,246 km road length has been approved for development of Economic Corridor in the Northeast in the 5,301 km approved for improvement.[103] So there is much to look forward to.

---

102 Pradir De, Sunetra Ghatak & Durairaj Kumarasamy, 'Assessing Economic Impacts of Connectivity Corridors: An Empirical Investigation, RIS, 2018, New Delhi at http://aic.ris.org.in/sites/default/files/Publication per cent20File/Assessing per cent20Economic per cent20Impacts per cent20of per cent20Connectivity per cent20Corridors_Report-5 per cent20July-min.pdf Accessed 30 July 2018

103 Lok Sabha Unstarred question 3644, 8 Aug 2018 at http://loksabhaph.nic.in/Questions/QResult15.aspx?qref=72667&lsno=16 Accessed 30 July 2019

According to a recent ICRIER study:[104]

> India's Northeast region's border trade with its neighbouring countries is quite small. In 2017-18, NER's border trade with its neighbouring countries was \$197 million, accounting for only 0.002 per cent of the region's total trade with its neighbouring countries. Bangladesh is India's most important border trading partner accounting for 87 per cent of the border trade, followed by Bhutan with a share of 11 per cent.

Clearly, there remains immense potential but at this present juncture the border trade facilities in NER are still inadequate, incapable of leading to any significant rising trade volumes. As per a report, the NE's share in India's trade with Bangladesh, Bhutan and Myanmar is less than one per cent at present.[105] Although dated, the World Bank study points to many of these issues; there has not been much difference in the overall trend. India accounts for 16.4 per cent of Bangladesh's imports but NER's share is only 1.2 per cent. It had reasons to grow. Given Bangladesh's import basket, NER can be a major trading partner, with the 28 per cent (\$15 billion) of Bangladesh's import demand being for products which can be manufactured using local resources of the region. The region needs to diversify its product mix and increase its processing capacity to serve the ASEAN and BBN markets.[106]

---

104 Nishta Taneja *et al*, 'India Myanmar Border Trade', *Working Paper 378*, ICRIER, New Delhi, 2019 https://icrier.org/pdf/Working_Paper_378.pdf Accessed 30 July 2019

105 FICCI & PWC Report titled '*Gateway to the ASEAN: India's north east frontier*', p11

106 Report, 'Development and Growth in the North-East, Strategy Report 36397 IN', World Bank, June 2007 p24

In other words, NER needs drastic improvement in border infrastructure, to increase its border trade manifold in particularly vis-à-vis trade with Bangladesh and Myanmar. Success of connectivity corridors will happen only when border infrastructure is upgraded to facilitate trade and investment at the border.[107] This is not to suggest that the scope is limited. Rather the possibilities have been well established. The region's comparative advantages in producing fruits, vegetables and other horticulture products can be tapped by setting up small-scale processing units for the local market which will also boost rural employment. This set-up is economically viable as well as doable, as a small processing unit requires little capital. The region produces a large amount of spices such as chillies, gingers, mustard seeds, fruits and vegetables which can be processed and marketed locally.[108] NER has also seen changes with growth of local capability in handling high-value projects like highway building as well as rise of start-ups that relates to the local situation, starting from agricultural product aggregation and low-cost eye care to software product development.[109] But it is yet to benefit from investment inflows and despite some attempts including hosting the NE-ASEAN business summits and Assam government organising the first 'Global Investors Summit' in Guwahati in 2017, investment interest in industries remains low.

The region offers skilled English-speaking human resources who could prove an asset in regular hospitality sectors as well

107 Pradir De, Sunetra Ghatak & Durairaj Kumarasamy, op cit

108 Report, India's North-East Diversifying Growth Opportunities, ICC- PWC 2013 at https://www.pwc.in/assets/pdfs/publications/2013/north-east_summit-2013.pdf

109 Pratim Ranjan Bose, A new North-East on the horizon, *BusinessLine*, 30 July 2019

as emerging sectors like geriatric care for ageing societies. Again, its potential goes across the borders.[110] While the Indo-Bangladesh border economy has been stable, the cross-border economy with Myanmar is yet to take off. The cross border connectivity and infrastructure is underway and once completed will change the economic landscape.

Conclusion

Evidently, a plan for creating a network of transportation corridors is underway, with corresponding expectations of greater economic momentum in this region. But despite the potential that exists, the problems on the ground are many. Incomplete planning and lack of synchronisation of the hardware and the software linkages continue to impede actualisation of the promise. At the domestic level, to expect realisation of increased industrial activity and greater production levels is unrealistic within a short time frame. The previous experiences should provide realistic pointers Although several policies and schemes have been put in place because of various other factors at play, they tend to stymie a high level of economic growth in the region. As is evident, the region will witness a slow incremental growth that is supported by the ecosystem and the prevailing environment. Also, as of now, given the low level of cross-border trade facilitation, the economic transformation in the region is unlikely to emerge from such areas. In fact, as the lack of trade flows discussed in the following chapters reveals, there

110 Ram Madhav, North East India: The Centre of Gravity in 'Act East' Policy, *Open Magazine*, 20 Jul 2018 https://openthemagazine.com/columns/guest-column/north-east-india-the-centre-of-gravity-in-act-east-policy/. Accessed 30 July 2018

are limited attempts to coordinate the planning or understand the ground realities. The new policies and thrust on indigenous industry and creation of supporting infrastructures is the first step but there are several measures required at various levels to tap the fuller economic and commercial possibilities. The lack of coordination at the various required steps are often missing. There seems to be increasing evidence that small size firms that grow into medium scale enterprises provides greater source of job creation. That being so, the potential in this region is remarkably high, which needs greater identification and measures to support and encourage such growth.

Mizoram has seen widening and upgradation of roads including two-lane road with paved shoulder configuration and geometric improvements on Aizawl-Tuipang section of NH-54 with JICA loan assistance. The World Bank has undertaken projects to link Mizoram with Myanmar and Asian Highway projects. Currently, World Bank has undertaken a $107 million project to widen 81 km of roads. This would facilitate transportation of cargo to Chattogram port, reducing the transportation time and the costs involved. NHIDCL has undertaken three projects in Mizoram.

Sikkim has seen some major road building and improvement projects being undertaken. In the aftermath of the Dhoklam developments, India decided to improve road access in Sikkim. In November 2018, the construction of nineteen roads was proposed along with twenty-nine permanent integrated buildings and other critical infrastructure along the Indo-China border in Arunachal and Sikkim.[20]

The National Highways and Infrastructure Development Corporation is building a 250-km new road from NH-31C near Bagrakote to Gangtok as an alternative to NH-10, that is invariably affected by the monsoon. In Gangtok, the upgradation of the 10-km-long Indira Byepass-Bojoghari road was to be completed by mid-2019. Another NHIDCL project has also been undertaken. Three major road construction projects amounting to around Rs 710 crore are being undertaken in Sikkim. The projects are: a 1.8-km viaduct across Rangpo

20 'India to build projects worth Rs 250 bn along China border in AP, Sikkim', *Business Standard*, 19 November 2018, https://www.business-standard.com/article/economy-policy/india-to-build-projects-worth-rs-250-bn-along-china-border-in-ap-sikkim-118111900395_1.html Accessed on 7 Dec 2019.

river connecting Sikkim and West Bengal, Rhenock-Pakyong road (27 km), Singtam-Tarku-Rabongla (32.5 km).[21] As per a newspaper report, the total length of National Highways in Sikkim is 492 km. Out of this, 351 km has been declared as new National Highways after 2014 to improve road connectivity in the state. Among these road stretches, 148 km is with the state PWD, 281 km is with NHIDCL and 63 km with the Border Roads Organisation.[22] These roads, once completed, will improve Sikkim's linkages with West Bengal and the rest of India.

Infrastructure Grants to NE States

States	2014-15	2015-16	2016-17	2017-18	2018-19	2019-20
Arunachal Pradesh	243.89				151.12	
Assam	249.96				231.69	
Manipur	173.44				208.52	
Meghalaya	96.84				65.29	
Mizoram	86.16				126.79	
Nagaland	155.18				94.40	
Sikkim	125.49				134.86	
Tripura	99.72				35.02	

21 'NHIDCL road projects gather pace in State, Rangpo viaduct stares at delay', *Sikkim Express,* 10 Feb 2019 at http://sikkimexpress.com/NewsDetails?ContentID=64123 &SectionID= Accessed on 7 Dec 2019.

22 'Road projects worth Rs 710 cr under progress in Sikkim', *Sikkim Express*, 25 March 2018, at http://www.sikkimexpress.com/NewsDetails?ContentID=9458&Section ID= Accessed on 7 Dec 2019.

Ground Issues

The above data points to huge road networks being planned and several initiatives being undertaken but that does not reflect the ground situation. The problem remains beyond the matter of delays, from approval to sanctioning to the actual implementation of the project. Not only will roads need to be built timely but more importantly they need to be maintained and they need to be connected to one another. In India this remains a challenge and more so for NER. Delays are more the norm than the exception and timely completion is celebrated as exceptional. There are some issues that come in the way of their becoming fully functional;

- While roads are being built, there are several issues surrounding their maintenance. The road development is uneven or patchy.
- There have been several issues including delays and quality of roads
- Many of the highways are not connected with the interior rural sector. The faulty planning is due to projects being awarded without ensuring land availability.
- Delays in the completion of projects are aggravated by weak finances of many top contractors, corruption within the agencies and sheer lethargy to push the projects through.
- The wide number of different stakeholders with different roles and linkages in the creation of road infrastructure is another critical issue and besieged with problems. Usually the funding is from the World Bank, the Asian

Development Bank and the Central Government for road infrastructure development, while it is the state stakeholders who implement development projects by appointing contractors. They tend to influence the dynamics of planning and location of the projects of the funders.[23]

- The sudden rise in vehicles has created further chaos without any serious planning taking place and unplanned parking system. Just building of roads is not enough to address issues of transport convenience. More importantly, the state authorities are seemingly unmindful of many of these issues.[24]
- As often pointed out, it is the pressure from Delhi that is keeping the projects going.[25] Regional interest and incentives seem to be as low as in the past.
- The widening work in the forest areas often remains embroiled in issue pertaining to public holding land, issues over the Right of Way being 100 feet. Locals often claim that they have been only paid compensation for 54 feet, following which work has been halted along the stretch.

23 Raile Rocky Ziipao, 'What Are the Impediments to Road Infrastructure in Manipur?' *EPW*, Vol. 54, Issue No. 14, 6 Apr 2019 https://www.epw.in/engage/article/what-are-impediments-road-infrastructure-manipur. The various stakeholders are; (i) World Bank and ADB, who collectively comprise the international stakeholders; (ii) Government of India (GoI), Ministry for Development of North Eastern Region (DoNER), North Eastern Council, and Border Road Organisation form the national stakeholders; (iii) state stakeholders include the Government of Manipur, ministers and members of the legislative assembly, bureaucrats, insurgent groups, elites, contractors, civil society; and (iv) key ethnic stakeholders, who are the Meiteis, Nagas, Kukis, and Zos, among others.

24 'Perforated roads and smart city bid', *The People Chronicle*, 19 July 2019 at http://www.thepeopleschronicle.in/daily/english/279 Accessed on 7 Dec 2019.

25 Pratim Ranjan Bose, 'Patchy pace of North-East highway projects', op cit

As the NEC also notes, the cost of maintenance of these roads is also much more than the national average due to the terrain, soil types, high rainfall, long duration of monsoon and shorter working season of maximum five months or so. The region is prone to landslides and earthquakes, which further add to the cost of maintenance.[26]

The air transport sector has seen visible improvement in recent times.

Airports

A significant number of airports have been added in NER since Independence. But while the construction of many is complete, the weather conditions and terrain have made it difficult to maintain the operability of many of these airports. In fact, largely because of its difficult physical terrain, this region did not for long have many airports but there has been a substantial rise in recent times. However, their operability remains a question. In 1970, Assam had Dibrugarh, Guwahati, Jorhat, Lilabari, Silchar and Tezpur (six), Manipur had one at Imphal, Nagaland had one at Dimapur, Tripura had Agartala, Kailashahar, Khowai, Kamalpur (four), making a total of twelve for NER. This became eighteen stations in the 1980s: Meghalaya had one in Shillong and Arunachal Pradesh had five: Along, Daparizo, Pasighat Pasighat, Tezu, Ziro. In 1990s, air service continued in Assam, Manipur, Mizoram, Nagaland and Tripura; Arunachal and Meghalaya had services discontinued as Vayudoot helicopters stopped functioning.[27]

26 Report, Transport and Communication 12 March 2020 at http://necouncil.gov.in/nec-project-sector/transport-and-communication Accessed on 7 Dec 2019.

27 Air Connectivity in NER, 7 May 2007, DONER, at https://mdoner.gov.in/contentimages/files/5_3.pdf Accessed on 7 Dec 2019.

Presently, there are a total of twenty-three airports in NER, out of which eleven are operational. These are: Agartala, Aizawl, Dibrugarh, Dimapur, Guwahati, Imphal, Jorhat, Lilabari, Shillong, Silchar and Tezpur. (The airport at Lengpui, Aizawl is owned by the state government.) The twelve non-operational airports are: Along, Daparizo, Kailashahar, Kamalpur, Khowai, Pasighat, Rupsi, Tezu, Tura, Tuirial, Ziro and Shella.

That apart, three greenfield airports are to be developed at Itanagar, Cheithu and Pakyong.[28] Under the Udaan (Ude DeshKa Aam Nagrik) schemes, small and big towns in Arunachal Pradesh would be connected with helicopter, seaplanes and passenger drone services.[29]

NER Airports

S.no	Operational Airports	Non-Operational	Greenfield Proposed
1.	Agartala	Along	Itanagar
2.	Aizawl	Daparizo	Cheithu
3.	Dibrugarh	Kailashahar	Pakyong
4.	Dimapur	Kamalpur	
5.	Guwahati	Khowai	
6.	Imphal	Pasighat	
7.	Jorhat	Rupsi	
8.	Lilabai	Tezu	
9.	Shillong	Tura	
10.	Silchar	Tuirial	
11.	Tezpur	Ziro	
12.		Shella	

28 Report, 'The Working Group Om Improvement and Development of Transport in the North East for the National Transport Development Policy Committee', *DoNER* June 2012 at https://mdoner.gov.in/contentimages/files/Final_Report_13-6-2012.pdf Accessed on 7 Dec 2019.

29 'Arunachal's new Hollongi airport to have better facilities than Sikkim's Pakyong airport', *Financial Express,* 1 Oct 2018, at https://www.financialexpress.com/infrastructure/airlines-aviation/arunachals-new-hollongi-airport-to-have-better-facilities-than-sikkims-pakyong-airport/1332832/ Accessed on 7 Dec 2019.

As often seen as in the past, helicopter services have been irregular. Although Pawan Hans Helicopters Ltd has deployed various categories of helicopters in four states of Meghalaya, Tripura, Sikkim and Arunachal Pradesh, their services have been erratic and often are temporarily suspended. Apart from incremental weather there are many causes.

The NEC is funding upgradation of infrastructure in twelve operational airports. Some of them are undergoing upgradation activities too. These are Dibrugarh, Dimapur and Tezu. So are the three international airports in the region: Guwahati, Imphal and Agartala. Pakyong Airport in Sikkim was inaugurated by Prime Minister Narendra Modi on 24 September. Situated around 30 km from Gangtok, the airport is built over an area of over 200 acres atop a hill at 4,500 feet above sea level, making it one of the five highest airports in the country. Developed at a cost of about Rs 605 crore, the airport has a 1.75-km runway. Tezu Airport will be operational soon. Connectivity to neighbouring districts like Lower Dibang Valley, Anjaw, Namsai and Dibang Valley, is expected to improve greatly. The runway extension works will be taken up by the NEC in Umroi (Shillong) Airport, to enable bigger aircraft to land.

A greenfield airport at Hollongi (Itanagar) has also been sanctioned at an estimated cost of Rs 645.63 crore. The greenfield airport at Pakyong has been constructed at a cost of Rs 553.50 crore and is now operational.[30]

Under the Udaan scheme, the Ministry of Civil Aviation announced the opening of 92 air routes in November 2017. The Centre proposed an estimated expenditure of Rs 500 crore

30 Lok Sabha Unstarred Question 2762, 'Projects for North Eastern Region' , 10 July 2019

at Agartala airport, with the AAI to spend Rs 2,500 crore in NE states in the next three years.[31] Bidders snapped up six airports——Rupsi, Jorhat, Lilabari and Tezpur in Assam, and Tezu and Pasighat in Arunachal Pradesh. But of the twelve new routes that were to start in this region only two are operational—Jorhat-Kolkata and Lilabari-Kolkata serviced by Indigo Airlines and SpiceJet. Air India started a flight between Guwahati and Pasighat in May 2018, Rupsi and Tezu airports are yet to be operational.

This sector, as mentioned earlier, has seen distinct progress, but the difficult and unpredictable weather conditions often have a bearing on the smooth functioning of these airports. Despite the development, there are several outstanding issues over ensuring smooth flights from this region. Airports have been built but given the difficult terrain and unpredictable weather conditions, aircrafts have faced problems. Some sectors in NER have been able to use helicopter services more effectively. The first 'Air Dispensary' based in a helicopter has also been proposed and the DoNER Ministry has already contributed Rs 25 crore as part of the initial funding for this initiative.[32]

Associated Problems

- While Mizoram's Lengpui airport became one of the busiest airports in the region, private airlines have not

31 PIB, 'Government laying emphasis on improving connectivity in the Northeast: Dr Jitendra Singh' , 1 January 2018 At https://pib.gov.in/newsite/PrintRelease.aspx?relid=175095. Accessed on 7 Dec 2019.

32 PIB, 'Government laying emphasis on improving connectivity in the Northeast: Dr Jitendra Singh,' 1 Jan 2018 https://pib.gov.in/newsite/PrintRelease.aspx?relid=175095. Accessed on 7 Dec 2019.

been able to sustain their routes, and it has been serviced only by national carrier Air India. The non-viability of routes due to fuel price hike, depreciating rupee value and difficult pricing environment are some of the recurring issues affecting smooth flight operations.[33]

- The track record for aircrafts taking off in Shillong has been rather bleak. Unpredictable weather conditions have played havoc with schedules.
- As aviation experts have suggested, the scheme has not been able to take wing because it is aimed more at reaping political benefits than increasing connectivity. Furthermore, it does not have enough incentives for airlines to ignore the issue of viability.[34] In the words of an expert, 'There is a very strong line between making an announcement for political and electoral reasons and actually making a scheme work…some of these airports, which were announced as part of the scheme, are not even ready,' said Martin. Apparently, routes were announced without terminals.
- As has been pointed out for many of the projects, the involvement of too many agencies–the Centre, the State, the Airport Authority of India–have also complicated the issue.
- Commercial viability has always been another issue to affect smooth running of air traffic. The increasing of

33 Rahul Karmakar, 'In northeast, air links shrinking', *The Hindu*, 9 Feb 2019 https://www.thehindu.com/news/national/other-states/in-northeast-air-links-shrinking/article26224980.ece. Accessed on 7 Dec 2019.

34 Rahul Karmakar, Ibid

fuel price is one such major problem.[35]

In recent times, Railways have been the most successful of the transport sector in NE. Once completed, the proposed railway tracks will be able to open up the inaccessible areas to people's movement.

Railways

The first known railway connection in this region was the railway line between Dibrugarh and Sadiya way back in 1881. It was only in 1958 that Northeast Frontier Railway was formed with headquarters at Maligaon, Guwahati. There were five divisions of Katihar, Alipurduar, Rangia, Lumding and Tinsukia in the region, which has now expanded to all the eight NE states. Apart from passengers, essential goods like coal and petroleum are transported through these lines. In 2011, the rail network covered around 2,602.35 route km out of which 1,454.16 km were broad gauge (BG) and the remaining 1,148.19 km on metre gauge.[36] This sector has seen substantial improvement.

In recent developments, under North-Eastern Railway Zone 4 gauge conversion and seven doubling projects were sanctioned in 2016-17, 2018-19 and 2019-20).[37] Subsequently,

35 'Into thin air: What happened to the Modi government's promise to increase flights in the North East? *Scroll.in 18 July 2019* https://scroll.in/article/911568/into-thin-air-what-happened-to-the-modi-governments-promise-to-increase-flights-in-the-north-east. Accessed on 7 Dec 2019.

36 Report, Planning Commission, p.14 March 2011, at http://planningcommission.gov.in/sectors/NTDPC/Working%20Group%20Reports/NER/Report%20of%20Working%20Group%20on%20North%20East_Submitted%20to%20the%20Govt%20on%20July%204th,%202012.pdf. Accessed on 7 Dec 2012

37 Lok Sabha Unstarred Question No: 2965, answered on 11 March 2020

the railways have added 150 km in the region.[38] According to Prime Minister Narendra Modi, the Centre is committed to put all the state capitals of the Northeast on the rail map and is executing fifteen new projects of 1,385 km length at a cost of over Rs 47,000 crore in the region.[39]

Further, in 2018, Ministry of Defence had identified fourteen projects across the country of which four were selected as priority corridors, three of which are within NER. The Central Government has since 2014 aimed at quick execution of infrastructure and safety projects and funding to the infrastructure projects has increased. The average annual expenditure in New Line/Gauge Conversion/Doubling infrastructure projects was Rs 1,527 crore during 2009-14. The average allotment for NE states was Rs 2,121 crore per year from 2009-14. However, it increased 161 per cent to Rs 5,531 crore per year for this region during 2014-19.[40] The Centre allocated nine per cent of the total budget for the NE states.[41] Expansion of the railway network is bound to have positive reverberations and enable the people to connect better with the region and outside. Apart from increased mobility, this would

---

38 Report, Planning Commission, p27 at http://planningcommission.gov.in/sectors/NTDPC/Working%20Group%20Reports/NER/Report%20of%20Working%20Group%20on%20North%20East_Submitted%20to%20the%20Govt%20on%20July%204th,%202012.pdf

39 PIB , 'Government laying emphasis…' op cit

40 PIB, 'Execution of Work of Linking Northeast States under PPP Mode', PIB, 28 June 2019 at https://pib.gov.in/PressReleasePage.aspx?PRID=1576183 Accessed on 7 Dec 2019.

41 9% of total railway budget 2020 allocated to North Eastern states: Assam Governor', *Economic Times*, 20 February 2020 at https://economictimes.indiatimes.com/industry/transportation/railways/9-of-total-railway-budget-2020-allocated-to-north-eastern-states-assam-governor/articleshow/74194286.cms?from=mdr Accessed on 7 Dec 2019

also allow increased trade and commerce to develop and result in growth of greater competitive manufacturing units too.

Beginning with the railway line (19.7 km) from Mendipathar in North Garo Hills to Dudhnoi in Goalpara district in Assam, the two states were connected in February 2014. This was followed by the second railway line connecting Itanagar, Arunachal Pradesh, during April 2014. The NE states after long are being connected through the railway network. Five NE states—Meghalaya, Arunachal Pradesh, Manipur, Mizoram and Tripura—have been converted to broad gauge and as many as twenty-nine new trains were introduced in the region in a span of just one year (2016-17). In February 2016, the first passenger train from Naharlagun, 10 km from Arunachal Pradesh's capital Itanagar to New Delhi via Guwahati began. The much acclaimed Shatabdi service between Naharlgun and Guwahati was also initiated in 2017.

While Meghalaya, Tripura and Mizoram have railway networks now, there are further plans to provide a railway link for the NE states through twenty major railway projects, encompassing thirteen new lines, two gauge conversions and five doublings with a length of nearly 2,624 km. One of the landmark developments was the inauguration of the Bogibeel Bridge, India's largest railroad bridge, in December 2017. The 5-km bridge will connect Dibrugarh in Assam and Dhemaji district bordering Arunachal Pradesh, reducing travel time by four hours.

A total thirty-four railway projects are proposed for NER with an allotment of Rs 90,000 crore and with a deadline of 2020. On their completion, 5,158 km railway line would be added. Fourteen projects were completed by early 2019, three are awaiting clearances, and four are in initial stages of planning.[42] Some of the new railway projects include:

Construction of a broad-gauge railway line between Bairabi and Sairang that will connect capital cities of the NE states is underway. Under the Northeast Frontier Railway Zone, the 51-km long rail link was expected to be operational by 2020. The project will also be accompanied by the construction of twenty-three tunnels spanning 9 km, along with thirty-six major bridges and 147 minor bridges. The railway line will include three stations viz. Hortoki, Kawnpui and Mualkhang, which will be equipped with contemporary facilities like escalators, foot over-bridge, etc. An express highway project along the Brahmaputra River, costing Rs 40,000 crore and spanning 1,300 km, is proposed. This will resolve connectivity issues within Assam.

Similarly, Arunachal Pradesh has seen a boost in railway tracks. Three railway lines at Naharlagun railway station near Itanagar were announced in 2017: the 378-km Bhalukpong-Tenga-Tawang line. Two others are the 248-km line to Aalo and the 227-km line to Parasuramkund in the southeastern part of the state. That apart, two more railway lines linking the rural to the mainland markets have also been proposed in 2018. Survey of eleven new railway lines is in progress in Arunachal Pradesh while two other surveys have been completed. The railway line connecting the Bhalukpung-Tenga-Tawang is scheduled for completion in 2025. Travel time to Tawang, a sacred site for Buddhists and also a popular tourist destination, would

42 'Northeast State Capitals to get broad gauge links by 2020,' *Economic Times,* 01 March 2019. https://economictimes.indiatimes.com/industry/transportation/railways/north-east-state-capitals-to-get-broad-gauge-rail-link-by-2020/articleshow/68222078.cms?from=mdr Accessed on 7 Dec 2019.

be reduced through the railway line of 166 km, drastically reducing the road distance between the same points of 285 km.

The Railways have also have been connecting the remaining capitals of NE states i.e. Meghalaya (Shillong), Manipur (Imphal), Nagaland (Kohima), Mizoram (Aizawl) and Sikkim (Gangtok). A latest status update on NE states includes: [43]

- In Arunachal Pradesh, a broad gauge railway line was commissioned in February 2015 between upto Naharlagun (suburb of Itanagar) to New Delhi. As mentioned earlier, the Bogibeel Bridge on Brahmaputra river was completed in 2018 leading to further reduction of travel distance from Dibrugarh to Naharlagun (Itanagar) by 705 km via Guwahati.
- In Tripura, the first broad gauge trial train to Tripura (Agartala) was done in January 2016, and the passenger train to Delhi from Agartala was started on 31 July 2016.
- In Manipur, the broad gauge between Jiribam to Imphal (110.62 km) in Manipur State was sanctioned in 2003-04. The latest anticipated cost of the project is Rs 13,809 crore and expenditure of Rs 6,969.49 crore had been incurred on the project till April 2019.
- The section from Jiribam to Vangaichungpao (12 km) was commissioned in March 2017 and works from Vangaichungpao-Tupul-Imphal (98.62 km) have been taken up throughout the length. The work of land acquisition has been completed on 102.62 km length

43 PIB, 'Execution of Work…' op cit

of the project and work of acquisition of balance land of 8 km length has been taken up. Once the entire land area is handed over, the railways will complete it in three years.

- In Mizoram, the broad gauge line between Bhairabi and Sairang (51.38 km) in Mizoram was sanctioned in 2008-09. The latest anticipated cost of the project is Rs 4,968 crore. Expenditure of Rs 1,958.09 crore has been incurred on the project till April 2019. Eighty per cent work on the tunneling has been completed and the work on six tall bridges has been taken up. But land acquisition of the balance 53.90 hectare of land needs to be done, and Railways would only complete the project two years after that acquisition.
- In Nagaland, the broad gauge line between Dimapur (Dhansiri) and Zubza (Kohima) (82.50 km) in Nagaland was sanctioned in 2006-07. The latest anticipated cost of the project is Rs 3,000 crore and the expenditure of Rs 626.67 crore had been incurred on the project till April 2019. The rail network in Nagaland covers only 13 km. Surface transport is the main mode of travel. However, road transport has been handicapped by inadequate development and poor maintenance of roads
- In Meghalaya, two projects of broad gauge line have been taken up for connectivity of Meghalaya. A new broad guage line from Teteliato Byrnihat (21.50 km) in Meghalaya was sanctioned in 2006-07. The latest anticipated cost of the project is Rs 1,532 crore and. Ten km length of the project falling in Assam from Tetelia to Kamalajari

got completed in October 2018 and expenditure of Rs 515.82 crore had been incurred till April 2019.

- The rail connection from Byrnihat to Shillong (108.40 km) was sanctioned in 2010-11. The latest anticipated cost of the project is Rs 6,000 crore and the expenditure of Rs 252.68 crore was incurred on the project up to 31 March 2019. The target date for completion is once again dependent upon when the land is acquired and physically handed over to Railways. In Sikkim, the broad gauge line connectivity from Sivok to Rangpo (44.39 km) was sanctioned in 2008-09. The latest anticipated cost of the project is Rs 4,085.69 crore and expenditure of Rs 554.46 crore had been incurred on the project up to April 2019. Due to non-availability of encumbrance-free land (77.78 hectare forest land after cutting of trees) to be given by West Bengal, it is delayed.[44]

Related Issues

While this sector has witnessed significant improvement, it has also experinced several problem areas. The physical terrain, narrow hills, steep slopes and different railway gauge line has been an engineering issue to be reconciled for the different sectors. The lack of coordination with other ministries or departments has led to lack of the last mile connection. In one instance, one of the key railway projects of the broad gauge Lumding-Silchar line in March 2015 faced some challenges. Post the inauguration of this line with a goods

44 PIB, 'Execution of Work…' op cit

train, it was declared unsafe. The Commission of Railway Safety, independent of the Railway Ministry and under the administrative control of the civil aviation ministry, announced this line specifically (the Lumding-New Haflong section), as unsafe for passenger traffic. Despite an estimated Rs 5,500 crore being spent on upgradation, it recorded nine derailments and fourteen instances of track-subsiding in the four months that this line was opened for goods traffic.[45] While these problems were eventually sorted, questions about quality of construction remain.

As mentioned earlier, in some states, the progress of new line projects of capital connectivity has been affected mainly due to delay in land acquisition and law and order issues. All the capital connectivity projects being in the hilly terrain of Himalayas involve building of large numbers of tunnels and major bridges, including very tall bridges in a very challenging geological environment.[46]

Given the terrain, many of the functional lines face periodic floods and disruption in services. But more importantly, many of the projects beg the larger question of accountability and coordination. While new projects are announced and initiated, the gap between fully functioning lines and turf wars continue to raise issues for smooth functioning of sanctioned projects.

---

45 Bibek Debroy, 'Problems of Indian Railways in the Northeast', *Business Standard,* 22 Oct 2015 https://www.business-standard.com/article/opinion/bibek-debroy-problems-of-indian-railways-in-the-northeast-115102200826_1.html. Accessed on 7 Dec 2019.

46 Multiple railway projects to link Northeast state capitals. 5 facts you need to know Jun 29, 2019 https://www.timesnownews.com/business-economy/industry/article/multiple-railway-projects-to-link-northeast-state-capitals-5-facts-you-need-to-know/445528. Accessed on 7 Dec 2019.

The financial implications are huge, no doubt, and have several implications for the future of these projects.

While most people welcome the growth of transport infrastructure, local sensitivity often poses an issue in NER. In the past, there have been protesters in Arunachal Pradesh over the train services in April 2014 and over the possibility of 'influx' of people from outside the state without the requisite Inner Line Permit (ILP).[47] Similarly, without local consultations, the railway line was started from Mendipathar in North Garo Hills to Dudhnoi in Goalpara district in Assam linking it to Meghalaya. Initially, the 19.7 km long railway line that was announced in the 1992-93 railway budget, and integrated with the rail network in February 2014 was stalled in the initial stages due to opposition from the Khasi Student Union fearing population influx.[48] As seen in the past, local population is often unable to understand the new development and how it will benefit them and there is very limited attempt to create a greater awareness of these issues of development and governance.[49] Also notable is the deep nexus between transporters that prevents the smooth operation of the newly commissioned rail routes for a variety of reasons, the revenue that would shift to other means being one of them. The one

47 David Gao, Railways and the Issue of Inner Line Permit in Arunachal Pradesh: Can the Two Function Together?, *EPW*, Vol. 50, Issue No. 8, 21 Feb, 2015 at https://www.epw.in/journal/2015/8/reports-states-web-exclusives/railways-and-issue-inner-line-permit-arunachal-pradesh. Accessed on 7 Dec 2019.

48 Ashwani Gupta, 'Infrastructure Development in Northeast India: Ushering Peace in the Region, *CLAWS*, 19 April 2014.

49 Meghalaya proposes railway connectivity between Shillong, Sohra, 16 June 2017 at https://zeenews.india.com/news/meghalaya-proposes-railway-connectivity-between-shillong-sohra-2015955.html. Accessed on 7 Dec 2019.

means of transport that was robust in the past and begs for revival is the inland waterways.

The transformation moment in the region, however, came with the introduction of cargo trains from the Northeast to West Coast in 2018. Fresh produce and other commodities from the region would be able to reach the markets of Maharashtra, Karnataka and other states from Guwahati. The Parcel Cargo Express Train from Guwahati to Kalyan in Mumbai will be able to carry consignment equivalent to fifty-two trucks.[50] This would bring down the unit cost of the product and also find greater market access for many goods like fruits and other agro and horticulture produce as well as cane and other local produce. Subsequently, in the early months of 2020, the Northeast Frontier Railway started operating freight trains for most of the NE states, including Tripura, Arunachal Pradesh, Nagaland, Manipur and Mizoram. This would have a greater impact on the commerce of the region. Competitive cargo movement will not only prove beneficial for the region but enable a greater momentum in economic activities. Earlier, the traditional cargo movement in the region used to occur through the inland waterway.

Inland Waterway

Both Central and state governments have been focussed on improving inland waterways in India, particularly in the NE region. It is estimated that NER has about 1,800 km of

50 PIB, 'Parcel Cargo Express Train (PCET) begins operation, connecting Northeast to the West Coast', 18-May-2018 athttps://pib.gov.in/newsite/PrintRelease.aspx?relid=179396

river routes that can be used by steamers and large country boats. As has been documented, the inland waterways in the Brahmaputra and smaller rivers, such as the Kaladan in Mizoram and Barak in Assam, became virtually non-functional after Partition.[51] As DoNER notes, NER being riverine offers immense scope for development of Inland Water Transport (IWT), which has not received its due importance in the scheme of transport planning, fund allocation and policy priority after Independence.[52] Currently, of the existing 111 national waterways, twenty are in the NE. [53]

In 2016, after the National waterway Act was passed, twenty waterways of NER were declared as National Waterways. These include one existing and nineteen new NWs (eleven in Assam, five in Meghalaya, one each in Arunachal Pradesh, Mizoram and Nagaland). Brahmaputra river between Dhubri (Bangladesh border) and Sadiya (Assam) was declared as NW-2 in the year 1988 and several projects for developing IWT infrastructure, namely fairway terminals and navigation aids, have been completed by Inland Water Authority of India (IWAI) thereon. Many projects are also under implementation. The Barak river (NW-16) is being developed and feasibility

51 Report, Planning Commission, 4 July 2012 p10. at http://planningcommission.gov.in/sectors/NTDPC/Working%20Group%20Reports/NER/Report%20of%20Working%20Group%20on%20North%20East_Submitted%20to%20the%20Govt%20on%20July%204th,%202012.pdf Accessed on 7 Dec 2019.

52 Inland Waterways In NER https://mdoner.gov.in/infrastructure/inland-waterways-in-ner, Accessed on 7 Dec 2019.

53 National Waterways Projects in the North 26 July 2018. East http://pib.nic.in/newsite/PrintRelease.aspx?relid=181103. Accessed on 7 Dec 2019.

studies for the remaining eighteen NWs is underway.[54] Manipur has also been promised its Loktak Inland Water ways improvement project at a cost of Rs 25.58 crore.[55]

These NWs together provide hinterland connectivity to states of Assam, Nagaland, Tripura, Manipur, Mizoram and Arunachal Pradesh and connect these states with mainland India through Indo-Bangladesh Protocol route. North Eastern Waterways also hold significant importance in terms of enhanced trade and commerce across neighbouring countries such as Bangladesh, Bhutan and ASEAN.[56]

The Brahmaputra now has several small river ports, including Sadiya, Dibrugarh, Neamati, Tezpur, Guwahati, Jogighopa, and Dhubri and there are more than thirty pairs of ferry ghats (crossing points) on the Brahmaputra, transporting both passengers and cargo. The Barak also has small ports at Karimganj, Badarpur and Silchar and ferry services at several places across it. As per a World Bank study, the major tributaries of the Brahmaputra (the Lohit, Dhansiri and Subansiri), the rivers of Tripura (the Gumti and Haora), the Tizu River in Nagaland, and the Kolodyne River in Mizoram have immense navigation potential that can be developed for both cargo and passenger movements.[57] Further, according to DoNER, the

---

54 ·100% subsidy is being provided by Ministry of Shipping under Central Sector Scheme for development of IWT infrastructure in North Eastern States

55 PIB, Project of Rs 25.58 crore approved for Development of Loktak Inland Waterways Project in Manipur, 28 Nov. 2019 https://pib.gov.in/PressReleaseIframePage.aspx?PRID=1593939. Accessed on 7 Dec 2019.

56 Report, North Eastern Waterways, at http://iwai.npglobal.in/departments/north-east-region-cell/north-eastern-waterways. Accessed on 7 Dec 2019.

57 Background Paper 7. Perspectives of Inland Water Transport Development In the Northeast, Inland Waterways Authority of India, *World Bank* Jan 2007, p7

present challenge is to recreate those routes by combining both investment and multi-modal planning similar to the integrated economic market that existed earlier between undivided Bengal and NER using the riverine transport system for movement of cargo and passengers.

Given the terrain and weather conditions, NE rivers as a mode of transportation had a clear advantage over roads and railways and historically have been used widely. The Brahmaputra river served not only as a major means of conveyance for people connecting the large rural population in the state, but also was the sole mode to connect to the mainland for those living on the small alluvial formations in the mid channels, called *chars*. Brahmaputra was declared as National Waterway-2 in 1988 for a distance of 891 km from Dhubri to Sadia. Brahmaputra cruises have now become a major attraction for both domestic and international tourists.

Feasibility studies are also being undertaken on NW-2 providing connectivity with mainland India through Indo-Bangladesh Protocol route, thereby reducing congestion on the Siliguri Corridor (the only direct corridor connecting mainland India with NE). The waterway is operational with permanent jetties at two locations viz. Pandu and Dhubri and floating jetties at eleven locations viz. Hatsingimari, Jogighopa, Pandu, Tezpur, Silghat, Biswanathghat, Neamati, Bogibeel, Sengajan, Dibrugarh and Oriumghat. Pandu, being a multimodal terminal, is connected with a broad gauge railway line. For development and maintenance of fairway (navigation channel), IWAI undertakes river conservancy measures namely, dredging and bandalling during non-monsoon months of October-

November and March-April every year.[58]

While NW-2 is already operational, development work on NW-16 on Barak river, (121 km from Lakhipur in Cacher district of Assam to Bhanga, Karimganj) has been initiated. Both these rivers are also part of the India-Bangladesh Protocol Routes for Trade and Transit, Kolkata-Shilghat and Kolkata-Karimganj respectively.[59] As per recent records, developmental works at a cost of Rs 76.01 crore for Phase-1 from Silchar to Bhanga has commenced, including maintenance, dredging, upgradation of terminals at Badarpur and Karimganj. At present, the inland waterway is operational with limited infrastructure facility.[60]

Limited Cargo Movement

Currently, trade volume in NW-2 is minimal compared to NW-1 as there are no major industries in NER along the river bank. Commodities like tea which were transported through waterways during the colonial period are now being transported through roadways as it takes considerably lesser time to reach Kolkata by road and is also perceived to be more secure and predictable in terms of supply chain management factors.

As identified by a CUTS study:

> With regard to NW-2, there is no observable dedicated cargo that could be transported through the Brahmaputra other than ODC [over dimensional cargo]. At present

58 Report, 'Expanding Tradable Benefits of Inland Waterways Case of India', *CUTS, Dec 2017 at* https://cuts-citee.org/pdf/IW_India_Report.pdf Accessed on 7 Dec 2019.

59 MEA, 'Protocol on Inland Water Trade and Transit', 6 June 2015 at https://www.mea.gov.in/Portal/LegalTreatiesDoc/BG15B2421.pdf Accessed on 7 Dec 2019.

60 Lok Sabha question, 'Development Work Currently Underway on 10 NWs, PIB 18 JUL 2019, http://pib.nic.in/PressReleasePage.aspx?PRID=1579340 Accessed on 7 Dec 2019.

> in Assam, 52 Pandu is the only port on NW-2 that has a cargo handling facility, multimodal connectivity (rail, road and air connectivity) and storage capacity. Another impediment to developing waterways on Brahmaputra is that, unlike on the Ganga, there are no identifiable commercial industries along the Brahmaputra. Absence of return cargo from the Northeast region, partly due to low traffic of operators in states such as Assam, no cargo would move through NW-2.[61]

Furthermore, conflicting interests and political turmoil were witnessed in Assam, especially with the truckers lobby that have also contributed to the negligence of waterway development for transport.[62]

Still, the scope for project-based cargo via this route is projected to be high as there are several hydro and thermal power plants coming up in upper Assam and Arunachal Pradesh. A joint study by IWAI and RITES has estimated that there will be significant movement of cargo by 2031-32 at Joghighopa (10.03 million tonnes, comprising mostly of coal) and Pandu (14.63 mt consisting of food items, cement, coal, fertiliser and building material). The transit cargo movement through Kolkata–Karimganj route largely consists of significant quantities of fly ash and food grains are transported whereas it is mostly ODC that is transported via Dhubri, in addition to food grains. [63]

The study also noted that a considerable volume of

61 Expanding Tradable Benefits of Inland Waterways Case of India , *CUTS, Dec 2017 at* https://cuts-citee.org/pdf/IW_India_Report.pdf p51-52 Accessed on 7 Dec 2019.

62 Ibid

63 Veena Vidyadharan and Prithviraj Nath, 'Connectivity gains for India's North East via waterways', *The Third Pole,* 15 Dec 2017 at https://www.thethirdpole.net/2017/12/15/connectivity-gains-for-indias-north-east-via-waterways/ Accessed on 7 Dec 2019.

commercial goods is already being transported across shorter stretches along the NW-2 in Assam which is dominated by the unorganised sector. For instance, in lower Assam, which is marked by a number of small islands, day-to-day necessities are transported by the unorganised sector for the stretches from Dhubri to Hatsinghimari and Phulbari near Meghalaya. As per estimates by the Central Government, unorganised sector contributes to 23.21 per cent of the total passenger and goods transport in Assam.[64]

Meanwhile, the Rs 169.59 crore Multi-Modal Terminal (MMT) being built at Varanasi by IWAI under Jal Marg Vikas project is set to be completed by November this year. This would be a major landmark for the project. Construction of the Rs 280.90 crore MMT at Sahibganj was to be completed by May 2019, and the one at Haldia being constructed at a cost of Rs.517.36 crore was scheduled to be completed by December 2019. In addition to this, the Rs 359.20 crore state-of-the-art navigational lock at Farakka was to be completed by June 2019. Contract for maintenance dredging in the Farakka-Kahalgaon stretch of the river at a cost of Rs 150 crore was awarded in April 2018, and work on this has already started.. The Multi Modal Terminals (MMTs) will connect this area to Haldia (in Kolkata) to NE states via Bangladesh by river-sea route and then further to the Bay of Bengal. The Sahibganj terminal will also connect India and Nepal through the waterways and facilitate quicker cargo movement.

The Rs 5,369 crore World Bank-aided Jal Marg Vikas project on National Waterway-1 (Ganga river), is aimed at increasing the navigational capacity of the Varanasi-Haldia

---

64 Ibid

stretch of the river, to enable commercial navigation of at least 1,500-2,000 tonne vessels. The project includes construction/ setting up of MMTs at Varanasi, Sahibganj and Haldia, IMTs, navigational lock, Roll on/Roll off terminals, jetties, river information system, vessel repair and maintenance facilities, fairway development, channel marking, river training and conservancy work.[65]

The DoNER Ministry also suggests that cargo movement in NER will improve with the large power projects being implemented by various private sector companies along with the National Hydroelectric Power Corporation Ltd (NHPC), North Eastern Electric Power Corporation (NEEPCO), National Thermal Power Corporation (NTPC) on various tributaries of the Brahmaputra, particularly in Arunachal Pradesh. These developments are expected to generate cargo movements of about 50-100 mt over a period of 20 years (2.5-5 million mt per annum).

Other identified cargo movements include coal from Meghalaya, fly ash from Farakka to various destinations in the Northeast, limestone for cement plants, petroleum products from Numaligarh refinery, bitumen from Haldia, and food grains from Kolkata to various destinations in NER for the Food Corporation of India (FCI).[66]

The IWAI report suggested that out of 8 million mt per

---

65 Inland waterways projects get underway in North Eastern region, *The Sentinel*, July 22, 201 https://www.sentinelassam.com/news/inland-waterways-projects-get-underway-in-ne/ The study on 'Modal shift of cargo passing through Siliguri Corridor destined for North East and neighbouring countries to IWT'in 2017 based on the study, suggested 49 mmtpa of cargo moves in and out of NER and 30 mmtpa within the region

66 Report, 'Inland Waterways In NER', at https://mdoner.gov.in/infrastructure/inland-waterways-in-ner, Accessed on 7 Dec 2019.

annum of divertible cargo, 3 million destined for Northeast can be easily diverted to inland waterways. They would benefit from freight incentives, service level offerings, development of adequate infrastructure on NW-2, effective integration with NW-1 and regulatory interventions. NW-16 would provide penetration to hinterlands of lower Assam, Manipur, Tripura, Mizoram and Nagaland and would facilitate exim cargo movement to/from Bangladesh for key commodities such as fly ash and food grains.[67] It was projected that with further development of NW-2, 6 million mt would be transported by 2020, a seven-fold increase compared to 2004, and the projected increase in economic activity as a result of the development of inland water transport would create an additional 27,000 jobs. Related development and multiplier effects in the hinterlands, as a result of this increased activity, have not been projected, but are estimated to be significant.[68]

While every Union ministry has to spend 10 per cent of its budget in NE, infrastructural development remains limited. Causes for delay can also be attributed to difficult geographical conditions, technical issues and corruption. While building infrastructure is one aspect, there are challenges to effectively utilising the waterways in the region. This include heavy siltation, shifting channels, lack of adequate depth of water during the lean season, constraints in night navigation and absence of other navigation aids in many parts of the channels in Brahmaputra and Barak rivers. Also needed are links to

67 Cargo potential of waterways in north east, IWAI, http://iwai.npglobal.in/departments/north-east-region-cell/cargo-potential-of-waterways-in-north-east. Accessed on 7 Dec 2019.

68 Report, 'Development and Growth in the Northeast, Strategy Report 36397 IN', *World Bank. June 2007*

other forms of connectivity, such as roads and railways as well as digital connectivity (mobile, phone, internet) the last mile connectivity that can help optimise the benefits of the waterways in the region.[69]

IWT has been seen as the most economic option for cargo movement. Not only does it free the road for passenger movement and also provides environment-friendly options, the problem as seen from the present limited cargo movement is not only a suitable handler but also maintenance of rivers, that often prove almost impossible to manage. The financial implications and efforts often cross out the benefits this mode of transport offers. Thus, despite the proposed potential, the ground situation does not provide for a viable option. Also, for reasons of being politically correct, no government is able to call the bluff. An interesting study points to how for a variety of factors, the decisions are based on optimistic estimates rather than on a rational weighting of gains, losses and probabilities. 'They overestimate benefits and underestimate costs. They spin scenarios of success while overlooking the potential for mistakes and miscalculations. As a result, managers pursue initiatives that are unlikely to come in on budget or on time—or to ever deliver the expected returns.'[70] Indeed given that the past is indicative how the revival of this form of movement has been limited, the motive to continue lies in past memories and not future realities.[71]

---

69 Veena Vidyadharan and Prithviraj Nath, Op cit

70 Dan Lovallo and Daniel Kahneman Delusions of Success: How Optimism Undermines Executives' Decisions, *Harvard Business Review*, July 2003 at https://hbr.org/2003/07/delusions-of-success-how-optimism-undermines-executives-decisions, Accessed on 7 Dec 2019.

71 PIB, Ibid

S. No	Name of the Waterways	State/ Location	Length (Km)	Status
1	National Waterway- 2[1]	(Dhubri to Sadiya)	891 km	Operational
2	National Waterway- 16[2]	Silchar to Bhanga	71 km (Phase 1)	Under Phase -1, the stretch between Silchar to Bhanga (71 km) has been taken up for development. Waterway is operational with limited infrastructure facility.
3	SUBANSIRI RIVER (NW-95)	Assam	111	Stage-I: Feasibility study completed, DPR received.
4	DHANSIRI / CHATHE RIVER (NW-31)	Assam	110	Stage-I: Feasibility study completed
5	TIZU - ZUNGKIRIVERS (NW-101)	Nagaland	42	Stage-I: Feasibility study completed
6	LOHIT RIVER (NW-62)	Assam & Arunachal Pradesh	100	Stage-I: Feasibility study completed.Not found technically feasible.

7	AAI RIVER (NW-6)	Assam	71	
8	BEKI RIVER (NW-18)	Assam	73	
9	DEHING RIVER (NW-30)	Assam	114	
10	DIKHU RIVER (NW-32)	Assam	63	
11	DOYANS RIVER (NW-33)	Assam	61	
12	KOPILI RIVER (NW-57)	Assam	46	
13	PUTHIMARI RIVER (NW-82)	Assam	72	Field work completed. Draft hydrographic survey reports received.
14	TLWANG (DHALESWARI) RIVER (NW-102)	Assam & Mizoram	86	
15	GANGADHAR RIVER (NW-38)	Assam & West Bengal	62	
17	JINJIRAM RIVER (NW-50)	Assam & Meghalaya	49	
18	UMNGOT (DAWKI) RIVER (NW-106)	Meghalaya	20	
19	SIMSANG RIVER (NW-93)	Meghalaya	62	
20	KYNSHI RIVER (NW-61)	Meghalaya	28	
	TOTAL		1213km	

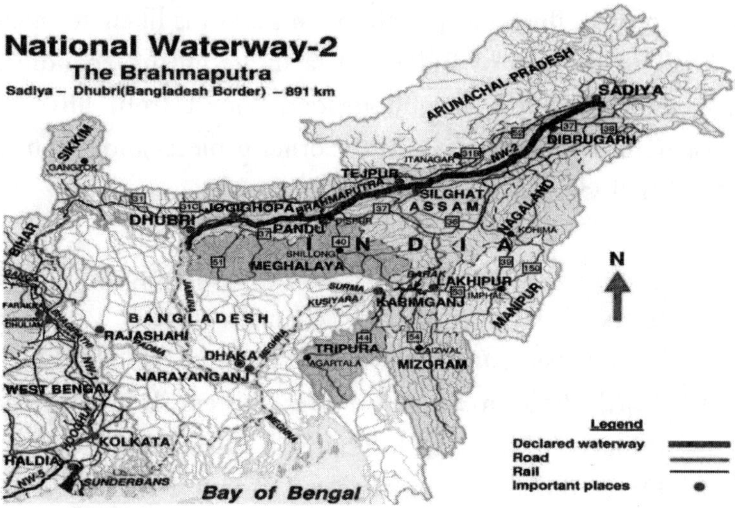

Source: IWAI 2016

NER Schemes and Projects

Infrastructure projects need to be complemented with social infrastructure. As it has been pointed out, 'The direct relationship between sustainable growth and development with both physical and social infrastructure is well documented. Thus, we in government must expedite the development and growth of infrastructural facilities to augment the pace of the economic development of our country'.[72] There seems a definite lack in the area and despite many of the schemes and projects listed, the benefits seem unevenly distributed.

There exist a plethora of schemes and projects for the region. Under the Bharatmala Pariyojana, the development of the Northeast Economic Corridor and the proposal to build the first multi-modal logistics hub (with road, rail, waterways and

72 Role of Physical and Social Infrastructure in Development, *The Sentinel*, 21 May 2018

air transport facilities) at Jogighopa in Assam is likely to open up NER to the rest of India and facilitate greater economic engagement with the neighbourhood. Apart from physical infrastructure projects, some of the other projects and schemes in NER include:

- Comprehensive Telecom Development Project (CTDP) for NER, Comprehensive Scheme for strengthening of Transmission and Distribution Systems (CSST&DS),
- North Eastern Region Power System Improvement Project (NERPSIP), Special Accelerated Road Development Programme for North East (SARDP-NE), Bharatmala Pariyojana (BMP),
- Projects under Swadesh Darshan Scheme for Integrated Development of Tourist Circuits and PRASAD Scheme for tourism infrastructure, National Sports University at Imphal, development of Brahmaputra and Barak for inland waterways.
- The other schemes are North East Road Sector Development Scheme (NERSDS), Schemes of North Eastern Council (NEC) and North East Special Infrastructure Development Scheme (NESIDS).[73] The NESIDS was approved by the Government of India as a new Central Sector Scheme in December 2017. This involves developing physical infrastructure relating to water supply, power and connectivity, enhancing tourism and social infrastructure in education and health sectors. Until early 2019, fifty projects with total

73 Lok Sabha Unstarred question 1834, 'Progress of Projects in North Eastern Region' 03 July 2019

estimated cost of Rs 1,673.94 crore were identified.[74]

- Funding under the new scheme of NESIDS for different states of NER.[75]
- Under the NESIDS, the Government also approved North East Special, an outlay of Rs 1,600 crore for the period 2017-18 to 2019-20.[76]
- Earlier the NLCPR Scheme was responsible for the 1,643 infrastructure projects at cost of Rs 16,366.57 crore. But with the introduction of the NESIDS, the NLCPR scheme will be discontinued although the projects were provided funds till March 2020.[77]
- The Centre proposed an allocation of Rs 695 crore for the North East Special Infrastructure Development Scheme. The agriculture ministry was allocated Rs 50.01 crore for organic value chain development in the Northeast.[78]
- Under Swadesh Darshan Scheme of Ministry of Tourism, projects worth Rs 1,400.03 crore have been sanctioned for the North East Region in the last five years and Rs 896.12 crore has been released for the same.[79]
- As decided in 1998, the Central Ministries had to allocate 10 per cent of their Annual Plan Budgets for

---

74 Lok Sabha unstarred Question 501, 6 Feb 2019 at http://loksabhaph.nic.in/Questions/QResult15.aspx?qref=78850&lsno=16

75 Report, DoNER, https://mdoner.gov.in/activities/nesids-background

76 Lok Sabha unstarred Question 3079, 14 March 2018 at http://loksabhaph.nic.in/Questions/QResult15.aspx?qref=64761&lsno=16

77 PIB, 'Cabinet approves continuation of NLCPR scheme for North East till March 2020', 15 Dec 2017 https://pib.gov.in/newsite/PrintRelease.aspx?relid=174377

78 PIB, ' North Eastern Region Vision 2020', 25-July 2019 at https://pib.gov.in/newsite/PrintRelease.aspx?relid=192227

79 PIB, 'North Eastern Region Vision 2020', PIB 25 July 2019 at https://pib.gov.in/newsite/PrintRelease.aspx?relid=192227

NER to address the development deficit, outlining a number of measures for its development under the 'New Initiatives for the North Eastern Region'. The Planning Commission had created a Central Pool of Resources for the Northeast out of the unspent amount of stipulated 10 per cent of Gross Budgetary Support to support infrastructure development projects in the Northeast.[80]

- The Centre had also established a Border Areas Development Programme (BADP), in the mid-1990s. It was initially meant to support the Border Security Force for building infrastructure at the international borders including that of NER. This scheme also gradually included developing socio-economic structures. BADP initially designed to facilitate development strictly from the boundary inwards has now included skill development programmes, promotion of sports activities in border areas, promotion of rural tourism, border tourism, protection of heritage sites, construction of helipads in remote and inaccessible hilly areas, without road access.

This region has seen support and funding from multilateral Institutions, World Bank (WB), ADB and Japan International Cooperation Agency (JICA). In fact, grants worth $1.4 million (over Rs 8 crore) were extended to twelve organisations for various developmental projects in Assam, Meghalaya and Mizoram by the World Bank in 2014.

80 'Frequently Asked Questions on 10% GBS for NER', DoNER, at https://mdoner.gov.in/print/activities/faqs

Several NE development projects have been funded by Asian Development Bank (ADB) under various schemes. One of them included the SASEC Road Connectivity Investment Programme for expanding about 500 km of roads in north Bengal and NER. The ADB also assisted NESRIP, a centrally sponsored scheme implemented over a period of five years at a revised cost of Rs 2,144.56 crore from the earlier approved cost of Rs 1,353.83 crore for construction/upgradation/ improvement of 433.7 km long state roads in Assam, Manipur, Meghalaya, Mizoram, Sikkim and Tripura, along with extension of project period till August 2022.[81]

Asian Development Bank

ADB asisted Project: North Eastern States Roads Investment Programme (NESRIP)[82]

S. No	Agency	Amount (Rs. Crores)	Amount (US$ Millions)	Share Percentage in Tranche-I	Share Percentage in Tranche-II
1	M/o DONER	378.40	88.30	24.9	14.2
2	State Govts.	67.42	14.90	6.8	6.1
3	ADB	908.01	200.00*	68.3	79.7
	Total	**1353.83**	**298.20**	**100**	**100**

81 PIB, 'Cabinet approves revised cost for the Asian Development Bank assisted North Eastern State Roads Investment Programme now called the North East Road Sector Development Scheme; 28 Feb 2019 at htt://pib.gov.in/Pressreleaseshare.aspx?PRID=1566720 Accessed 10 Dec 2019

82 'Northeastern Road Investment Program', DoNER at https://www.mdoner.gov.in/activities/nesrip-project-details. Accessed 10 Dec 2019

Tranche-I:

- Effective from October 2012
- Cost – $74.8 million (Rs 339.592 crore)

S. No	Name of Road	State	Length in Km.	Approved Cost (Rs. in Crores)
1	Kalitakuhi to Barpeta (AS- 37C)	Assam	58.30	169.94
2	Bilasipara (NH-31) to Fakiragram (AS-II)	Assam	16.20	
3	Garobada to Dalu (MLN-I)	Meghalaya	93.40	196.82
4	Meli (from Km.17.00) to Nayabazar (SK-01)	Sikkim	9.50	95.39
5	Nayabazar to Namchi (SK-02)	Sikkim	19.70	
	Total		**197.10**	**462.15**

Tranche-II:

- Effective from May 2014
- Cost – $125.2 million (Rs 568.408 crore)

S. No	Name of Road	State	Length in Km.	Approved Cost (Rs. in Crores)
1	Tamirpur to Paneri (AS-02)	Assam	43	292.57
2	Paneri to Udalguri (AS-03)	Assam	18.6	
3	Major bridges (AS-02-03)	Assam	1.3	
4	Tapul to Kasom (MN-06)	Manipur	97.925	277.01
5	Serchhip to Buapuri (MZ-02)	Mizoram	55	167.90
6	Udaipur to Melaghar (TR-02)	Tripura	20.3	69.16
	Total		**236.125**	**806.64**

Closely linked to the infrastructure development taking place, the government is considering a Rs 5,400 crore in viability gap funding for a proposed Northeast gas grid. The 1,656-km North-East Natural Gas Pipeline Grid will connect Guwahati in Assam to major cities in the region such as Itanagar, Dimapur, Kohima, Imphal, Aizwal, Agartala, Shillong, Silchar, Gangtok, and Numaligarh.[83]

World Bank Assistance

The World Bank's support to NER has intensified since the announcement of the Act East Policy. The Bank is now focused on financing major infrastructure projects across NE, including road projects in Mizoram, the 400 KV high voltage transmission and distribution lines and mining in Meghalaya. On 24 June 2016, it had approved a $470 million loan to support six states in NER to augment their transmission and distribution (T&D) network. The World Bank will aid in setting up a Northeast centre for excellence in water management, which will serve as a hub to manage floods and other growing water issues of the region, under a National Hydrology Project, estimated at $175 million. Their interests also include installation of new hydromet stations in NER.[84] Word Bank has recently selected nine innovative organisations to fund up to $150,000

---

83 Govt mulling Rs 5,400 cr funding to Northeast gas grid, *Business Standard*, 28 Aug 2019 at https://www.business-standard.com/article/pti-stories/govt-mulling-rs-5-400-cr-funding-to-northeast-gas-grid-119082800604_1.html (the pipeline grid is to be implemented by Indradhanush Gas Grid, a joint venture of state-owned GAIL India, Indian Oil Corp (IOC), Oil and Natural Gas Corp (ONGC), Oil India Ltd (OIL) and Numaligarh Refinery Ltd (NRL)

84 Roopak Goswami, 'World Bank Aid for NE hub', *The Telegraph*, 21 April 2017 , at https://www.telegraphindia.com/states/north-east/world-bank-aid-for-ne-hub/cid/1430826

(Rs 1 crore approximately) for capacity development programmes in Assam, Mizoram, and Meghalaya.[85] Essentially, WB has invested in a cross section of sectors in NER. Some of the significant roads connecting the state capitals in the region have been undertaken by them. Besides the ADB and the World Bank, Japan has played a very important role in many infrastructure projects in Northeast India.

The World Bank assisted North East Rural Livelihood Project has four major components:[86]

- Social empowerment
- Economic empowerment
- Partnership development & management and
- Project management.
- Duration – Five years
- Total estimated cost: Rs 683.2 crore ($144.4 million).
- World Bank contribution: Rs 614.8 crore ($130 million) (90 per cent) as IDA soft loan
- Ministry of DoNER contribution: Rs 68.4 crore ($14.4 million) (10 per cent)

(*Source: Ministry of Development of North Eastern Region*)

Japan (JICA)

Japan brought to India FDI of $26 billion during the period 2000-2017, constituting 8 per cent of the total FDI in India. The number of Japanese companies grew by about 5 per cent

85 'World Bank gives Rs 1 crore in grants to expand operations in North East India', 19 June 2014, *Economic Times* at https://m.economictimes.com/small-biz/sme-sector/world-bank-hands-out-1-4-mn-grants-in-ne-india-through-development-marketplace/articleshow/36819758.cms

86 https://www.mdoner.gov.in/activities/nerlp-project-details

State	District
Mizoram	Aizwal and Lunglei
Nagaland	Peren and Tuenang
Sikkim	South, West and 15 Panchayat Poorest districts of East Districts
Tripura	West and North

per year, rising from 1,156 in 2014 to 1,441 in 2018; the total number of all Japanese establishments grew from 3,961 in 2014 to 5,012 in 2018. A substantial amount of this has been towards improving infrastructural and other projects in NER. India and Japan had decided to set up the Act East Forum in September 2017. This bilateral cooperation was strengthened with the two sides, signing five loan agreements during Prime Minister Modi's visit to Japan in October 2018, of which three were for projects in NER, including loans of $66.5 million.

Interestingly, other than the multilateral institutions, Japan was the only state to be engaged in the North East. This began in 2004 with the Overseas Development Assistance (ODA) coming through in 2010, and which was further consolidated after the Modi Government came to power in 2014. In April 2017, JICA signed an agreement to provide over 67 billion yen ($610 million) for Phase I of the NERNCIP, focusing on projects in Meghalaya and Mizoram. It has also contributed ODA loans for NH51 in Meghalaya and the NH-54 in Mizoram. Among others, JICA will also support the expansion and upgradation of the Shillong-Dawki strip in Meghalaya and the construction of a new bridge in Dawki (on the border with Bangladesh).[87]

87 Rajiv Bhatia, Japan in India's Northeast, 22 Aug 2019, Gateway House, at https://www.gatewayhouse.in/japans-in-indias-northeast/

In addition, other Japanese organisations, such as the Nippon Foundation have financed the construction of the Imphal War Museum in Manipur in Northeast India in memory of the nearly 70,000 Japanese soldiers who perished in the Battles of Imphal and Kohima during the Second World War..[88] In addition, JICA will be financing the construction of India's longest bridge between Dhubri in Assam and Phulbari in Meghalaya, spending 25.5 billion yen.

Some of the other projects include:

The renovation and modernisation of a hydro-electric power station in the state of Meghalaya (Rs 315 crore), and 12.3 billion yen for a sustainable forest management project in Tripura.

Japan had extended a loan of Rs 22.39 billion (S$430 million) to India last year for the ongoing NERNCIP to upgrade NH-40 and construct a bypass on NH-54. This project forms part of a larger Indo-Japan corridor for the Indo-Pacific region extending to eastern Africa under the Asia-Africa Growth Corridor.[89]

The Government of Japan has decided to invest an amount approximately Rs 13,000 crore in several ongoing as well as new projects in different states of NER. Some of these are:[90]

- Guwahati Water Supply Project and Guwahati Sewerage Project: Assam

88 Rupakjyoti Borah, 'Japan in the Infrastructure Sector of Northeast India', *ISAS Insights* No. 556 – 29 Mar 2019

89 Skand Tayal, 'Japan's investments in India have not been without pitfalls', *The Asian Age* 16, 2019, at https://www.asianage.com/india/all-india/150419/japans-investments-in-india-have-not-been-without-pitfalls.html

90 PIB, Ministry for DoNER 'Japan to invest Rs 13,000 cr in Northeast', 12 June 2019

- Project on Capacity Enhancement for Sustainable Agriculture and Irrigation Development: Mizoram
- Forest Environmental Improvement and Poverty Alleviation Project: Tripura
- Capacity Development for Forest Management and Personnel Training Project: Assam, Mizoram and Nagaland
- Biodiversity Conservation and Forest Management Project: Sikkim
- Forest Resource Management Project: Nagaland Japan has also initiated the IRIS programme for the young of NER to visit Japan. Buddhist affinities are likely to impart momentum to the process, which has taken off under the Modi government's AEP.

JICA (Ongoing) Projects

S. No	Project Name	State	Sector	Type of Cooperation	Loan Amount (Millions)
1	Guwahati Water & Sanitation Supply Project	Assam	Water & Sanitation	ODA loan projects	29,453
2	Guwahati Sewerage Project		Water & Sanitation	ODA loan projects	15,620
3	Project on Capacity Enhancement for Sustainable Agriculture and Irrigation Development	Mizoram		Technical Cooperation Project	

4	Tripura Forest Environmental Improvement Project	Tripura	Forestry	ODA loan projects	7,725
5	Nagaland Forest Management Project	Nagaland	Forestry	ODA loan projects	6,224
6	Sikkim Biodiversity Conservation and Forest Management Project	Sikkim	Forestry	ODA loan projects	5,384

Conclusion

The NEC report called for inclusive governance and rural development and identifies the single biggest constraint to accelerated growth as poor infrastructure, affecting all the sectors of transport including road, rail, air, inland waterways, power and cyber and telecom connectivity.[91] Evidently, there has been in recent times a focused attempt to address that anomaly although the entire transport network will take time to fully develop and be fully operational. However, the pitfalls are many. Not least is the concern over corruption. As seen over past decades, much of the lack of growth can be attributed to the entrenched corruption and systemic problems in many of the states. It is thus pointed out that the bane of the region is the politician-bureaucrat-contractor nexus, which 'licks its

91 Report, Northeastern Region Vision 2020, *NEC/DONER*, May 2018 at http://necouncil.gov.in/sites/default/files/Vision_2020.pdf.

lips every time the region gets monies'.[92] Indeed corruption, delayed projects, lack of implementation, have been the blight of NER.

Implementation of a fully developed transport corridor is the key element towards making NER a stakeholder in India's outreach of its immediate neighbours. Undoubtedly, accessibility through development of wide network of quality road and rail network will lead to greater economic opportunities. The internal and cross-border transport infrastructure development is the first step of the Act East Policy, moving the region to South Asian and pan-Asian regional integration. The work pace has certainly increased and the tangibles are there for all to see. Given the magnitude of these projects, the transport corridors continue to be a work in progress, and for them to be fully functional and dovetail into each other will take time.

Not only that, corresponding efforts are needed to synchronise the software issues and introduce ground reforms alongside. Further, while many projects are being implemented, it is critical to optimise their potential. Last mile connectivity becomes crucial for full, effective implementation of the route. Planning should start when the project is ongoing, not when it is completed and awaits being fully commissioned.

While airports have been built, the number that are operational is limited. Given the vagaries of nature and geographical conditions, the cost and benefits of these investments will never really balance. Maintenance and

---

92 Jaideep Mazumdar, 'Budgetary allocation to Northeast Hikes, But Governments Should Plug Leaks' *Swaraj*, 6 July 2019. https://swarajyamag.com/politics/budgetary-allocation-to-northeast-hiked-but-government-should-plug-leakages

operating costs are likely to be much higher and if some other services are not provided like hotels and hospitality centres, their popularity will not meet expectations.

Similarly, for the roads sector, despite some of the newly made roads being four- lane highways, if passenger and tourism sector is to be encouraged, they need to be freed from cargo movement. The number of vehicles is growing and the pressure on the road infrastructure will increase with each passing day. The maintenance of roads is high and difficult too, as the soil is loose and frequent rain in the region makes it very vulnerable to breakage and cracking.

Railways, although not widespread as yet, show the best potential to provide mobility for a larger number of people and, more importantly, provides transportation at more competitive rates as compared to other options. The introduction of freight train will provide greater access to markets and also give a boost to local produce. This would also provide greater incentive to apply and use aggregators to ensure producers can build an agro loop with similar agro products. While airports have been built, the number that is operational is limited.

Many of the social sector schemes and projects seem less visible on the ground than on paper. Earlier, many of the schemes and projects existed but there is almost no available data to understand how they have been accessed by the population and how many have benefitted from the schemes. Rural employment schemes have seen uneven implementation; the governance issues vary from state to state and results are also equally varied.

Better centre-state coordination would improve with greater accountability and efficiency in the administration systems. There is equal interest on all sides to ensure that roads, railways and airports all prove beneficial to the people of the region and others too. Once the cobweb of transport network falls in place, it will certainly get the region closer to other parts of India and vice versa.

Energy Potential

Need of the hour is effective water management in the Northeast. We need to harness solar and wind energy potential in the region

—Narendra Modi, 2014

AS PER Government data, NER accounts for less than 8 per cent of the nation's power generation requirement. Per capita power consumption, at 258 kWh, is less than one-third of the national average (883 kWh).[1] Energy consumption in most of region is for domestic and subsistence needs. Accordingly, for the most part, biomass is the predominant source of fuel.

An estimation dated 31 March 2020 suggests that 70 per cent of the total energy consumption in the region is in the domestic sector. Over 90 per cent of households use firewood as the only source of energy for cooking and space heating. No wonder, NE states have one of the lowest per capita

1 Hydrocarbon Vision 2030 for North East Region https://www.satp.org/satporgtp/countries/India/document/papers/visiondoc2030.pdf

electricity consumption rates in the country: there are still roughly 4.85 million households—more than 50 per cent—that do not have access to electricity. In fact, the per capita electricity consumption in the region is as low as some of the least developed nations.[2]

Despite the present limited demand, there have been many studies pointing to the potential available. While electrification projects are bringing light to a greater part of the rural areas in the region, under-production and possibilities of capacity addition have led to the belief that this region could contribute substantially to the emergent energy grid in the South Asian neighbourhood.

Arguably, energy sector development can be a major means of integrating NER with economic centres in neighbouring South and South-east Asian countries. Lower tariffs and more reliable supplies are distinct incentives for countries like Bangladesh, India and Myanmar to import power from Bhutan and Nepal. NER could play a three-dimensional role in sub-regional energy security.[3]

This chapter will examine the energy capacity that exists and the various plans that are under way for enlarging this sector, highlighting some of the projects as well as governmental initiatives. The possibility of an energy grid in NER will also be discussed. While many studies have projected the possibility of

---

2 National Power Portal, ' Location wise North Eastern region state-wise installed capacity as on 31/03/2020', 31 March 2020, at https://npp.gov.in/public-reports/cea/monthly/installcap/2020/MAR/capacity2-North per cent20Eastern-2020-03.pdf

3 Venkatachalam Anbumozhi, Ichiro Kutani & Mahendra P Lama, *Energising Connectivity between Northeast India and its Neighbours*, Economic Research Institute for ASEAN and East Asia, 2019, p2

energy trade with the neighbourhood through the Northeast, tangible bilateral trade exists with Bangladesh. There are other possibilities but as yet not much development has taken place.

Energy Potential Estimation

One of the latest government initiatives in developing larger energy projects is outlined in Hydrocarbon Vision 2030. Measures to leverage the hydrocarbon sector for development of the region are discussed. Indeed as detailed in its study, the Ministry of Petroleum and Natural Gas (MoPNG) has consciously and constantly focused efforts towards making hydrocarbons a tool to enable social and economic development.[4]

Despite the low level of tapped energy, as many studies have pointed out, this region has tremendous potential. Given the presence of many perennial rivers and water bodies, hydro-power can be generated in the states of Arunachal Pradesh, Sikkim and Meghalaya. In 2014, it was estimated that the total hydro-power potential of NER is about 58,971 mw but only 2.4 per cent had been harnessed till February 2019.[5] Growth in installed capacity is even lower at (0.17 per cent).[6]

In 2019, there were only eighteen projects above 25 mw capacity under construction across the Northeast. Of these, 10 are suffering from time overrun due to various challenges.[7]

---

4 PIB, Petroleum Minister releases Hydrocarbon Vision 2030 for North-East , 9 Feb 2016, at https://pib.gov.in/newsite/printrelease.aspx?relid=136255

5 PIB, 'NEEPCO Emerging as the Major Power Producer in the North-East', 22 Aug 2013 https://pib.gov.in/newsite/PrintRelease.aspx?relid=98534

6 Report, 'Power Potential in the North Eastern Region', NEEPC at https://neepco.co.in/projects/power-potential

7 Jaya Thakur, 'Exploring the hydropower potential in India's Northeast', ORF Issue Brief, March 2020 at https://www.orfonline.org/research/exploring-the-hydropower-potential-in-indias-northeast-61853/. Accessed 30 April 2020

Another 2,600 mw of hydro-power is under construction. The balance of about 93.17 per cent is yet to be exploited. Contribution of North Eastern Electric Power Corporaton Ltd (NEEPCO) in the hydro installed capacity of NER is 925 mw i.e. about 65 per cent. During his visit to Arunachal Pradesh in February 2015, Prime Minister Narendra Modi spoke about the immense hydropower potential of over 50,328 mw of installed capacity. Hydro-power potential of the state is the highest in the country. But, about nearly 95 per cent of potential in terms of installed capacity is yet to be developed.

For natural gas, the potential estimated is 151.68 billion cubic feet which is capable of generating 7,500 mw for 10 years As for coal, NER has 864.78 million tonne reserves against 186 billion tonne of reserves in the country. With these reserves, approximately 240 mw per day can be generated for the next hundred years.[8]

More importantly, as brought out in a World Bank report, the concerns and issues differ from state to state. Rivers have different potential depending on the flow and geographical contours:[9]

> Arunachal Pradesh's concerns are development of hydropower and avoidance of resettlement, whereas Assam's concerns are primarily flood management. Arunachal's preference is for single-purpose run-of-the-river projects, whereas Assam would benefit most from largely multipurpose reservoirs. There is currently little systematic exploration of the tradeoffs and mechanisms

---

8 Report, 'Power Potential...' op cit

9 Report, 'Development and Growth in the Northeast, Strategy Report' 36397 IN, *World Bank June 2007 p41.*

for a development program that would take full account of the multiple benefits and costs.

Apart from estimation of potential, studies have been undertaken about the demand for power in NER, which estimates a rise up to 4,000 mw in the next five years with increase in electrification. A report by the North Eastern Regional Power Committee in October 2017 had stated that power requirement for the region was 2,553 mw with availability of 2,525 mw, resulting in a shortfall of 1.1 per cent (28 mw).[10] Given the new electrification projects being undertaken, according to North Eastern Council economic adviser W Synrem, 'It is projected that the demand of power in the region will substantially increase to the tune of 3,500-4,000 mw in a span of five years, as we progress towards electrification in villages and increase the number of industries'.

By March 2017, 40,140 villages (96 per cent) out of the 42,435 villages in the region had been electrified, even as Sikkim and Tripura achieved 100 per cent, while in Arunachal Pradesh it stood at 77 per cent.

Despite this progress, it must be pointed out that only three per cent potential has been tapped till date, according to the Central Electric Authority, which has indicated that only 2,000 mw has been generated from a total capacity of 63,257 mw.[11] Although on 28 April 2018, when Leisang, a tiny hamlet in the Manipur, was connected to the power grid, it

10 'Power demand in North East region to rise by 4,000 mw in 5 years, says official', *Financial Express*, 5 Sept 2017 at https://www.financialexpress.com/industry/power-demand-in-north-east-region-to-rise-by-4000-mw-in-5-years-says-official/842635/

11 'Power demand…' *Financial Express*, ibid

was announced that all Indian villages have electricity, there still remain many pockets in the region where households are yet to get electricity.[12]

Renewable Energy

Apart from the above, NER has substantial potential for renewable energy from solar power units (particularly in Assam), biogas and small and micro hydro-power projects. There is much focus on adding solar energy to the basket and new studies reveal the huge potential. India aims to increase its renewable energy capacity by 175 gw by 2022, including 100 gw from solar power, 60 gw from wind, 10 gw from bio-power, and 5 gm from small hydro-power plants (with capacities of no more than 25 mw).[13]

Special attention is being given to the development of renewable energy in the entire NER. In 2018-19, budgetary support for renewable energy programmes in the region stood at Rs 504.53 crore. The state-wise status of grid-connected installed renewable energy capacity as on 3 March 2019 was 0.394 per cent.[14]

As for solar energy, as estimated by the Ministry, NER as a whole has a potential of setting up 62 gw capacity. While current

---

12 A village is considered electrified if 10% of its homes and all public buildings are connected to the grid.

13 Venkatachalam Anbumozhi, Ichiro Kutani, and Mahendra P. Lama, *Energising Connectivity between Northeast India and its Neighbours*, Economic Research Institute for ASEAN and East Asia, 2019 p69

14 J Kumar and Majid, Renewable energy for sustainable development in India: current status, future prospects, challenges, employment, and investment opportunities, *Energy, Sustainability and Society,* 2020, 10:2 pp1-36

installed capacity is less than 50 mw, the Ministry of Renewable Energy has put forward a target of 1.2 gw by financial year 2022 (as against the national target of 100 gw).[15] The Central Government is keen to support the production of solar power in this region just as it has undertaken all over India.

The Assam Energy Development Agency (AEDA) will provide Central Financial Assistance (CFA) of 70 per cent for the development of grid-connected rooftop solar photovoltaic (PV) projects across the state.

The AEDA is implementing this programme to develop 14 mw of grid-connected rooftop solar PV projects atop various buildings spread across residential, institutional and social sectors of the state.[16]

It was decided that a solar park over 340 acres would be set up in 2019 in Assam, with production life of 25 years as well as research and development facilities. Also, Agartala, capital of Tripura, is all geared up to be NE's first solar city. In 2012, 700 hamlets and 50 villages in remote areas were provided solar energy, benefiting more than 35,000 families, mostly tribals.

Of India's 60 proposed solar cities, eight cities have been identified in NER by the Ministry of Non-Renewable Energy (MNRE). They are Itanagar in Arunachal Pradesh, Agartala in Tripura, Guwahati and Jorhat in Assam, Aizawl in Mizoram,

---

15 Niti Ayog, Report of the Expert Group on 175 of GW RE by 2020, Dec 2015 at https://niti.gov.in/writereaddata/files/175-GW-Renewable-Energy.pdf

16 Saumya Prateel, 'Assam to Provide 70 per cent Central Financial Assistance for 14 MW Rooftop Solar Projects', MERCOM. 14 Feb 2018 at https://mercomindia.com/assam-cfa-rooftop-projects/

Imphal in Manipur and Kohima and Dimapur in Nagaland.[17] The Ministry is implementing the Grid Connected Rooftop and Small Solar Power Plants Programme which is providing subsidy upto 30 per cent of benchmark cost for the general category states and upto 70 per cent of benchmark cost for special category states, i.e. NE states, including Sikkim.[18]

The Central Government had in September 2016 launched Atal Jyoti Yojana for better street lighting as well as solar lights in NER.[19] The Solar Study Lamp Scheme' was launched for the states of Arunachal Pradesh, Assam, Manipur, Meghalaya, Mizoram, Nagaland, Sikkim and Tripura to provide solar lamps for school children. While solar energy has greater scope in the region, there is a debate about hydro energy and the capacity to generate more. There remains question marks over environmental costs, financial implications and the social impact that they have on the local population, especially those they displace.

Indeed, the government has also recorded success in commissioning of 1 mw Zhangdongrong small hydro-power plants in West Kameng district of Arunachal Pradesh. It will benefit nineteen villages with nearly 4,000 population.[20] While all this certainly points to the improvement of electrification

17 '16 hydropower projects under construction in northeast', *Business Standard*, 6 August 2015 at https://www.business-standard.com/article/news-ians/16-hydropower-projects-under-construction-in-northeast-115080601511_1.html

18 Annual report 2018-19, The Ministry of New and Renewable Energy, Government of India, 2019 at https://mnre.gov.in/img/documents/uploads/0ce0bba7b9f24b32aed4d89265d6b067.pdf

19 Ibid

20 Annual Report, 2018-19, MNRE, ibid

and other aspects of providing energy to the rural Northeast, it also points to the fact that there is some but not overwhelming potential for energy in trade. However, Tripura is the exception, for it has been in forefront of successful bilateral energy trade, as discussed in the next section.

Large Dams

In 2001, the Central Electricity Authority (CEA) conducted a preliminary study of the hydro-electric potential of various river basins in India, ranking the Brahmaputra basin with the highest potential in the region.[21] In 2003, the Ministry of Power launched a hydro initiative of 50,000 mw with a major focus on NER. In January 2007, the Pasighat Proclamation on Power was adopted at the Northeast Council's Sectoral Summit on the power sector, identifying the region's hydro-power potential as a priority area with regard to India's energy security.

In 2001-02, Sikkim became the first state in the region to kickstart the hydro-electric boom, followed by Arunachal Pradesh. Soon to follow were states of Meghalaya, Manipur, Mizoram and Nagaland. The government of Arunachal Pradesh had already allotted 132 projects to companies. By 2019, there were only eighteen projects above the capacity of 25 mw under construction across NER. Of these, ten are suffering from time overruns due to various challenges.[22] A total of eight hydro-electric

21 'Power Potential in the North Eastern Region', NEEPC, April 2019 at https://neepco.co.in/projects/power-potential

22 Jaya Thakur, 'Exploring the Hydropower Potential of India's Northeast', ORF Issue Brief No. 341 l March 2020 at https://www.orfonline.org/wp-content/uploads/2020/03/ORF_Issue_Brief_341_Hydro-Northeast.pdf P10

projects aggregating to 3,733 mw are under construction.[23] Heavy investment has been made in power transmission, with two projects covering all the eight states, the sanctioned total cost being Rs 9,865 crore.[24]

Traditionally, hydro projects have found favour with governments and such large projects have been commissioned with their support. In continuation of this policy, the Central Government has offered several incentives for developing power projects in the region. The Centre offers greater incentives to setting up plants under the Mega Power Policy to NER as compared with the rest of the country. Also, the qualifying threshold capacity for NER is lowered to 350 mw for hydro-power plants, compared with 500 mw in the rest of the country.[25] With the 60-mw Tuirial hydro-power project, Mizoram became the third power-surplus state in NE after Sikkim and Tripura. The Tuirial project, which was sanctioned in 1998, was the first major central project to be successfully commissioned in Mizoram.[26] But such success stories have not been many, given the lack of new projects being commissioned in the region.

---

23 Lok Sabha Unstarred Question 196, North East Gas Pipeline Grid, 3 Feb 2020

24 PIB, Industrial Development in North-Eastern Region, Ministry for Development of North-East Region (28 July 2016) at https://pib.gov.in/newsite/mberel.aspx?relid=147899

25 Office Memorandum, 'Revised mega power project policy'. No.A-118/2003-IPC Government of India Ministry of Power, 14 Dec 2009 at https://powermin.nic.in/sites/default/files/uploads/Revised_Mega_Power_project_policy.pdf

26 PIB, Northeast emerging as new StartUp destination: Dr Jitendra Singh, 16 Oct 2017 https://pib.gov.in/newsite/PrintRelease.aspx?relid=171739

Many studies have pointed to the benefits of dams and hydro-power projects. As Pranab Kumar Das notes:[27]

- Dams are a sustainable source of energy
- There is no outflow of foreign exchange
- Hydro-power is no-inflation power, as water, the raw material, is free
- Environment-friendly–zero carbon emulation rate
- Hydro-power projects enhance socio-economic development of remote areas with the development of project site
- They have become a very cost-effective and renewable form of energy.
- There are additional benefits like irrigation, flood control, tourism and transportation.

While the above are advantages, there are factors that weigh against building such large projects.

The Dibang Multipurpose Project with 165 proposed dams received a go-ahead from the National Green Tribunal (NGT) after a long legal battle in 2018. The court case is helpful in understanding the complexities involved in such projects. The project was proposed for NER in 2000. Hailed as 'clean and cheap' these dams, mainly situated in the state of Arunachal Pradesh, would purportedly help sustain India's energy and environmental security in the era of climate change by adding more non-carbon power to electricity grids.

---

27 Pranab Kr Das, 'North-East: The Power House of India: Prospects and Problems', *IOSR Journal of Humanities And Social Science* (IOSR-JHSS) Vol 18, Issue 3 (Nov-Dec. 2013), pp36-48

However, these projects proposed by the Central Government have been unpopular. Ministerial approvals based on expert appraisals took years. Collective opposition was so effective that these projects did not materialise for fifteen years, except for the half-built Lower Subansiri Dam.[28]

The building of large dams is increasingly being opposed by environmentalists as well as the local population in the region. As Deepak Mishra noted in 2015, the proposal for commissioning of just three ongoing hydro-power projects in the state was estimated to earn Rs 445 crore ($66 million) annually as revenue from 12 per cent power supplied by the projects free for the state to sell. The Dibang Multipurpose Project would also meet 40 per cent of India's power demand and help the country graduate from severe dependence to financial self-sufficiency but did not find approval. Local apprehensions made the project unfeasible. There were two specific roadblocks to completion: first, environmental clearances—the state's own procedures protecting the Himalayan ecosystem and societies immediately engaged with it; second, civil society demands for compensation and political mobilisation against dam construction in Assam and Arunachal Pradesh.[29]

Das writes that despite some of the tangible benefits, the development of hydropower in NER should not be encouraged for several reasons. Many of the north bank tributaries are

---

28 https://in.boell.org/en/2019/05/08/infrastructure-development-northeast-hydropower-natural-resources-legal-and-institutional

29 Deepak K Mishra, 'Himalayan "hydro-criminality"? Dams, development and politics in Arunachal Pradesh, India' in Barbara Harriss-White & Lucia Michelutti Ed, *The Wild East,* UCL Press, 2019, p118.

of Himalayan origin, fed by glaciers in their upper reaches. The Brahmaputra is a trans-boundary river and the subject of conflicts between China, India and Bangladesh. Within India, the total basin area of this river spreads over the states of Arunachal Pradesh, Assam, some part of Sikkim and West Bengal. Due to its international status, there are several issues regarding sharing the Brahmaputra waters.[30]

Apart from the above issues concerning the environment, nature of the source of the water and actual implementation of river projects pose serious issues.

- Resettlement and rehabilitation issues: The land acquisition situation is difficult due to inaccurate and incomplete data of land ownership. There is a need for sustainable resettlement options to be conceptualised by Central and state governments.
- Environmental concerns: Because of biodiversity in NER, getting clearances from Environment Ministry has become a challenge in the past. It has been suggested that the state governments and Ministry of Power need to collaborate so that faster clearances can be obtained for genuine, useful projects from the Environment Ministry.
- Riparian issues: Most of the NE river systems are transnational and hence full potential of the river streams cannot be utilised due to inadequate agreements and disputes regarding water sharing. The Central Government, along with state governments may put in

30 Pranab Kr Das, 'North-East, The Power House…' op cit

place a mechanism to resolve outstanding border and share allocation issues.

- Transmission and Distribution: Due to dispersed demand in the region, the per unit cost of transmission in NER is higher compared to other parts of the country. Further, difficult terrain and hostile weather coupled with lack of qualified manpower results in inadequate development of Transmission & Distribution (T&D) System, adversely affect the reliability of power supply in the region. The Central Government should sponsor schemes for inter-state and intra-state T&D projects.
- Physical Infrastructure: Power projects generally require massive infrastructure backing, especially roads, railways and airways which needs to be developed in the region.[31]
- Effect on livelihood patterns: As pointed out by Mahanta, areas where such large-scale dams are planned are mainly inhabited by indigenous tribal people. Their livelihood is dependent on the ebb and flow of the rivers and forest resources. 'Hydropower dams also have a great impact on the traditional practice of *jhum* or shifting cultivation. Clearing forests and agricultural land due to large infrastructure development projects have often had an impact on agricultural practices in the region'.[32]

---

31 Conference on Energising North East 5 Sept 2017, Shillong, Meghalaya https://www.indianchamber.org/wp-content/uploads/2019/05/Brochure-1-1.pdf

32 Chandan Mahanta, 'India's North East and Hydropower Development: Future Security Challenges', *South Asian Survey*, 2010, 17:131 p135.

- Lack of investment: Due to the risks involved, there is very little interest among private players.

As a study by Jaya Thakur succinctly points out:[33]

'Despite their significance, the viability of hydropower projects has come under scrutiny in North-East India. Private players seem uninterested in investing in the business due to difficulties they face in reaping economic returns within the expected timeframe. To ensure project viability, all possible hidden costs—including those of losing ecosystem services—must be factored into the projected cost of a plant before national resources are allotted. The time overrun of the current hydro-power projects in the Northeast is an important reminder of the importance of ecological and human issues, which must not be neglected in favour of quick benefits.'

To recall briefly, in the past India was keen to develop the Tipaimukh project (1,500 mw) over the Barak river in Manipur. But apprehensions surrounding it stemmed not only from the local population but also Bangladesh, that voiced concerns about the project disrupting the seasonal rhythm of the river system and having an adverse effect on downstream agriculture and fisheries. The Barak river enters Bangladesh as the Surma and Kushiara, which play an important role in keeping the ecological balance in the greater Sylhet region dotted with hundreds of water bodies. Thousands of fishermen and farmers are dependent on the river. This project for now seems shelved.[34]

---

33 Jaya Thakur, 'Exploring the Hydropower Potential of India's Northeast' ORF Issue Brief No. 341, 1 March 2020, p14 https://www.orfonline.org/wp-content/uploads/2020/03/ORF_Issue_Brief_341_Hydro-Northeast.pdf

34 Srd

To address the impediments and difficulties involved in building large dams, there has been increasing move towards building alternative hydro-projects, smaller in scale and without the attendant challenges.

Mini Grids

Considering all the issues surrounding big dams, the idea of mini grid is gaining traction.

As per one report, the NER has good potential to develop small hydro-power projects, and Arunachal Pradesh has the highest potential followed by Sikkim, Meghalaya and Mizoram. Their emphasis on developing small hydro projects in NER is premised on these projects efficiently providing energy demands without much major maintenance or dependence on weather.[35]

Similarly, the proposal for mini grids model in NER presents the possibility of moving towards a clean energy future.

For long, discussions have centred on NER contributing substantially to the South Asian energy grid. India has 8 per cent deficit on an average whereas during peak hours it is about 11 per cent, in Nepal it is about 9 per cent and in Bangladesh it is about 20 per cent, making them dependent on other countries for the supply of electricity. Thus energy security for this sub-region emanates from interdependency for electricity. Energy cooperation for enhanced power trading is essential to cater to the burgeoning demand for electricity of this sub-region, one of the largest, most populous and growing economies.[36]

---

35 Renewable energy in North Eastern Region, Annual Report 2018-19,

36 'Opportunities and challenges for electricity trade in the BBIN Sub-Region', CII report

II

Regional Grid

While proceedings in the Bangladesh Bhutan India Nepal Motor Vehicle Agreement (BBIN MVA) are set to start shortly, the idea of this sub-regional process has also led to possibilities of several other interlinked initiatives. The idea of developing an energy grid is receiving greater traction and is also being discussed at various levels. India is also preparing a draft agreement for regional energy trade. Apparently, a more tangible initiative of energy trade seems in the offing amongst India, Nepal and Bangladesh. Presently India buys 1,450 mw from Bhutan and sells 660 mw and 150 mw to Bangladesh and Nepal respectively. But both Nepal and Bangladesh still experience severe shortage of around 550 mw and 10,000 mw, respectively. Whether NER has potential to contribute to this energy trade is the key consideration here. While there remains no legal problem surrounding this possibility of energy trade, the problems arise out of geographical constraints and socio-economic factors that may stymie the potential that is being discussed often at various levels and forums.

It was in 2018 that India issued a new guideline that created scope for Bangladesh to import power from other neighbouring countries like Bhutan and Nepal by using the Indian power transmission system and cross-border interconnections. The new guidelines had also opened up opportunity to purchase power through power exchange, which is not available in the existing guidelines of cross-border power trade. The guidelines will now allow any company in Bangladesh to enter into agreements with Indian companies as well as with companies in the neighbouring countries to facilitate power trade.[37] This has all the portents to change the face of cross-border regional energy trade.

India-Bangladesh Bilateral Energy Trade

India and Bangladesh's energy trade covers explorations for oil and natural gas, building more coal-based power plants and importing power and coal.

Indeed, one of the most tangible and immediate benefits that accrued between India and Bangladesh in the last decade was in the energy sector, a priority for the Sheikh Hasina government given its daily shortage of up to 1,500 mw against installed capacity of 15,379 mw.[38] Drawing from a basket of types of trade in energy, the bilateral cooperation has covered a lot of ground from the first bilateral trade in 2013.

During Bangladesh Prime Minister Sheikh Hasina's visit to India in 2010, a year after she came to power, two agreements were signed regarding purchase of electricity and expansion of trade and commerce, changing the face of bilateral trade. In its first goodwill gesture, Bangladesh allowed India to facilitate one-time movement of Over Dimensional Cargo (ODC) for construction of a power plant in Tripura through the Ashugunj port near Palatana. Bangladesh received its first 250 mw of power supply in 2013.

---

37 'Indian Transmission System can Lead to Import Power from Bhutan, Nepal', *New Age*, 26 Dec 2018, http://www.newagebd.net/article/59909/indian-transmission-system-can-be-used-to-import-power-from-bhutan-nepal

38 Bangladesh has a demand of over 5,000 mw energy while its present supply hovers around 3,646 mw. The deficit has led to cuts in its industries affecting its quantity of export. Incidentally, Bangladesh government had plans to generate 7,000 mw by 2013 and 20,000 by 2021; 7,0000 mw by 2015

Apart from this, India and Bangladesh have been able to initiate other forms of energy trade. There was a mutual decision about exchange of power to be made in adjoining areas. In areas close to Bangladesh where India has surplus, it will transfer a certain specific amount to Bangladesh while India will draw similar amount from Bangladesh in areas in India which suffer a deficit. In accordance with this, India and Bangladesh have signed a deal for 35 years. Bangladesh Power Development Board (BPDB) will buy 500 mw power from different power plants of India and India will export it through the Power Grid Corporation of India Ltd (PGCI) regional transmission system. Energy cooperation benefitted both countries and was quick to get off to a great start. Tripura was in the forefront of this energy cooperation. The Tripura Monarchak power project of North Eastern Electric Power Corporation Ltd is planning to increase supply from of 68 mw to 101 mw shortly.[39]

Additionally, the Numaligarh Refinery Ltd in 2017 signed a 15-year agreement with Bangladesh Petroleum Corp (BPC) for export of diesel to Bangladesh. The export quantity will be increased gradually from 0.25 to 0.40 mmtpa over a period of 15 years.[40] In fact, within two years, India was able to send through two Bangladeshi barges—Hangang-1 and Darashako— carrying about 1,400 tonnes of high speed diesel

39 Sreeradha Datta, 'Indo-Bangladesh in an Evolving World', *Revista UNISCI / UNISCI Journal*, No. 49 (Enero/January 2019) p196.

40 NRL enters diesel export pact with Bangladesh, *Business Standard*, 23 Oct 2017 at https://www.business-standard.com/article/pti-stories/nrl-enters-diesel-export-pact-with-bangladesh-117102300986_1.html

(HSD) from Silghat, which has been declared as the Port of Call in Indian territory for onward shipment to Baghabari in Bangladesh (which is the latter's Port of Call), along the river via Dhubri in lower Assam. Two more barges, Naharkatia and Barauni, both Indian vessels, were used to carry 2,100 tonnes of HSD for loading at Silghat.[41]

There is greater possibility for bilateral collaboration as argued by Amit Bhaduri. The four oil refineries in Assam have the capacity to produce 7 mt of petroleum products.

> The consumption of petroleum products in the seven north eastern states is only 2.88 million tonnes. Exporting petroleum products from Assam to Bangladesh via a pipeline makes economic sense for both sides: it is cheaper than moving them by ship, as is currently done by Bangladesh. This will lower the logistics cost for Bangladesh. For India, it will be cheaper to pipe these products to Bangladesh than to transport them to other Indian or overseas markets.[42]

Several other bilateral projects have been initiated. Some of them are the Maitre Super Thermal Power Project at Rampal, Bagerhat of Bangladesh, by Bangladesh-India Friendship Power Plant Company Pvt Ltd, which is also progressing well. Under this project, 1,320 mw power will be produced. Alongside, a solar power project at Rampal is also under progress with a capacity of about 180 mw.

---

41 'Assam begins diesel export to Bangladesh', *Indian Express*, 17 Dec 2019 at http://archive.indianexpress.com/news/assam-begins-diesel-export-to-bangladesh/251374/

42 Amit Bhandari, *North East Energy for Bangladesh*, 6 June 2014, Gateway House, HTTPS://WWW.GATEWAYHOUSE.IN/NORTH-EAST-ENERGY-FOR-BANGLADESH/

Subsequently, in 2016, Indian Oil Corporation Ltd (IOCL) and Bangladesh Petroleum Corporation (BPC) agreed to set up an LPG terminal in Chattogram. This would make it possible for Bangladesh to receive gas and would facilitate supply of liquefied petroleum gas (LPG) to NE states, including Tripura, thereby benefitting both the countries. Private enterprises like Adani Energy and Reliance Group have also been engaged in bilateral cooperation in energy trade. It's a robust engagement that has been very beneficial to the two neighbours.[43]

India exports a small quantity of coal to Bangladesh (approximately 1.5 mt) and India currently supplies 660 mw of electricity to Dhaka daily. Of the total, 500 mw is supplied through the Bheramara border in Murshidabad, West Bengal and the rest from Tripura.[44] They are both also exploring the possibility of another 500 mw through this Behrampur-Bheramara inter-connection, which is under construction. Bangladesh has signed an agreement with India to import additional 160 mw from Tripura state.

Such an overture can catalyse other economic gains for India, such as improved access to the NE states if Bangladesh allows transit rights. This has already happened in a limited way in the energy sector in Tripura. The state has gas reserves with limited local use, and transporting them to other parts

43 For details see India-Bangladesh Joint Statement during the State Visit of Prime Minister of Bangladesh to India', 8 Apr 2017 at https://mea.gov.in/bilateral-documents.htm?dtl/28362/india++bangladesh+joint+statement+during+the+state+visit+of+prime+minister+of+bangladesh+to+india+april+8+2017

44 Pratim Ranjan Bose, 'India to double its power supply to Bangladesh,' *BusinessLine*, 21 Feb 2018 at https://www.thehindubusinessline.com/economy/india-to-double-its-power-supply-to-bangladesh/article22808443.ece

of India is not feasible. Converting the gas into electricity and transmitting it via power lines is easier.[45]

Bangladesh has also shown interest in signing a mutual Power Trade Agreement with Nepal and has proposed to invest $1 billion in Nepal's hydro-power sector. During a visit to India, the Bangladesh Prime Minister had expressed willingness to facilitate cross-border energy trade between Bangladesh and Nepal.

The most recent progress in this field has been the possibility of trilateral agreement in this sector. The idea of developing an energy grid is receiving greater traction and is being discussed at various levels. India is also preparing a draft agreement for regional energy trade. Apparently, a more tangible initiative of energy trade seems in the offing amongst India, Nepal and Bangladesh. An Indian company was in discussion for long with the Nepal government to build the Upper Karnali project in western Nepal and is in the final stages of acquiring permission for constructing the 600-mw Upper Marsyangdi-II project in central Nepal Bangladesh will import 200 mw from the Upper Marsyangdi-II project and the remaining 300 mw will be imported from Upper Karnali. Bangladesh has been making several proposals to Nepal for purchase of electricity and India will provide the transmission lines needed to cross over to Bangladesh through India. [46]

This commitment was in fact reiterated by Bangladesh's Ambassador in Nepal. In 2018, 'India is positive and has

45 Amit Bhandari, op cit

46 News Report: 'GMR India to sell 500 mw power to Bangladesh from Nepal', *Nepal Energy Forum* , 14 August 2018, at http://www.nepalenergyforum.com/gmr-india-to-sell-500-mw-power-to-bangladesh-from-nepal/

agreed to allow transmission of electricity to Bangladesh from Nepal. We are ready to import electricity from Nepal after meeting Nepal's requirements as much as Nepal can export to us.' Thus, after several rounds of discussion a 500-mw hydro-power plant in Nepal is under construction for the export of electricity to Bangladesh, using Indian transmission lines and will be operational within the next five years. The three neighbours, however, will need to resolve the trading and tariff modalities. While for long, political differences had prevented energy trade between India and Nepal, the bilateral Bangladesh–Nepal energy trade will allow the process to start. Maybe, with the improvement of bilateral atmosphere, India and Nepal will be able to embark on similar cooperation too. Thus simultaneously a cooperative framework amongst three neighbours is developing with a distinct sub-regional momentum being seen in this region.[47]

Currently, the main electricity trade flows in these regions are as follows: Bhutan to India, India to Bangladesh and India to Nepal.

India's NER can connect to these two grids via transmission lines and gas pipeline connections through Myanmar. India's electricity grid is already connected to Bangladesh's grid, and Bangladesh is planning to link its grid with Myanmar's. As countries recognise the multiple benefits of interconnectivity, significant discussions have arisen over a potential Myanmar–Bangladesh–India natural gas pipeline. India and Myanmar have also revived a discussion concerning a proposed gas pipeline

47 Sreeradha Datta, 'Bangladesh the Much-Coveted Neighbour,' *ISAS Insight* 4 August 2020 https://www.isas.nus.edu.sg/papers/bangladesh-the-much-coveted-neighbour/

connecting India and Myanmar through Bangladesh.[48] Various design options are being considered, including a land route via the states of Tripura and Mizoram, an offshore route through the coastal areas of Bangladesh and a deep-sea route. In the future, India will be able to access not only electricity and gas from Myanmar but also gas from faraway fields in Indonesia, Malaysia and Brunei, as well as electricity from the Lao People's Democratic Republic.[49]

Hydrocarbon Vision 2020 also identifies the possibilities for energy trade with neighbours.

> Total demand for all petroleum products in the Northeast region is around 3.2 mmtpa. Taking into consideration the expansion proposed along with existing refinery capacity, the region will have more capacity than demand. Already a net exporter of petroleum products, India can utilise this excess capacity to service demand in neighbouring nations such as Bangladesh, Myanmar, Sri Lanka and Bhutan. Bhutan and Nepal present export opportunities to replace firewood by cleaner sources of energy, i.e., natural gas and LPG. Myanmar is an exception with excess capacity in natural gas production. Therefore, the option to import gas from Myanmar through NER may be considered once the gas pipeline network in the region is developed and

48 Sanket, Sudhir Kulkarni and Ameya Pimpalkhare, 'Exploring cooperation between India's Northeastern gas grid and Myanmar', *ORF Raisina Debates*, 7 June 2019 for more details.

49 Venkatachalam Anbumozhi, Ichiro Kutani, and Mahendra P Lama, *Energising Connectivity between Northeast India and its Neighbours*, Economic Research Institute for ASEAN and East Asia, 2019 http://www.eria.org/uploads/media/ERIA_Book_Energising_Connectivity_Northeast_India(NER)_2019.pdf

> linked to the national gas grid. Development of a gas grid in the region will provide opportunities for setting up industries such as power and petrochemical plants which, in turn, will bring in investment and provide employment opportunities to the local population.[50]

Further, this report adds:

> Another important issue that needs to be addressed is the effective utilisation of oil and gas resources available. An energy corridor needs to be developed in NER for utilising the resources available, producing POL products and exporting to the rest of India as well as Bangladesh, Myanmar and Nepal. This will fuel overall growth in the region. A corridor is envisaged to connect Paradip to NER region for imported crude oil in Phase I and to Chittagong for export of products in Phase II. This will facilitate uninterrupted and economic transportation of hydrocarbons.[51]

According to Renewable Energy Minister Raj Kumar Singh, India has to set up a regional grid that will be leveraged to create a common electricity market for nations in India's neighbourhood. This proposed market would include Myanmar, Sri Lanka, Nepal, Bhutan and Bangladesh. While India has been procuring hydropower from Bhutan, it is also supplying electricity to Bangladesh and Nepal.[52]

---

50 Hydrocarbon Vision 2030 for North East Region at https://www.satp.org/satporgtp/countries/India/document/papers/visiondoc2030.pdf

51 Ibid

52 Utpal Bhaskar, 'In push for neighbourhood-first policy, India plans a common electricity market', *Live Mint*, 5 Mar 2020, https://www.livemint.com/

Another report identifies the potential that exists and highlights the various transmission lines that are being planned and implemented that hold great promise for a regional grid. A domestic grid project is underway: The North East Gas Grid project of Indradhanush Gas Grid Ltd (IGGL) with Viability Gap Funding (VGF) / Capital Grant at 60 per cent (Rs 5,559 crore) of the estimated cost of Rs 9,265 crore. This 1,656-km-long North East Gas Grid will connect all eight NE states.[53] This would complement the earlier comprehensive scheme of transmission, sub-transmission and distribution. Interstate transmission was implemented by the Powergrid Corporation of India at the cost of Rs 113.48 billion during 2015-16. The new lines being developed would connect the NER grid to the National Gas Grid.[54]

However, a recent study also points to the lack of energy demand in NER as well as the challenges involved in financing cross-regional energy infrastructure projects connecting NER with neighbouring economies. Even in a robust regional energy trade scenario, NER will play an important role as a transit corridor but its ability to buy power would be limited due to its low production facilities.[55]

---

53 Lok Sabha Unstarred Question No.196, North East Gas Pipeline Grid, 3 Feb 2020. Apart from North East Gas Grid Pipeline Project, several infrastructure projects have been taken up by oil and gas companies which inter-alia include gas pipeline, gas compressor stations, secondary tank farm project, refinery projects, petroleum product depots and LPG bottling plants

54 'Natural Gas Scenario', Ministry of Petroleum and Natural Gas. 17 Sep 2019 at http://petroleum.nic.in/natural-gas/about-natural-gas

55 Venkatachalam Anbumozhi, Ichiro Kutani & Bhupendra Kumar Singh, 'Energy Market Integration in Northeast Region of India: Efficiencies, Vulnerabilities and Strategic Implications for Asia', *Journal of Asian Economic Integration 2(1) 82–96, 2020*

Many of these projects are in the planning stage and the various other developmental projects will contribute to the growth and integration of NER. For now, the effort to provide electricity to the population within the region assumes priority. Regional grid plans are in place. The ongoing bilateral energy projects will need to be strengthened over time.

Conclusion

Many of the responses for greater generation of energy have stemmed out of available resources and ideas and methods relevant for the region. The attainment of energy self-reliance remains a major goal. While there are several Government schemes and projects to augment NER's energy capacity, it is increasingly becoming clear that the potential that exists will take time to be actualised. Questions have been raised about the cost effectiveness of these projects. There is no clarity as yet. For now, a few projects that are already underway, like the one in Tripura may be augmented to slightly greater capacities. Whether these projects will be able to deliver to the mainland or even the neighbouring states seems doubtful. Indeed for now, NER needs to increase its capacity to provide for its own population. Towards this goal, many of the schemes that are underway need to increase and find greater implementation and higher efficacy. Under the present circumstances, NER being a substantial contributor to the neighbourhood energy cooperation remains confined to the domain of ideas.

While there are several initiatives for development of industries in NER, policies and programmes are directed towards development of infrastructure, entrepreneurship skills, markets and flow of credit to entrepreneurs. Until they develop industries based on local resources, and industries in the medium and small-scale sectors, NER is still a long way from becoming a source of export for the Act East Policy. Indeed North Eastern Development Finance Corporation Ltd has undertaken techno-economic studies and resources mapping for the development of industries in the NER in sectors like medicinal and aromatic plants, agriculture, livestock and poultry development, tourism, software development, handloom and handicrafts and food processing.[56] Regional energy trade seems to be full of promise but until it gets off the ground, there is limited capacity for NER to become a robust partner in the Act East Policy. Hopefully, with the full implementation of the new reforms and new regulations, each state's capacity for energy absorption will be greater as the economy broadens its base. It has taken long, but hopefully a beginning has been made.

According to an article in the *Journal of Asian Economic Integration,* due to the geographical location of the neighbouring countries, energy exports will mainly be directed to the NER; however, as these exports will far exceed the NER's import requirements, most of the imported electricity will be sent to the rest of India and Bangladesh. As such, the NER will play an important role as a transit corridor.[57]

Due to high costs and the necessary multiplicity of projects as well as human capacity constraints, a sequenced approach based on priorities is required. However, financing cross-

---

56 PIB, Industrial Development in North-Eastern Region, Ministry for Development of North-East Region (28-July, 2016 16:21 IST) at https://pib.gov.in/newsite/mberel.aspx?relid=147899

57 Venkatachalam *et al,* op cit

regional energy infrastructure projects—connecting NER with neighbouring economies—would remain a challenge. There are sizeable economic, environmental and social benefits to be gained from greater energy connectivity among NER and its neighbouring economies. To close coordination gaps among the NER states, its South Asian neighbours and ASEAN, it may be necessary to retool existing institutions and create new ones to facilitate cross-border energy trade and economic links. The cost vulnerability and carbon reduction analysis also suggest that the benefits of greater energy market integration far outweigh the costs, especially since they will spread the benefits of economic development to isolated areas of the NER. This will likely require cooperation among the NER states in implementing coordinated energy and economic sector policy reforms.[58] The energy expansion plans for domestic consumption is essential but to rush to try and put the Northeast on the international regional grid map till the other ground logistics are worked out seems unnecessarily ahead of times.

58 Ibid

Tenuous Political Stability

We are constantly working to improve the ease of living of people of Assam and the Northeast

—Narendra Modi, 2019

THE NORTHEAST Region is not new to either political turmoil or economic backwardness. While many of the states have now settled into a stable political order, there remain pockets of violence and ongoing struggle. Many political settlements and regional peaceful conditions have emanated from negotiations and agreements between regional stakeholders and the government. The fault lines in the region remain. While much has been achieved in terms of establishing a stable political order, it still remains a work in progress given the complexities that abound.

What is new is that NER has now been discovered for what it has to offer, moving away from the past narratives. There has been a distinct shift in the narrated perspective about the region in the decade starting 2010.

Once characterised as remote, the region has become a vital land bridge between South Asia and South East Asia, the two regions that the Indian government is deeply engaging with in recent times. As has been discussed earlier, NER now assumes a pivotal role and position for many of India's new foreign policy overtures. Whether Neighbourhood First or Act East Policy (AEP), many of Indian policies undertaken in the past decade have introduced a new relevance to the region. Inevitably, development trajectories and economic growth are necessarily incumbent on political stability and diffusion of internal turmoil.

While most of the large political issues have been settled within the region, a few outstanding issues remain. The demand for Greater Nagaland and the activities of National Socialist Council of Nagaland continue to fester, although apparently at manageable levels. In November 2019, an eleven-member delegation of the National Socialist Council of Nagaland, Isak-Muivah faction (NSCN-IM) held a meeting with the chairman of the Ceasefire Monitoring Group (CFMG), Nagaland. The meeting that dwelt upon ceasefire monitoring and other ground rules is said to have ended positively, although details were not revealed. As per latest media reports, the talks are progressing well.

A few other minor irritants apart, there is credible peace and stability in most parts of NER. Gradually and incrementally, the region is moving away from the security-driven narrative towards a larger imperative for development, growth, progress and prosperity.

There is a concerted effort to position the region to join the Indian growth story—a process in which it was for a greater period of time largely uninvolved. There are growing expectations about NER, now poised for a bigger role and unprecedented dividends. Indeed, much of the developmental plan unpacked for the region is unprecedented and points to a new journey that NE states have embarked upon. For a region that was not even internally well connected and with minimal connectivity with the rest of India, this is now considered the key geographical and physical entity to link India with its neighbours. Hopefully, the large connectivity corridors and developmental plans underway are poised to take the region to another level of growth and prosperity. Not only is the domestic environment expected to undergo a change but its engagement with the neighbourhood is likely to alter drastically. As the projects and schemes unfold, India is leaving no stone unturned in ensuring that NE is part of the big picture in the Indian journey to bigger international recognition.

Some of the domestic policies undertaken in recent times have, however, been under scrutiny and have faced severe criticism both within NER and outside the borders too. Herein lies the dilemma.

The recent issue of National Register of Citizens (NRC) and Citizenship Amendment Act (CAA) has brought forth a sense of insecurity and restlessness that the region was trying to put behind (*See Annexure 1*). If Northeast is going to be positioned as a stake holder in the AEP, then the contradictory voices within India are certainly not supporting the case. This chapter will thus seek to examine political developments in contemporary times in NER. It will discuss the issues of NRC and CAA within the Northeastern context and assess how the internal dissonance impacts upon the foreign policy moves of India.

The last section will highlight how insiders view the

developments taking place around them. There appears a political fatigue in what would seem as a panacea for the region. The political journey of the region has left it with some complexities that often seem bewildering. One set of issues seem resolved and another raises its head. There appear no straitjacket solutions, and often those dealing with the region from a distance seem unable to fathom the way ahead. NE has its own political narrative that remains embroiled in the idea of space and identity and the political narrative.

This chapter revisits the question of ethnicity and migration in the present context of the debate about the NRC and CAA. The next section also highlights the mixed signals it seems to be sending to the neighbours. The last section also examines some of the writing from the region that questions the kind of development that is taking place and the cost and the consequences the region have to bear for that.

I

A brief journey into political developments

Ethnicity and Migration

While a linguistic criterion was adopted for the reorganisation of the rest of India, the reorganisation of the Northeast was guided by ethnicity. Even when administrative considerations might have worked in favour of maintaining the status quo, despite initial reservations, the Centre eventually conceded to the political demands of prominent ethnic groups. As discussed in the first chapter on Economic Potential, the Centre has adopted several economic measures for the development of the region and its integration with the Union. After Independence,

India sought to integrate the hill areas and the princely states of the Northeast into the Indian Union. The constitutional formula for managing the diversity of tribal identities, historical specificity of the hill areas and the need to assuage the fears of the hill communities were incorporated in the Sixth Schedule, that conferred local autonomy on the formerly excluded areas. As per BG Verghese:[1]

The Constituent Assembly felt that the checks and balance mechanism provided for the states of the Union was inadequate to meet the special needs of the Northeast. Hence, it provided additional safeguards including:

1. The creation of autonomous district councils to address social, economic and secondary criminal and civil issues;
2. Restrictions on Indian citizens to acquire properties in these district councils; and
3. The creation of tribal belts and blocs in the plains.[2]

The reawakening of the ethnic identity in the Northeast coincided with the modernisation process while the states' reorganisation witnessed politicisation of various ethnic groups. Despite the formation of separate states based on distinct ethnic and tribal identities, the region remains heterogeneous. Even at the micro level, there is lack of

1 BG Verghese, *India's Northeast Resurgent Ethnic Insurgency, Governance, Development,* Konark Publishers, New Delhi, 2nd edition 1997, p42

2 BP Singh, *The Problem of Change: A study of North-East India,* Oxford University Press, New Delhi, 1987, pp.21-22

homogeneity.[3] Ethnic differences, conflicts and oppression were neither new nor unusual in NER. They, however, were not central to the regional dynamics until after the departure of the British, when independent India sought to integrate the region with rest of the country. Ethnic history is often a product of political memories, myths and emotions and much of the inter-ethnic conflicts in the Northeast are rooted in such conflictual portrayals. Undoubtedly, much of the political developments in Northeast, from reorganisation to protracted violence, are intrinsically linked to the question of ethnicity. The ethnic debate is further compounded by tribal identities that provide a sense of belonging to the people.[4] One of the measures to address the outstanding issues was the formation of Autonomous Councils.

Autonomous Councils were primarily aimed at granting autonomy to various ethnic groups. Unfortunately, the ethnic group for whom such an arrangement is made often do not live exclusively in that particular area. For instance, the formation of Autonomous Council for Nagas excluded vast number of Nagas who lived outside the Council. When the Council was transformed into a separate state of Nagaland, the problem persisted, as sizeable numbers of Nagas live in areas outside the Naga homeland.

The story is the same for the Bodo Autonomous Council as large numbers of the Bodos live outside the autonomous area. This in turn led to the Bodo resurgence and the demand

---

3 Sreeradha Datta, *The Northeast Complexities and Determinants*, IDSA-Shipra, 2004, New Delhi. p23

4 Sreeradha Datta, Ibid, p27

for a separate Bodoland.[5] The land witnessed a new agreement in early 2020, carving out the Bodoland Territorial Region, a journey that began with an Autonomous Council in 2003.

This apart, the government has also been able to successfully resolve long outstanding ethnic issues including the one surrounding the settlement of the Bru-Reang people in Tripura. For 23 long years, more than 30,000 members of this community lived as refugees in relief camps there, having fled their homes in Mizoram in the wake of ethnic clashes. This latest agreement will now pave the way for the safe rehabilitation of those refugees in Tripura who wish to stay back and also provide for an enabling environment for those who desire to return to Mizoram.[6]

Usually, the ethnic linkages do not have a clear demarcation and often spill over into neighbouring states, thereby creating tension and conflictual situations. Manipur has a sizeable population of Nagas, Kukis and allied Mizo tribes. The formation of Nagaland and Mizoram states has generated a sense of affinity and loyalties of those clans to their ethnic community outside Manipur. This in turn has sharpened and intensified the internal divisions in Manipur, with rival ethnic communities forging linkages with Nagaland and Mizoram respectively and giving rise to one of the largest movements within the region.[7]

---

5 Anup Dutta, 'Modernisation and ethno-national identities: State-civil society conflict in North East India, in Phukonand Dutta E*d Politics of Identity and National Building*, 1997. South Asia Publishers, p18

6 Rajesh Singh, 'Game Changing Pacts for the North East', *VIF Commentary*, 3 Feb 2020 at https://www.vifindia.org/2020/february/03/game-changing-pacts-for-the-north-east

7 Anup Dutta, op cit, p28

The formation of a separate state of Nagaland and the Shillong Accord of 1975 brought waves of moderates into the political process. However, key Naga leaders such as Zapu Phizo and Thuingeland Muivah denounced the accord as a betrayal and vowed to continue the struggle. The formation of Nagaland and Mizoram states has generated a sense of affinity and loyalties of those clans to their ethnic community outside Manipur. This in turn has sharpened and intensified the internal divisions in Manipur with rival ethnic communities forging linkages with Nagaland and Mizoram respectively.[8]

The Naga National Council (NNC) formed in 1946 proclaimed independence on 14 August 1947, maintaining that the Nagas have never 'acceded' to India, and that they were not an Indian or sub-continental entity and started a war of independence with the active backing of Pakistan. Massive counter insurgency measures launched by the security forces failed to crush the insurgency, leading to a series of political concessions to the Nagas. At present, a ceasefire exists and a dialogue is underway. However, the continuation of the larger Nagaland demand and ground conditions necessitated declaring Nagaland a 'disturbed area' for six more months. The AFSPA Act empowers security forces to conduct operations anywhere and arrest anyone without any prior notice, for a period of six months with effect from 30 December 2019.[9] For obvious reasons, this an unpopular move that finds little support from the ground.

8 Ashok Kumar Roy, Constraints of nation building and ethnic autonomy: A Northeastern experience, in Girin Phukon and NL Dutta, *Ed. Politics of Identity and National Building in Northeast India*, New Delhi: South Asia Publishers, 1997, p71

9 Entire Nagaland Declared 'Disturbed' for 6 More Months Under AFSPA, T*he Wire* https://thewire.in/government/nagaland-afspa-disturbed

While the reawakening of the ethnic identity in NER coincided with the modernisation process, the states' reorganisation witnessed politicisation of various ethnic groups and the migratory impulses in the region have led to further complications. Beginning with British rule, the region has been witnessing regular and at times accelerated phase of economic migration. This influx from within and outside India and the demographic changes brought about by immigration are often the immediate source of conflict. The resentment over large-scale unchecked migration into the region, both from different parts of India as well as from Nepal and East Pakistan/Bangladesh were brewing much before the anti-foreigner outburst in the late 1970s.[10]

Most of the population in NER either have roots outside India or have migrated to the region from different parts of the Indian heartland. In the pre-British era, major population flows were from east of the region, from south-west China and upper Burma. During colonial rule, there was large-scale influx of Bengali-speaking people, followed by Nepalese and tribal people from central India. The British economic ventures absorbed Bengali clerks and officials and the central Indian tribal people and Bihari labourers were absorbed in tea gardens and oil fields. The Bengali migrants, particularly Muslim, farmers made substantial contribution to the agricultural development of Assam.[11] The Census of 1911 described these migrant farmers as 'hardy and prolific cultivators working

---

10 BG Verghese, op cit, p42

11 Sabari Bandopadhyay and Debesh Chakraborty, Migration to the Northeastern region and problems of security in Sanjukta Bhattacharya and Rochana Das Ed. *Perspectives on India's Northeast*, Calcutta: Bibhasa, 1998, pp.94-116.

their way northwards. These people are accustomed to the risk arising from deluvian and devastating floods which other cultivators are unwilling to face.'

Likewise, the 1931 Census reported: 'At first the local people did not accept them joyfully. But as they came to see their knowledge of agriculture, their contribution to the general prosperity of the district, the prejudices and dislikes are beginning to disappear.'[12] Clearly, while migrant labours may not have been necessarily welcomed but their usefulness was certainly seen and their services were utilised appropriately by the locals.

Initially, the settlement and development of the wasteland was considered a positive fallout of the migration but before long the influx began to undermine the economic interests of indigenous people. The new entrants created acute economic problems since mid-thirties as they began to settle down in forest land, particularly in the tribal areas. Increased population pressure on land aggravated the problem of landlessness among the indigenous people. Unplanned clearing of the forest aggravated the problem of soil erosion in the hills and consequent floods in the plains. Trade and commerce were monopolised by the more enterprising capital-owning migrants, who cornered modern professions in large numbers. The ensuing trouble was waiting to erupt. The demographic changes caused by migrant movements resulted in acute conflicts over language, education and employment policies, leading to the fear of being overwhelmed demographically, culturally and economically.

---

12 Sreeradha Datta, 'The Northeast Turmoil: Vital Determinants', *Strategic Analysis, 23(12) March 2008, pp2123-33*

The crises that developed in Assam from the 1950s alarmingly pointed to consequences of such developments.

The presence of a large number of migrants shook the foundation of the Assamese social structure and created a sons-of-the-soil solidarity among Assamese. The percentage of the Assamese-speaking population considerably declined while the share of the Bengali-speaking population has risen considerably. Cleavages also developed between the indigenous Assamese and tribal population. Soon after India's independence, with the apprehension of losing identity and culture in the hands of the Bengali migrants, Assamese language and anti-migrant movements germinated in the 1950s. This is what is commonly known as the Assam movement, and it became more convoluted in the early 1960s when the Bengalis and the other indigenous tribes started counter movements.

Consequently, in the 1970s, most of the peripheral hills separated from Assamese domination and this continued till 1980s. At the same time, mass movement against the migrants intensified in the 1980s with the rise of the All Assam Students' Union (AASU) backed by the Assam Gana Sangram Parishad (AGSP). Unfortunately, the Assam movement, which brought about a massive political mobilisation in the 1960s, became an opportunity for certain sections of the middle class Assamese society with radical leanings to take a militant turn.[13]

The lack of common ground often led to violent confrontation between various ethnic groups and many grew into militant outfits. Thus, the region was plunged into a

13 Komol Singha, 'Ethnicity-based movements and state's response in Assam', *Asian Ethnicity* (2017): 1469-2953

series of insurgency movements by militant outfits. Over the years, through a combination of military measures, political accommodation and understanding between the region and the rest of India, the region settled down to normalcy. Apart from the Naga SCN, the other militant outfits remain under a certain degree of limitations and the region incrementally moved towards a path of growth and development. But the introduction of National Register of Citizens (NRC) and Citizenship Amendment Act (CAA) plunged the region into series of protests and instability. PM had to cancel two visits to the region in wake of the protest and agitation that shook Assam.[14] As the situation unfolds, the region is thrown into disarray once again.

Close on the heels of Assam, the states of Tripura and Meghalaya have been caught up in the throes of NRC reaction. The following section would try and examine the NRC and why it has elicited such a strong reaction?

II

National Register of Citizens

What is the NRC? To explain briefly, it is essentially an official record of those who are legal Indian citizens. 'It includes demographic information about all those individuals who qualify as citizens of India as per the Citizenship Act, 1955. The register was first prepared after the 1951 Census of India

14 PM plans to inaugurate the youth games called *Khelo India* in Guwahati January 10 2020 was cancelled as was the summit with Japanese Prime Minister Shinzo Abe scheduled for Dec 2019.

and since then it has not been updated until recently' when the recent process was initiated.[15]

The citizen of India is defined, identified, verified and distinguished from infiltrators under a set of three laws; the Citizenship Act of 1955 (amended many times; the latest version emerged in the recent winter session of Parliament 2019), the Foreigners Act of 1946 and the Passport Act of 1920.[16]

As per the protocol, the NRC registers were kept in the offices of the deputy commissioners and sub-divisional officers.[17] It contained the names of all genuine Indian citizens and recorded relevant information of those included which would subsequently help detect non-citizens. Maintained by the Registrar General of India, it was meant to be updated every decade. Assam is the first state in India to update the NRC since 1951.[18] The pilot projects for updating the NRC started in two blocks (in Kamrup and Barpeta districts) in June 2010 but were stopped the following month because of law-and-order problems.

In July 2011, the state government set up a cabinet sub-committee to simplify the procedure. In May 2013, the apex court directed the Centre to finalise the modalities by 16 July

15 'What is NRC: All you need to know about National Register of Citizens ', *India Today*, 18 Dec 2019 at https://www.indiatoday.in/india/story/what-is-nrc-all-you-need-to-know-about-national-register-of-citizens-1629195-2019-12-18

16 Prabhash K Dutta , 'CAA NRC Confusion Explained', *India Today* December 26, 2019https://www.indiatoday.in/news-analysis/story/caa-npr-nrc-confusion-connection-explained-india-1631534-2019-12-26

17 Everything you wanted to know about NRC, *The Telegraph*, 30 July 2018 at https://www.telegraphindia.com/india/everything-you-want-to-know-about-the-nrc/cid/1352646

18 Pranjit Agarwala. 'The Mess in Assam NRC', *Organiser*, 18 Sep 2019 at https://www.organiser.org//Encyc/2019/9/18/The-Mess-in-Assam-NRC-.html

2013.[19] In 2014, the Supreme Court directed the government to resume updating the NRC and monitored the process too

The NRC List

Preparation of this list took seven years involving 50,000 people and costing close to Rs 1.5 billion was finally fraught with severe problems.[20] The name of all NRC applicants was published on 31 August 2019. The list included names of all the 3.30 crore applicants as per draft NRC and a supplementary list of inclusions and exclusions (final NRC). More than 19 lakh people were left out from the final NRC published list. They could of course appeal before the foreigners' tribunals.[21] According to the Central Government guidelines, these excluded people who can approach one of the 400 foreigners' tribunals and appeal against their exclusions within 120 days of the publication of the final list. The tribunals set up the government would hear their appeals as well as issue certificates to the excluded people and explained why they were not included in the final list of NRC. And if that process was not fruitful, then the individual could approach the High Court and eventually the Supreme Court.

Undoubtedly, for those excluded from the list, they are confronted with a situation that is fraught with fear and worry

---

19 'Everything you wanted to know about NRC', *The Telegraph, 30 July 2018 at* https://www.telegraphindia.com/india/everything-you-want-to-know-about-the-nrc/cid/1352646

20 Sanjoy Hazarika, 'Indian Citizenship question and the never ending Assam Imbroglio', *Al Jazeera,* 15 Sept 2019 at https://www.aljazeera.com/indepth/opinion/india-citizenship-question-assam-imbroglio-190914153846262.html

21 A total of 19,06,657 people have been excluded from the total of 3,30,27,661 applicants. Thus 5.77% of the applicants have been left out in a long process that was undertaken from February 2015 under the direct supervision of the Supreme Court of India.

about the uncertainties ahead. Not only because they had submitted whatever relevant papers were available with them, but also they were hardly equipped to handle the long- drawn and cumbersome procedural and legalities ahead. There are many instances where the anomalies seem glaring. A block with 21,700 households across 75 villages had at least one member whose name was not in the final published list.[22] More importantly, as many pointed out, while bona fide citizens were excluded, there was no clarity about how many illegal immigrants were identified in the exercise, which essentially asked every resident to prove their Indian citizenship.[23]

The proponents of the NRC found the 'opposition to National Register of Citizens is stupefying'. Which country, with some semblance of order, doesn't have a citizen's register in one form or the other? As they argued, yes, there are migrants in large number of countries, but do they get same rights as the local populace?[24] This very factor, indeed, has been the centre of past movements in Assam, as mentioned earlier. But the controversy is rooted in larger questions that are difficult to dismiss. Clearly this list will have far-reaching implications for a very large number of people. Ironically, Hazarika raises the question: Did the NRC serve the purpose it was meant for? He asks whether

---

22 Rahul Karmakar, 'Fear of statelessness haunts thousands rejected by NRC in Assam', *The Hindu,* 16 March 2020 at https://www.thehindu.com/news/national/other-states/fear-of-statelessness-haunts-thousands-rejected-by-nrc-in-assam/article31077342.ece

23 Prabhash K Dutta , 'CAA NRC Confusion Explained', *India Today* , 26 December 2019, at https://www.indiatoday.in/news-analysis/story/caa-npr-nrc-confusion-connection-explained-india-1631534-2019-12-26

24 Ratan Sharda, 'NRC Exposes Duplicity of Self Proclaimed Liberals', *Organiser* 01-Sep-2019 at https://www.organiser.org//Encyc/2019/9/1/NRC-exposes duplicity of self-proclaimed liberal.html

this extensive process was able to identify the settlers who had crossed borders into India and settled and live a life quietly.[25] There are as yet no adequate replies to these queries.

The intense outbursts pointed to the region with a point of view that seems at variance with Delhi's view. Political scientist from the region Deka, in fact, raises the point that before one attempts to find out 'who qualifies to be a citizen of India, there was another difficult question to be understood in Assam, about who is an Assamese?'[26] He reiterates, 'NRC is born out of a complex history and it gives rise to a set of complex questions and cannot be fit into the ideological straitjacket or ready-to-serve linear narratives'.[27] As the political narrative on both sides of the argument kept getting sharper, the possibility of finding a common middle ground became increasingly distant.

Similarly, expressing dissatisfaction about the inaccurate exercise, a technocrat from the region Subimal Bhattacharya says this NRC list was meant to be carried out as per an agreed premise, decided with the signing of the Assam Accord in 1985. He regrets that the government, having taken more than '30 years to actually do the exercise, that too under constant push of the SC and finally published a list to no one's satisfaction'. He further urges the government to work on an NRC list that is to the satisfaction of all concerned and so the next steps have to be diligently decided by the Union Government as

---

25 Sanjoy Hazarika, 'Indian Citizenship question and the never-ending Assam Imbroglio', *Al Jazeera,* 15 Sept 2019 at https://www.aljazeera.com/indepth/opinion/india-citizenship-question-assam-imbroglio-190914153846262.html

26 'Debates around NRC show the common thread of trauma that binds the people of Assam', *Scroll.in,* 3 Sep 2019 at https://scroll.in/article/936017/debates-around-nrc-show-the-common-thread-of-trauma-that-binds-the-people-of-assam

27 Ibid

well as Assam Government. While undertaking the whole exercise might not be feasible nor desired, he insists a correct list is crucial to gather public confidence after all the effort undertaken.[28] Ironically, as pointed out, this list that excluded 1.9 lakh includes 700,000 Muslims. The majority are Bengali Hindus, mostly those who would have come from Bangladesh, clearly not what was hoped for by the proponents of the NRC, the Bharatiya Janata Party, the Asom Gana Parishad and the Assam Students Union.[29] There was much confusion within Assam and the state government as well as within the Centre. Voices from the region point out how the agitation in Assam was largely a reaction to the perceived breach of this political commitment, given by the Government of India to Assam.

> At the base of this equation lies another cardinal political truth about Assam—that language has historically trumped religion as a primary marker of identity. This foundation quickly lapses into the argument that with the 'acceptance' of Bengali Hindu migrants, there appears a real possibility that the Assamese speakers and the other 'indigenous' communities will be turned into absolute minorities, linguistically and politically.[30]

The Ensuing Contradiction

Given the problems existing in the published list and how certain sections viewed the NRC, there was no scope for tempers

---

28 Subimal Bhattacharjee, 'Make NRC Exercise More Meaningful' 9 Sep 2019 at https://www.organiser.org//Encyc/2019/9/9/Make-NRC-Exercise-More-Meaningful-.html

29 Sanjoy Hazarika, op cit

30 Kaustubh Deka, Restiveness in Assam has come full circle with the Citizenship Amendment Act Updated 20 December 2019 https://indianexpress.com/article/opinion/columns/assam-citizenship-protest-nrc-1971-accord-6175661/

to cool down given the flip-flops within the Government. The contradictory statements by political leaders did not offer much assurance to the people of Assam, nor to others. While the Home Minster reiterated the Government plan to implement the NRC in other states as well, the Prime Minister said otherwise. The confusion that ensued was not very promising for the stability ahead. The two strong proponents, the Home Minister and the Prime Minister, spoke at cross purposes. It seems that either there were limited discussions at the highest level about the coordinated plan and policy ahead or it was a deliberate attempt to confuse and confound on part of the political leaders.

Significantly, a week after the publication of the final list of the NRC, Home Minister Amit Shah visited Guwahati during 8-9 September 2019 to inaugurate and attend the 68th plenary session of the North East Council and emphasised that the Centre respects Article 371 and it will not touch the Article which grants special provisions to the Northeast.[31] He also addressed the fears raised by three chief ministers of Meghalaya, Mizoram and Nagaland about the impact of the Citizenship Amendment Bill (CAB) on Inner Line Permits, Article 371 provisions and Sixth Schedule areas provisions of the Constitution.[32] To recall his pre-election speech in April 2019 at West Bengal's Raigunj, he unequivocally stated, 'The BJP would introduce NRC across the country and grant

31 PIB 2-day 68th Plenary session of North Eastern Council held in Guwahati, 9 Sep 2019 at https://pib.gov.in/newsite/PrintRelease.aspx?relid=193089

32 Subimal Bhattachrya, 'Amit Shah and North East - Energising NEC and NEDA', *Organiser*, 19 Sep 2019 at https://www.organiser.org/Encyc/2019/9/19/Amit-Shah-and-North-East-energizing-NEC-and-NEDA.html

citizenship to each and every Hindu refugee in the country.'[33]

Indeed, after assuming office in the Government, he stood firm on his earlier position while replying to the debate on Citizenship Amendment Bill (CAB) in the Lok Sabha on 10 November 2019. Amit Shah mentioned that there would soon be a pan-India National Citizenship Register and all citizen of India will figure in the NRC list.[34] On 20 November, he further stated in the Rajya Sabha that there was no need to create a background for NRC, 'We are clear the NRC ought to be done for this country'.[35]

While addressing the inaugural joint session of the Parliament on 20 June 2019, President Ram Nath Kovind unequivocally said, 'Government has decided to implement the process of NRC on priority basis in areas affected by infiltration.'[36] However, On 20 December 2019, the PM stated that the government had never discussed anything about the NRC apart from the one in Assam. 'I want to tell the 130 crore people of India that ever since my government came to power in 2014...from then until now... there has been no discussion on NRC anywhere...we only had

---

33 'Infiltrators are termites, BJP will weed them out, says Amit Shah', *Indian Express*, 12 April 2019 https://www.newindianexpress.com/nation/2019/apr/12/shah-infiltrators-are-termites-bjp-will-weed-them-out-1963206.html

34 'NRC will be applicable to entire India: Amit Shah in Rajya Sabha', *Economic Times*, 10 Sep 2019 at https://economictimes.indiatimes.com/news/politics-and-nation/nrc-law-applicable-to-entire-india-amit-shah-in-rajya-sabha/videoshow/72140627.cms?from=mdr

35 'Centre plans NRC exercise all over the country: Amit Shah' , *The Hindu* 20 Sep 2019 at https://www.thehindu.com/news/national/nrc-process-to-be-carried-out-in-entire-country-says-amit-shah-in-rajya-sabha/article30027083.ece

36 Vijaita Singh, 'Nation needs NRC Centre tell Supreme Court', *The Hindu*, 18 March 2020. at https://www.thehindu.com/news/national/nation-needs-nrc-centre-tells-supreme-court/article31101913.ece

to implement it in Assam to follow Supreme Court directives'.[37] While that may be so, questions are being raised in the wake of the Ministry of Home Affairs filing an affidavit in the Supreme Court, in the same month, stating that preparation of the NRC is a 'necessary exercise for any sovereign country for mere identification of citizens from non-citizens.[38]

The Assam NRC experience has shown how large numbers of people were required to devote huge time and undergo procedural harassment. Worse, lakhs excluded from NRC are still running from pillar to post though they are proposed to be included under CAB.[39] Reflecting certainly the majority Indian thought, the author writes, 'The motto remains clear—Not a single genuine Indian name has to be excluded and at the same time not a single illegal immigrant included.[40] But the issue became further embroiled in controversy given the Citizenship Amendment Act (CAA) being passed on 12 December 2019. For the ruling party, it has been a long-time intention for the BJP-led Government to undo what they perceive as 'injustice of history.'

---

37 Kaustubh Deka, Why PM Modi chose to contradict Amit Shah's NRC vow *India Today,* 23 Dec 2019 https://www.indiatoday.in/mail-today/story/why-pm-modi-chose-to-contradict-amit-shah-on-nrc-1630689-2019-12-23

38 Vijaita Singh, 'Nation needs NRC, Centre tells Supreme Court', The Hindu, 18 March 2020 at https://www.thehindu.com/news/national/nation-needs-nrc-centre-tells-supreme-court/article3

39 Sudip Kar Purkayastha, 'NRC and CAB: The Complimentary Twins', *Organiser,* 6 Nov. 2019 at https://www.organiser.org//Encyc/2019/11/6/NRC-and-CAB-The-Complimentary-Twins.html

40 Subimal Bhattacharjee, 'Make NRC Exercise More Meaningful', *Organiser* 9 Sep 2019 at https://www.organiser.org//Encyc/2019/9/9/Make-NRC-Exercise-More-Meaningful-.html

Citizenship Amendment Act

As author Amarjeet Singh points out, it was during an election rally held in Assam in February 2014 that Modi had promised to accommodate Hindus from Bangladesh in India if the BJP won the elections. According to Modi, there are two types of immigrants from Bangladesh in Assam: the immigrants who are part of a 'political conspiracy' forming a crucial vote-bank; and others who are harassed in Bangladesh. He stated, 'Infiltrators and those who have come with political objectives' have to be sent back as they have not only taken away jobs of locals but have come with political designs in mind. He stated: 'We have a responsibility towards Hindus who are harassed and suffer in other countries. Where will they go? India is the only place for them.[41] He would repeat similar lines during 2019 pre-election phase in Silchar: 'Citizenship Bill is not for anyone's benefit, but a penance against injustice done in past; hope it will be passed soon in Parliament.'[42]

It was during the Atal Bihari Vajpayee government period that the amendment to the Citizenship Act of 1955, Section 14A, had been inserted. Section 14A relates to issue of national identity cards. According to Section 14A of the Citizenship Act, 'The Central Government may compulsorily register every citizen of India and issue a national identity card to him.' It further says, 'The Central Government may maintain

41 M Amarjeet Singh, 'Narendra Modi and Northeast India: development, insurgency and illegal migration', *Journal of Asian Public Policy*, (2016) 9:2, 112-127, p121

42 'Penance against injustice done in past,' says Narendra Modi', *Hindustan Times*, 5 Jan 2019 at https://www.hindustantimes.com/india-news/pm-narendra-modi-in-silchar-live-updates-pm-to-launch-projects-address-public-meetings-in-northeast/story-K2XPWSmHlJ0tcbunQn6kZK.html

a National Register of Indian Citizens and for that purpose establish a National Registration Authority. 'The current NPR exercise was set in motion after the Narendra Modi government decided to update the NPR originally created after the Census 2011'.[43] The Citizenship Amendment Bill was passed in the Lok Sabha with 311 votes in favour. As per the new provisions, amnesty is offered to non-Muslim illegal immigrants from three countries—Pakistan, Bangladesh and Afghanistan.

- This bill amends India's 64-year-old citizenship law, which used to prohibit illegal migrants from becoming Indian citizens. This bill expedites the path to Indian citizenship for members of six religious minority communities—Hindu, Sikh, Buddhist, Jain, Parsi and Christian—if they can prove that they are from Muslim-majority Pakistan, Afghanistan or Bangladesh.
- They will now only have to live or work in India for six years, instead of 11 years before becoming eligible to apply for citizenship.[44]

Journalist Swapan Dasgupta, explaining the government's position, opines:

> The law is primarily aimed at tying up loose ends of the partition in Eastern India. And the primary beneficiaries are Bengalis from Bangladesh who came after the 1971

43 'CAA, NPR and NRC : Confusion and connection explained', *India Today*, 26 Dec 2019

44 'Citizenship Amendment Act: Court refuses to put controversial law on hold', *BBC*, 22 Jan 2020 at https://www.bbc.com/news/world-asia-india-51203104

> war. The CAA has no power to take away anyone's citizenship. It has the power to grant and fast-track certain processes to those who are either legal refugees or illegal immigrants. Secondly, the linkage of CAA to a yet-to-be-designed form---the NRC (National Register of Citizens), which is meant for identifying who is a citizen and who is an illegal immigrant–is also unfortunate. The linkage is also taking place in the light of the NRC in Assam, which was Supreme Court monitored; and which turned out to be horribly flawed.[45]

According to the Government, this was necessary to offer sanctuary to people fleeing religious persecution in the neighbourhood, but critics argue that it will marginalise India's Muslim minority.[46] The fears dig deep. As Hazarika says, the amendment of the Citizenship Act would give citizenship rights to migrants from other religious communities apart from Muslims, adding to the fear of the small states about legalising a large part of their population 'of settlers, and would only deepen the fault lines that exists between the locals and outsiders'.[47]

As explained, the scepticism stems from 2004, when another citizenship Amendment Act had been passed—the Citizenship Amendment Bill 2003. According to the Section 14A of the Citizenship Act, 'The Central Government may

45 Abhishek Law, 'CAA &NRC: BJP underestimated Political Opposition, its Communications Could have been better, says Swapan Dasgupta', *Business Line* 20 Jan 2020 athttps://www.thehindubusinessline.com/news/caa-and-nrc-bjp-underestimated-potential-opposition-and-its-communication-could-have-been-better-says-swapan-dasgupta/article30565399.ece

46 Citizenship Amendment Act: Court refuses to put controversial law on hold 22 Jan 2020, https://www.bbc.com/news/world-asia-india-51203104

47 Sanjoy Hazarika, 'Indian Citizenship question…' op cit

compulsorily register every citizen of India and issue a national identity card to him.'[48] This partly explains why in most parts of India, NRC and CAA have been clubbed together as testaments of communal politics targeting the Muslims, not understanding the local and historical contexts to it, according to Kaustubh Deka.[49] Indeed, as events unfolded, and as state and Central Governments grappled with trying to defuse the tension, it was increasingly becoming clear that Assam and the other NE states view this issue through a different lens, not necessarily through those viewed by the Government.

Nobel laureate economists Abhijit Banerjee and Esther Duflo reminds that Assam sees the migrant issue as a problem irrespective of their religion.

> In all of this conversation about citizenship, it seems to take as given that immigrants are a problem. In Assam, this idea has been taken to its logical conclusion—all immigrants, irrespective of religion, are a problem. This is why the CAA is anathema there and the NRC was unpopular for not finding enough foreigners.[50]

48 Prabhash K Dutta , 'CAA, NPR and NRC: Confusion and connection explained', *India Today*, 26 Dec 2019 https://www.indiatoday.in/news-analysis/story/caa-npr-nrc-confusion-connection-explained-india-1631534-2019-12-26

49 Kaustubh Deka, 'We will give blood, but not our land': The Citizenship Amendment Act protests in the context of Northeast India', 20 Dec 2019 at https://in.boell.org/en/2019/12/20/we-will-give-blood-not-our-land-citizenship-amendment-act-protests-context-northeast

50 Abhijit Banerjee, Esther Duflo, 'CAA, NRC introduce meddlesome officialdom into a question as fundamental as citizenship', *Indian Express* 1 Jan 2020 at https://indianexpress.com/article/opinion/columns/citizenship-amendment-act-caa-protests-nrc-abhijit-banerjee-esther-duflo-6193735/

Others have also questioned the opacity of the Act.

- Does it mean that those undocumented immigrants in these areas shall not be allowed to apply for citizenship under the provisions of the CAA?
- Or that those immigrants who have been granted citizenship under the new law shall not be allowed to enter and/or settle in these areas?
- In any case, what will stop the same immigrants from applying for citizenship in other areas or parts of the country which are not under the Sixth Schedule or BEFR/ILP (/Inner Line Permit).
- And once they have been granted citizenship, what will stop them—and their next generations—from entering or settling in any part of India's Northeast? Such critical issues have been left unexplained.[51]

Further as pointed out by sociologists, even if the CAA is held to be Constitutional, the protests are justified and should continue. If the CAA is held by the Supreme Court to be unconstitutional, the NPR and NRC should still be objected to, since they are exercises that will be extremely detrimental especially to the poor and the marginalised. The CAA widens and expands the pool of persons who can claim to be citizens of India.[52] That by no account is something that Northeast or other regions of India are looking forward to.

---

51 'The CAA Widens the Gap Between the Nation and Its 'Unintegrated Region' , *The Wire* at https://thewire.in/rights/assam-anti-caa-protests

52 Mihir Desai, 'CAA–NRC–NPR and Its Discontents', *EPW*, 15 Feb 2020, Vol lV 7, p25

Indeed, the complications do not stop here. As pockets in India were erupting in protests, a fresh controversy erupted over the updating of the National Population Register (NPR). The NPR is a register of residents of India where the enumerator collects demographic and biometric data of individuals living at the place of enumeration for six months or more. The West Bengal and Kerala governments announced suspension of NPR work. It is being argued that while the NPR and NRC provide the data and procedure for determining the final list of citizens of India, those not in this list will be treated as foreigners or stateless persons without substantial rights. And now while presently all three of these orders are linked, even independent of each other, they are dangerous and need to be opposed.[53]

This seems to be a common refrain:, several NE states have seen protests and debates. Tripura refuses to accept CAA, as it does not want to legitimise more outsiders. According to former Tripura Pradesh Congress Committee president, Pradyot Kishore Manikya Deb Burman, 'After implementation of CAA, a sizeable number of people coming from foreign countries would get citizenship, but none of them could be resettled in our state.'[54] Meghalaya and others seem to be discussing ushering in of the ILP to keep away outsiders from entering their states in future. Even Sikkim witnessed protests. As seen from previous experience, ILP has never contributed to any growth of economy and while it is often used as a political tool, it has held back the states from opening up. The new development has brought forth

53 Ibid

54 'New Citizens Won't Be Allowed to Reside in State: Anti-CAA Protests Rage in Tripura', *The Wire* https://thewire.in/rights/anti-caa-protests-tripura-pradyot

a renewed demand for this rather restrictive ILP. The CAA has been opposed by other states too. Political groups within Sikkim also have voiced reservations and have demanded that the state be given exemptions on the lines of other NE states.[55]

As reported by *Washington Post*, in the bigger cities like New Delhi, Hyderabad, Aligarh and Lucknow, protesters have turned out to object to what they see as the 'anti-Muslim' nature of the legislation. Students have been at the forefront of the urban protests, along with academics, authors and activists. Muslims, who reside in many Indian cities in large numbers, have also joined in. These demonstrators argue that by excluding Muslims, the CAA violates the country's secular principles—and risks turning India into a majoritarian state. Many also cite concerns that the country's Muslim community already experiences political and socio-economic marginalisation. One noticeable pocket has been the area around Jamia Milia Islamia.[56] Inevitably, a certain section saw these developments as a BJP-led government targeting the community to further the Hindutva agenda of the BJP.[57] Economists Banerjee and Duflo also bring out the inherent contradictions that have added to the recent political quagmire in NER. According to them, 'The NRC presumes that this woman would be able

55 Nistula Hebbar, 'Lok Sabha passes Citizenship Bill amidst Opposition outcry ', *The Hindu*, 10 Dec 2019 at https://www.thehindu.com/news/national/lok-sabha-passes-citizenship-amendment-bill/article30260415.ece

56 Aditi Malik, Shivaji Mukherjee and Ajay Verghese, 'In India, thousands are protesting the new citizenship law: Here are 4 things to know'. *India Express*, 31 Dec 2019 at https://www.washingtonpost.com/politics/2019/12/31/india-thousands-are-protesting-new-citizenship-law-here-are-things-know/

57 Sanjoy Hazarika, 'India's citizenship question and the never-ending Assam imbroglio', *Al Jazeera*

to provide enough details about her life to establish her true citizenship status. And if she cannot, there is the CAA—for migrant Hindus, or for Sikhs and Christians, Buddhists and Jains. But not for Muslims.'[58]

While for a long time, political stability was in deficit in NER, there has been certain progress in past decades. But since the NRC list was published and other developments correspondingly occurred, the stability of NER is being questioned again.

III

Having examined the political developments relating to NRC and CAA, it is apparent that NER, which has seen sustained unrest over the outsider issues, will not settle down till the Centre is clear about how it wants to tackle the CAA and any such related legislation. It is important to understand that states that are in the throes of internal discord can hardly be expected to be engaged with and contribute to a process that needs stability to usher in productivity, amongst many other activities. Two broad issues seek consideration. Within the domestic ambit, given the history of perceived neglect and indifference, any new unfavourable policy pertaining to the region is likely to hold hostage the developmental trajectory. The preoccupations will be diverted to issues that when seen through the larger prism of the Indian growth story will seem irrelevant and inopportune. NER states need investments, sustained activities that would catapult

58 Abhijit Banerjee and Esther Duflo, 'CAA, NRC introduce meddlesome officialdom into a question as fundamental as citizenship, *Indian Express* 1 Jan 2020 at https://indianexpress.com/article/opinion/columns/citizenship-amendment-act-caa-protests-nrc-abhijit-banerjee-esther-duflo-6193735/

then to a national level and allow for a level playing field at various levels of economy and social and cultural sectors. Sectors like education, tourism, health, all will be unable to sustain the spurt it was recently seeing in some of the states, without internal support and commitment.

Secondly, in the foreign policy domain, it seems mixed signals are being sent to the neighbours. While India wants to deepen the engagement, it also wishes to throw out the many believed to have crossed over illegally to India seeking jobs and livelihood. While the official stance has been to dismiss the domestic developments as an internal issue, it is not unrealistic to imagine that neighbours are deeply concerned, if not directly affected by the various other contradictory strands that are emanating within India. Contemporary history is replete with evidence of interplay of domestic and international factors. In today's world, it is simplistic to assume domestic policies are isolated from foreign policy, as clearly the policy flows are multi-dimensional and interrelated.

Many editorials in the Dhaka media stand testimony to their negative reactions to the now infamous 'termite' remark about Bangladeshi migrants. That apart, the official reaction was not very encouraging. India tried to control the damage when Indian Foreign Secretary Harsh Vardhan Shringla met Bangladesh Prime Minister Sheikh Hasina in Dhaka to convince her that the unrest over the citizenship laws was 'temporary' and the CAA will have no impact on Bangladesh. Earlier, in January 2020, the Bangladesh Foreign Minister, AK Abdu Momen, Home Minister Asasuzzaman Khan did not participate in the already scheduled meetings in New Delhi. The Speaker of Bangladesh Parliament Shirin Sharmin

Chaudhary also cancelled her visit to India. And its officials also boycotted the meeting in January 2020. Dhaka expects New Delhi to understand the country's concerns about recent developments in India over the CAA and NRC in Assam.

Indeed, Indian domestic and foreign policies seem to be cancelling each other out, as seen in recent developments. While there is no doubt the neighbourhood is keen to engage with India, sending mixed signals will hardly result in any positive movement. Also, while the leadership at the highest levels may be convinced of Indian intentions, the common people see the situation through a diverse lens. To be effective, policies need coherence and ground support. The Centre and states need to work together for common goals.

Given the tenuous political stability that exists in the region, there are also a few apprehensions and wariness about the nature of developments that are taking place. Thus, even apart from the CAA and NRC issue, the developmental paradigm needs to be viewed through a different lens.

Beyond the Development Matrix

Undoubtedly, the formulation of the AEP has led to NER receiving greater attention not only from New Delhi but also from the immediate neighbours. The Centre's intentions are clear. 'The next decade will be known as the decade of the Northeast and the concept of Act East Policy given by the Prime Minister will go down as one of the most illustrious achievements of the present government.'[59] Such a belief has been premised on two

59 PIB, 'Northeast key to Act East', Dr Jitendra Singh, 8 Nov 2016 at https://pib.gov.in/newsite/PrintRelease.aspx?relid=153384

primary considerations. First, NER's assets need to be exploited and utilised and secondly, the region can be better explored if it is integrated with mainstream India and with the countries to its East. Perhaps so, but not before the region has grappled with many of the remaining residual issues. This includes how it reacts to many of the undergoing projects. While at one level, NER with its vast resources and endowments will be willing to partner the large projects planned and implemented by the Centre, the region's uneven relationship with the Centre tends to cast a shadow its full implementation. The region has a substantial presence of large numbers of indigenous tribes and their traditional societies and economies are organised differently. Much of the workforce belongs to the realm of the unorganised sector. This contributes to the complexities that are inherent to the region and continues to influence many of the social and economic factors.

The previous chapters have examined some of the core factors that would make the NE a core component as well as a stakeholder of the Act East Policy but also points to many gaps that exist in the schemes, policies and projects. While the region holds great promise for making its way to higher levels of growth, there is a need to go beyond just economics and statistics. Importantly, the prism to examine success and development in the region is not necessarily the conventional one. For NER, the calculations and indicators need to assimilate more factors beyond what sheer statistics reveal and needs to be understood beyond the number of trucks and cargo movement.

Unlike how prosperity is understood in modern India, NER has an ethos that cherishes old world values and ethos, while they have also embraced development and modernity. But it is not to be achieved at the cost of the other. The need to balance the region's growth cannot be understood through only monetary transactions, there are several other factors that provide terms of reference for guiding growth and development. The fragile ecological environment, which is an integral part of the region, the close-knit societal framework, individual faith and beliefs play a significant role not only for their livelihood patterns but also their interaction with the state. As political scientist Chatterjee argues:

> India's Look East Policy at its imaginative best would most likely vacillate between the conventional spatial idioms of geo-politics and a form of liberalism coexistent with the cartographic certainties of our times. It is not fundamentally opposed to the market conception of space espoused by the liberals, but it puts the claims of community prior to those of the market.[60]

Essentially, markers based on market revenue methods do not have a great fit in NER. The people's resistance to drastic change is instructive for policies to be successfully planned and implemented in this region.

It has been argued that given the low industry base and commercial activities, with many infrastructure projects in various stages of completion, their ability to fuel greater momentum or draw in investments will take time to fructify. Given that NE shares extensive borders with the neighbours, the expectations for it to be a critical stakeholder in the Centre's foreign policy in the neighbourhood does not bear out. The rush

60 Shibashis Chatterjee, 'Conceptions of Space in India's Look East Policy: Order Cooperation or Community?' *South Asian Survey*, 2007, 14: 65 p80

to bring out the region and put it in the forefront of cross-border relations may not necessarily bring about the most optimum results. Ground conditions of the region are difficult to ignore or bypass. The transformational changes which are planned may not be necessarily welcome across the region. Indeed, they often refresh the fissures that already exist. Importantly, is the region prepared to accept the changes brought in through the big projects and infrastructure developments? As Deka points out, the NE is 'a geopolitical and geocultural unit that requires micro-adjustments to India's macro-projections.'[61]

This, in fact, has been the bane of the Northeast region. Given the diversity, it is not possible to find a single voice that speaks for all. While Assam, with its geographic location and its other advantages is predominant in the region, it cannot be representative of the other states. Each of the other states in their varied levels of development have options and opportunities that are often not similar. Their expectations also do not necessarily converge with the plans the Centre has designed for them. Inevitably, the Centre's planning and imagining for the region is not surprising nor unexpected, more so with the continued financial support that each state requires. This has become a double-edged sword. The region that for a longish time has been in a state of flux, is now once again having to undergo some major readjustment with the large projects that the Centre has planned.

61 Kaustubh Deka, 'Debates around NRC show the common thread of trauma that binds the people of Assam', *Scroll.in* 3 Sep. 2019 at https://scroll.in/article/936017/debates-around-nrc-show-the-common-thread-of-trauma-that-binds-the-people-of-assam

While the opening up of the economy and cross-border economy will be a welcome move for the region, the AEP and Neighbourhood First, two of the milestone policies for the present Government, depends on NE also being on board. The Centre's interest in the region is evident. In 2019, during his pre-election visits to NER, Modi had mentioned that Delhi was now closer to the Northeastern region. He had undertaken fourteen official visits to the region and almost an equal number as a party leader to campaign during the Assembly elections in Assam, Manipur, Tripura, Meghalaya and Nagaland. This has also led to greater familiarity and association with many planned projects and schemes. The number of BJP-led or coalition governments that are in NE now, also bears that out.

But can the Northeast partner the Act East dream? Or will it be confined to providing transit and become a physical gateway without having substantial role in ensuring India's AEP deepens through various sectoral ties?

The inherent complexities remain. As also pertinently brought out by Chatterjee, it seems that the Indian government wants the 'best-of-all' kind of an approach, resulting in uneasy compromises, awkward bottlenecks and policy indecisions. This trend is expected to continue till there is a conscious articulation of the underlying conceptual map to guide India's AEP to its desired destination.[62] The guideline for the Centre has been to close the physical gap and provide a bridge for the region to connect with its conjoined region as well as mainland India. But it also needs to ensure that NER understands and appreciates its goals and ambitions. However, as the previous

62 Shibashis Chatterjee, 'Conceptions of Space...' op cit p79

chapters have highlighted, given the level of development in the present phase, for the developmental projects to fructify and bring about not only substantial dividends to NER but also make it a significant partner in the AEP will take time and much greater effort, than what appears visible at present.

Notedly, notwithstanding the political rhetoric, the fatigue and indifference of NER about spurt in connectivity and physical infrastructure is well brought out through this passage by political scientist Kausubh Deka:

> Instrumental to understanding how the local population perceives the Act East road near my house that is now tarred with the rubber of burnt tyres, ringing with the uneasy silence of curfew and patrolled by army trucks, still bears the sign, 'Asian Highway 1'. People look at it and wonder what sense notions like the 'Act East' policy make when one is beneath the military boots? I thought of taking a picture of it recently to send it to a friend abroad, only to realise that internet services had been suspended. Perhaps 'normalcy' will be restored in a few more days, but by then, India would have taken a few strides backwards when it comes to acquiring the good faith of smaller 'nationalities' within the larger design of the nation-state.[63]

Sustaining of political stability runs beyond the negotiated settlement and reorganisation of the administration. While issues of governance remain fraught with gaps, people's unmet

63 Kaustubh Deka, 'Restiveness in Assam has come full circle with the Citizenship Amendment Act', *Indian Express*, 20 December 2019 https://indianexpress.com/article/opinion/columns/assam-citizenship-protest-nrc-1971-accord-6175661/

aspirations, unremitted demand and resultant discontent and frustrations spill over to another round of conflictual relations and a damaging narrative. The past has shown how steady flow of funds into hands of local elites discouraged local initiatives and did not lead to any generation of employment and creation of resources. The past is replete with examples and lessons that the present journey should be able to take into cognition and act upon accordingly. Suffice to say, the jury remains out on that as yet.

Growing Cross-Border Linkages

We are developing North East as the gateway to South East Asia

—Narendra Modi, 2 November 2019, Bangkok

IN RECENT years, India and many of her South Asian neighbours have been enjoying sustained and steady economic growth, despite a global dip that has affected them. But despite economic progress, it has not coincided with expansion of regional or bilateral trade within South Asia. Indeed, for India as well as other countries in the region, bilateral trade agreements have been the practised norm over regional arrangements. Undoubtedly, the limited and near-stagnant bilateral trade India shares within South Asia has been in sharp contrast to the quantum leap in India's trade with China and the US over the past decade. For long, the neighbourhood was not politically or economically attractive for India. It is only recently that India's neighbourhood policies have been articulated and there appears a concerted effort to improve its ties within the region.

The Government has undertaken several thorough measures in recent years towards strengthening neighbourly ties. This of course coincided with the coming to power of the NDA Government in 2014. These measures range from political to economic and presently are in various stages of conception, planning and implementation of various infrastructural projects. One of the visible and immediate efforts has been in ensuring better connectivity. Lack of regional connectivity has been identified as one of the major constraints hindering regional growth and several studies point towards connectivity bringing important benefits.[1]

One of the cornerstones of Prime Minister Modi's foreign policy articulation has been that of developing a zone of peace and stability with friendly neighbours. The case for developing close, peaceful and cooperative ties with the neighbourhood has been made at various levels. In view of this, India has undertaken several measures in recent years towards strengthening neighbourly ties.[2]

India's NE shares 98 per cent of its border with Bangladesh, Myanmar, China and Bhutan. The eight NE states—Assam, Arunachal Pradesh, Manipur, Meghalaya, Mizoram, Nagaland, Sikkim and Tripura—share long borders with Bangladesh, Myanmar, China and Bhutan and are linked with mainland India only through the narrow 21-km corridor known as 'Chicken's Neck'. The borders with Myanmar and Bangladesh

---

1 Report 'Trade and Transport Facilitation in South Asia Systems in Transition', Vol I: Summary and Main Report, World Bank, 23 June 2008 Report No. 44061-SAS, Washington DC and Haruhiko Kuroda, 'Regional Economic Cooperation and Connectivity: Regional Infrastructure Development' at the UNESCAP Distinguished Persons Lecture, 11 November 2010, United Nations Conference Centre, Bangkok, Thailand, at http://www.adb.org/documents/speeches/2010/ms2010108.asp

2 Ibid

are the longest and largely open for trade and travel, unlike the border with China.[3] This area, geographically distinct and culturally varied, has had a tenuous physical link with rest of India. For long, the fear of transgression by inimical neighbours or non-state actors virtually held hostage the idea of opening up this region, especially in the strategic and security community.

Given their geography and location, the NE states played a critical part in India's role in the neighbourhood, more so in its eastern region. NER not only has a critical international strategic dimension but is also a vital part of the nation's defence architecture. It is India's land bridge between South Asia and South East Asia and also a region richly endowed with a variety of natural resources such as uranium, coal, hydro-power, forests, oil and gas. In view of the cross-border geographical contours and length of the international border India enjoys with its neighbours, especially Bangladesh and Myanmar, invariably any developments in NER have implications for these two neighbours and vice versa.

Under Neighbourhood First and Act East Policy, South Asian economies, especially of Bangladesh, Nepal, Bhutan, Sri Lanka, Maldives and South East Asia, especially Myanmar and Thailand, have seen greater engagement with India in recent times. There is a visible thrust in India towards improving the physical connectivity with two immediate eastern neighbours, namely Bangladesh and Myanmar, as also Nepal and Bhutan. Indo-Myanmar relations have seen a marked improvement in the past decade while the present Indo-Bangladeshi bonhomie is reminiscent of the Indira-Mujib friendship era—in fact, stronger.

---

3 Myanmar 1,640 km, Bangladesh 1,596 km, China 1,395 km

While political relations seem strong, economic relations have improved but show potential to grow much more. Indo-Myanmar bilateral trade has risen from $12 million in early 1980s to $100 million in the last decade. Indo-Bangladesh trade has also seen a gradual growth to nearly $4 billion. Both these bilateral trade figures fall far below the potential that was expected.

The next few sections will examine the Indo-ASEAN economic engagement as well as the cross-border economy and growing linkages with Bangladesh and Myanmar under the specific ambit of AEP. This section will examine the possibilities of how the Northeast economy and South East Asian economies can work closely, which ideally should be a core element in making NE critical to the AEP. It will highlight the various infrastructural projects that are underway and the nature of cross-border trade. Before examining the opportunities that will arise out of this new infrastructure development taking place on both sides of NE, it will be useful to enumerate the number of projects that are being planned, firstly in India and then between India and Bangladesh on one side and with Myanmar on other side. This chapter will also discuss the linkages with Nepal and Bhutan but more within the eastern regional framework, as although these two Himalayan neighbours lie very close to the NER, their direct cross-border linkages remain limited. The last section would examine the scope of regional integration through the Motor Vehicle Act signed by Bangladesh, Bhutan, India and Nepal as well as energy trade.

Engagement with ASEAN

As has been articulated by the Prime Minister and many other high-level leaders periodically, ASEAN is central to India's

Act East Policy. Evidently, the Indian engagement with the South East Asia economies and ASEAN has seen substantial growth just as it has strengthened ties with Bangladesh with the implementations of several of the foreign policy overtures during the past decade. Trade volume with ASEAN has been growing manifold over the past two decades through the Free Trade Agreement (FTA) with ASEAN and India has alongside deepened its bilateral ties with the South East Asian economies. A study by Punjab Haryana Delhi (PHD) Research Bureau under the aegis of PHD Chamber of Commerce and Industry has suggested that that India's bilateral trade with the ASEAN economies would double by 2025 to $300 billion from the current level of $142 billion (2018).[4]

As statistics reveal, India-ASEAN trade and investment relations have been growing steadily, with ASEAN being India's fourth largest trading partner. India's trade with ASEAN stands at $81.33 billion, which is approximately 10.6 per cent of India's overall trade. India's exports to ASEAN stand at 11.28 per cent of our total exports.[5]

Further, according to the report, India's merchandise exports to ASEAN economies were to the tune of $38 billion, imports at $59 billion and total trade at $97 billion in 2018-19. In the services segment, India's exports to ASEAN economies stand at $24 billion, imports at $21 billion and total trade at $45 billion in the recent times.[6]

---

4 'India-Asean bilateral trade may double by 2025 to $300 billion: Study', *Business Standard*, 12 November 2019

5 MEA, 'India-ASEAN Relations', August 2018 at https://mea.gov.in/aseanindia/20-years.htm. Accessed 20 April 2020.

6 Ibid

An Exim Bank study also identifies the nature of traded commodities. About 60 per cent of India's exports to the ASEAN region include products like mineral fuels, mineral oils and products of their distillation, bituminous substances, mineral waxes, ships and related structures, organic chemicals, meat, animal fodder, nuclear reactors, boilers, machinery and mechanical appliances and parts thereof.[7]

About 60 per cent of India's imports from ASEAN countries include mineral fuels, mineral oils and products of their distillation, bituminous substances, mineral waxes, edible oils and animal fat products, electrical machinery and equipment and parts thereof, sound recorders and reproducers, television image and sound recorders and reproducers and their parts, nuclear reactors, boilers, machinery and mechanical appliances and their parts.[8]

The PHD Industry report also identifies measures for boosting India-ASEAN dynamic trade and investment relations. This ranges from enhancing the facilitation to exporters, increase services trade, undertaking continuous review of the ASEAN-India agreement on trade in goods, harmonising and simplifying customs procedures, promoting greater private sector engagement and also supporting greater financial inclusion towards improving access to financial services.

Undoubtedly, for India an important element for enhancing economic relations between the two regions is through creating regional value chains and production networks. Towards this end, at the ASEAN-India Summit in 2015, a Project

7 'Strengthening ASEAN-India Partnership: Trends and Future Prospects', Export-Import Bank of India, January 2018

8 Ibid

Development Fund with a corpus of Rs 500 crore for catalysing Indian projects in Cambodia, Lao PDR, Myanmar and Vietnam (CLMV), was announced. Besides, the Ministry of Commerce and Industries has financed over 14 trade promotional events in ASEAN member-states at a cost of Rs 767 crore during the year 2016-17.[9] There have been several more such efforts to tap the investment and commerce potential.

Going ahead, trade and investment opportunities lie in sectors such as infrastructure and fintech, culture and tourism, IT/ITES and e-commerce, education and skill development, healthcare, pharmaceuticals, agriculture and food processing, among others.[10]

Apart from trade and services, India has been supporting ASEAN, especially CLMV countries under the initiatives for integration with ASEAN which include a whole range of services.[11] However, none of the services have much scope for contribution by NER. Tourism and people-to-people interaction can be implemented in the region much earlier than the other projects but it would still need many services to be in place and many of the last mile connections required for

9 ibid

10 'India-Asean bilateral trade may double', op cit

11 MEA, 'India-ASEAN Relations', August 2018 at https://mea.gov.in/aseanindia/20-years.htm. Accessed 20 April 2020. This includes projects on training in English Language for Law Enforcement Officers in CLMV countries and training of professionals dealing with capital markets in CLMV by National Institute of Securities Management Mumbai, scholarships for ASEAN students for higher education at Nalanda University, Training of ASEAN civil servants in drought management, disaster risk management, sustainable ground water management etc. In the people-to-people sector, India has been organising various programmes including training programmes for ASEAN diplomats, exchange of Parliamentarians, participation of ASEAN students in the National Children's Science Congress, ASEAN-India Network of Think Tanks, ASEAN-India Eminent Persons Lecture Series, ASEAN-India Students Exchange programme, ASEAN-India Media Exchange programme, etc.

greater efficiency that seem to always run into rough weather in India. India is improving the country's port infrastructure and improving air connectivity with Vietnam, Indonesia, Myanmar and the Philippines, launching a new maritime policy but this hardly also involves NER in any comprehensive way.

As articulated by PM Modi, making NER a gateway to Indo-ASEAN relations is core to the Act East Policy. There has been a concerted effort to tap huge potential, but the ground challenges evidently have not allowed significant growth to take place as yet in the region. A quick look at the nature of commodities traded and services provided clearly reveals the limited role for the NER presently in engaging with AEP. The region has not been able to attract any investments too. Political fluidity does not help.

Yet Japan's presence is noticeable and the multilateral banks—World Bank and Asian Development Bank—have invested in NER infrastructure. NER is neither self-sufficient nor can it develop production lines on large scale that would open avenues to export or import. Cross-value chains are being attempted but as yet, the results have been insignificant. Given the smaller size of the economy, demand is also limited within the region. There is potential to create value chains in textiles between India and a few ASEAN economies, as the latter import cotton yarn (an input used in manufacturing of textiles) from India. Creating a value chain in fibres is another area of possible collaboration between India and ASEAN as well as in bamboo, which has shown huge potential for exports. As suggested, these trans-boundary value chains can create bona fide cross-border movement of labour and goods. But much of that as yet remains in the realm of possibility. Tariff and non-tariff barriers have stymied many such trade opportunities.

It has also been pointed out that while Bhutan, Nepal and CLMV could undertake production and market integration with India and the North East Industrial Development Scheme (NEIDS), whose provisions would provide them a first ladder of opportunity. However, commercial banks are unwilling to provide loans to Indian entrepreneurs in the absence of acceptable collateral. Goods produced with foreign investment also have difficulty getting access to 'green channels' in the ASEAN market.[12]

Several studies point towards potential for greater robust economic ties with both Bangladesh and Myanmar. Indeed, regional transport corridors have been argued to be a primary determinant of greater economic linkages. Improved regional connectivity facilitates the flow of goods and factors across borders which enables countries to benefit from a better relocation of resources. Further, transportation networks linking neighbouring countries enlarge market size and help national economies to grow.[13] Substantial amount of trade within South Asia is land based, adding to the cost, increasing the time factor as well as raising the probability of loss and damage.[14] India's initiation of border infrastructure development, with its neighbours Nepal, Myanmar and Bangladesh assumes greater relevance

12 Sujan Ghosh, 'Is the Indian Government Impeding Infrastructure Development in the Northeast', *EPW,* Vol. 54, Issue 17, 27 April 2019

13 Biswa N. Bhattacharya and Prabir De, 'Restoring the Asian Silk Route: Toward an Integrated Asia,' *ADBI Working Paper Series*, No. 140 June 2009, Asian Development Bank Institute, Japan

14 World Bank Report, op cit

in the backdrop of the bilateral and regional agreements that India has signed with them. The Indian government's attempt has been to showcase how 'the North East of India has bountiful opportunities for investment in development of various sectors mentioned above. With proper focus and investment, it can truly become the centre of gravity for India's Act East'.[15] While this would be the goal, given the ground conditions, the region is yet a long way away from participating in the commercial activity that takes place between India and South East Asia. The India-Myanmar-Thailand road corridor once fully functional will open windows of opportunity to the NER to engage in the South East Asian economics.

Connectivity Across Borders

A popular narrative surrounding the decision to facilitate border trade and connectivity is about its scope to not only lead to greater economic ties within NER, but also to bring about economic engagement within NER. For long, the NE has been typified as an economically backward, insurgency-infested region, unable to keep pace with the growth and development visible in other parts of India. Its geographic isolation compounds the problem of developmental gaps. This is also largely applicable to Bangladesh's eastern border and Myanmar's western borders.

Indeed, over the past years, several attempts have been initiated to draw this region out of its seclusion and the 'Look East Policy'

15 Ram Madhav, North East India: The Centre of Gravity in 'Act East' Policy *Open* Magazine, 20 July 2018 https://openthemagazine.com/columns/guest-column/north-east-india-the-centre-of-gravity-in-act-east-policy/

of 1992 launched by then prime minister PV Narasimha Rao aimed to usher in development in the Northeast by connecting it with South East Asia. A report 'Transforming the North-East: High Level Commission Report' prepared by the Planning Commission (March 1997) fleshed out the details in this study and outlined the contours India would pursue to engage with South East Asia.[16] While implementation of the Look East Policy did increase substantially India's engagement with South East economies and ASEAN engagement in the following decade, NER remained outside the ambit of the growing ties.

Post 2014 with the coming of the Modi-led NDA Government, the reformulation of this to Act East Policy essentially aimed at involving NER in India's outreach to its South East Asian neighbourhood. Complementing the 'Neighbourhood First' policy, outreach to the neighbourhood received greater attention. Exchange of visits, meetings, MoUs led to a flurry of bilateral activities with the neighbours; with India's focus on developing border infrastructure, NER involvement was inevitable. Modi's return in early 2019 meant further consolidation of the ongoing and unfinished programmes and projects which were initiated during the first term of his government. As envisaged, Modi's second term will provide greater scope and an enabling environment to work towards the larger regional goal that India is so keen to establish.

Clearly, India is keen to engage with the neighbours through a regional forum and regional organisations of BIMSTEC; sub-regional arrangements as well as regional trading arrangement

16 MN Karna, 'Conceptualising Social Change in Northeast India: Isolation and Integration', in C Joshua Thomas Ed. *Polity And Economy: Agenda For Contemporary North East India.* Bookwell Publication, 2005. p 111.

will be given greater thrust to make them more robust and deliver to the people the common goals of development, peace and prosperity.[17] Considering the above, the next few sections will examine the bilateral initiatives at the borders and how they have actualised the AEP.

Cross-Border Linkages

In the post 2014 period, the bilateral cooperative framework as well as scope for regionalism in India's extended neighbourhood grew substantially. Bilateral cross-border linkages with Bangladesh and Myanmar, two of India's eastern neighbours, are critical in making the AEP effective through the NER and this section discusses the linkages.

Bangladesh: New Trade Routes and Measures

Fragmented, insufficient transport networks due to historical, political and economic reasons and lack of cooperation among the member countries have been the bête noire for border trade in South Asia. In the past decade, India has been engaged in closing this gap but also building and creating infrastructural linkages for not only deepening trade and commerce but also people-to-people contact. Bangladesh received greater attention as there was convergence of several bilateral issues.

For long, India and Bangladesh have enjoyed air traffic. The major cities of India and Bangladesh are connected by both national and private carriers. On and off, there have been some changes in the number of flights and carriers. The

17 Sreeradha Datta, 'Modi's Second Term: Implementing the Neighbourhood First', *VIF Commentary*, 31 May 2019 at https://www.vifindia.org/article/2019/may/31/modi-s-second-term-implementing-the-neighbourhood-first

breakthrough in this sector came with Sheikh Hasina being voted to power in Bangladesh in December 2008.

Beginning with the Indo-Bangladesh Joint Communiqué signed in January 2010, the two neigbhours sought to engage closely. The importance of the communiqué has to be seen within the context of other developments that were taking place both on the bilateral front and within India's NER. Subsequent memoranda of understanding and agreements between the two sides added to the growing linkages. Beginning with the 2010 'Framework Agreement on Cooperation for Development', the Bangladesh PM's invitation to the Northeastern chief ministers to visit her country and finalise the modalities to further increase trade and connectivity ushered in a new era.[18] With cooperation in building roads, reviving railway links and increasing airport and coastal connectivity, India and Bangladesh unfolded a large cobweb of transport network between them. The two countries subsequently signed the Land Boundary Agreement and the neighbours were able to put aside this issue, that had plagued bilateral relations for long.[19] Over the years, India has extended three Lines of Credit (LoC), beginning from $1 billion in 2011; the next LoC of $2 billion was announced in 2015 and the third LoC of $4.5 billion in 2017. A substantial portion of these funds have been funnelled towards developing infrastructure in the field of railways, power, road transport, ICT, shipping,

18 Press Note, 'PM statement on eve of his departure to Bangladesh', MEA, 5 Sep 2011 at https://mea.gov.in/outoging-visit-detail.htm?411/PMs+statement+prior+to+his+departure+to+Bangladesh

19 For details read Sreeradha Datta, India Bangladesh Land Boundary Agreement: Follow up Concerns Need a Fair Approach, *ISAS Working Paper* No 219, Institute of South Asian Studies, Singapore 12 January 2016

health and technical education, energy trade, port development, connectivity (rail and road) and civil nuclear energy.[20]

Significantly, India and Bangladesh decided to open up their border to facilitate trade and commerce. For long, the majority of surface trade (about 70 per cent) between the two countries has taken place through the Benapole-Petrapole border in West Bengal. This is a highly congested Land Customs Station (LCS) with a road not broader than 5.5 metres. The alternative route has been through the NE states. Despite criss-crossing of over 54 rivers between India and Bangladesh, waterways have not been optimally utilised to further Indo-Bangladeshi trade. In view of this, the Indo-Bangladesh inland waterway treaty is now viewed as a critical component in Bangladesh's domestic transport.[21] Indeed, NER using the transit through Bangladesh could save 14-18 per cent of total transportation cost, approximately translating into Rs 300-400 crore.[22]

Inland Waterways

The inland waterways trade and transit between India and Bangladesh is regulated by the Protocol on Inland Water Transit and Trade (PIWTT) first signed in 1972. Subsequently, there has been extension of the PIWTT. The Protocol has been in force ever since it was agreed upon and is renewed regularly

20 Lok Sabha Question No. 2840, Infrastructure Development in Bhutan and Bangladesh', 10 July 2019 at https://www.mea.gov.in/lok- sabha.htm?dtl/31574/

21 Despite IWT being the cheapest and most environment-friendly option in Northeast, it is not been optimally used. Resource constraint and shoal formation in Brahmaputra has often been cited as a reason but that does not explain fully the underutilisation of this means of transport.

22 Report, 'Connectivity-led Development of Northeast India through BBIN Corridor', FICCI & AT Kearney, New Delhi 2017.

for periods of 2-3 years. At present, there are four routes under the PIWTT. Five Ports of Call have been identified in each country to provide facilities to the vessels of the other country engaged in inter-country trade. Vessels of either country plying under the Protocol are permitted to purchase fuels and essential stores at defined bunker points. [23] The routes will see expansion in the days ahead.

National Waterway One (NW-1) will connect the North East through the Indo-Bangla Protocol route. It will reduce the distance from about 1,700 km via Siliguri in north Bengal to about 500 km via Bangladesh. The issue of transit has assumed importance. Agartala is 1,650 km from Kolkata and 2,637 km from New Delhi via Guwahati, whereas the distance between the Tripura capital and Kolkata via Bangladesh is about 350 km. Flowing from this, India would be able use Mongla and Chattogram (formerly Chittagong) sea ports for movement of goods to and from India using both road and rail. From Tripura, the distance would be covered in 3-4 days via the Chattogram port through less than 100 km distance as against nearly 2,000 km away from Kolkata. And Bangladesh can also use the Haldia port for sending its cargo. Although this was agreed upon years ago, the final agreement was signed only in September 2018. This route will need dredging at an estimated cost of Rs 3,500 crore, to be shared 80:20 between India and Bangladesh. The 2018 agreement includes:[24]

23 High Commission of India, 'Connectivity', HCI, Dhaka, Accessed 15 April 2020

24 PIB, 'India and Bangladesh Sign Agreements for Enhancing Inland and Coastal Waterways Connectivity', 25 October 2018, https://pib.gov.in/newsite/PrintRelease.aspx?relid=184384

- Inclusion of Rupnarayan river (National Waterway-86) from Geonkhali to Kolaghat in the Protocol route and to declare Kolaghat in West Bengal as new Port of Call.
- Chilmari was agreed to as a Port of Call in Bangladesh. The new arrangement will facilitate movement of fly ash, cement and construction material from India to Bangladesh through IWT on Rupnarayan river.
- Badarpur on river Barak (NW-16) was declared as an Extended Port of Call of Karimganj in Assam and Ghorasal of Ashuganj in Bangladesh on reciprocal basis.
- The Indian side proposed extension of the Protocol routes from Kolkata upto Silchar in Assam.

For now, about 1.5 million metric tonne of traffic is transported via the Protocol routes per annum. Out of this about 1.495 mmt is inter-country trade cargo and about 0.005 mmt transit cargo. This cargo mainly comprises of cement, clinker and fly ash.[25] This is expected to increase substantially after the declaration of additional Ports of Call and extension of protocol routes. The NE states would get connected directly to the ports of Kolkata and Haldia in India and Mongla in Bangladesh through waterways which would facilitate cargo movement and would also reduce logistic costs. Apart from the wider movement of cargo and people, the declaration of river Barak as NW-16 by the Inland Waterways Authority of India and the navigational prospects of the Meghna river system have come into the limelight. According to economists Bipul Chatterjee and Veena Vidyadharan, the Meghna basin is fed by

25 High Commission of India, op cit

a number of rivers originating in the hills of Manipur, Mizoram, Nagaland and Tripura, and supports the lives of local riverine communities with its extensive system of wetlands, flood plains and fisheries. Inland navigation in these rivers would not only improve hinterland connectivity of this isolated landscape but would also integrate it with mainland India through the Bangladesh-India Protocol routes.[26]

In a first, fly ash has successfully reached Pandu Port in Assam via Bangladesh, through the longest distance IWT movement. The first load of fly ash reached Assam on 30 September 2018. About 1,235 of fly ash was transported from NTPC Kahalgaon to Pandu Port via Kolkata through National Waterways 1 and 2 via Indo Bangladesh Protocol (IBP) route. IWT was chosen to deliver fly ash to Assam due to the lack of railway facilities in NER.[27] Altogether 5.6 lakh tonne of cargo was moved through IWT in NER during 2017-18. To enhance access to NER through waterways, work has been initiated for awarding dredging along the two identified routes of Sirajganj-Daikhawa and Ashuganj-Zakiganj on the Indo-Bangladesh Protocol route.[28] The Indian government also provided support to the tune of Taka 10 crore to maintain the

26 Bipul Chatterjee and Veena Vidyadharan, 'Local Trade between India and Bangladesh', *Third Pole*, 24 July 2019 https://www.thethirdpole.net/en/2019/07/24/local-trade-between-india-and-bangladesh-in-the-meghna-basin/

27 First time ever! Longest inland water transport movement delivers fly ash successfully to Assam via Bangladesh *Financial Express*, October 6, 2018 https://www.financialexpress.com/economy/first-time-ever-longest-inland-water-transport-movement-delivers-fly-ash-successfully-to-assam-via-bangladesh/1339897/, Accessed 15 April 2020

28 PIB, 'Multi Modal Terminal on Ganga at Varanasi Nearing Completion', 20 July 2018 at http://www.pib.nic.in/PressReleaseIframePage.aspx?PRID=1539437, Accessed 15 April 2020

navigability of the IWT Protocol routes.[29]

Bangladesh and India are also discussing the option of using the PIWTT for operating cruise services and transporting passengers in addition to cargo. Both countries are keen to promote river cruise activities on inland waterways of the country by providing policy support and fiscal incentives for infrastructure and fleet augmentation (of inland tourism vessels) in a sustainable manner. One of the first agreements over river transportation signed between the two sides in November 2010 was over facilitating the transportation of heavy Indian equipment, including turbines for a power plant at Palatana, south Tripura. Indian cargo could move from West Bengal to Ashugang in Bangladesh's Brahmanbaria district through river way and then Ashuganj to Akhaura (49 km) by road.

Bangladesh waived off service fee for the multi-modal transit facility to India for this particular project, initially valid until June 2012. Ashuganj is now being considered as extended port of call between these two sides. Ironically, post the one-time offer when the Over Dimensional Cargo (ODC) was used to transport equipment for setting up the power plant at Palatana in Tripura, this has not been subsequently used. Although Bangladesh had subsequently agreed to India developing the port for future cargo movement and had even cleared local grounds, India made no moves to take on that offer although in principle it was agreed upon.[30]

The first trans-shipment cargo between India and Bangladesh was received at the Agartala (Tripura) Integrated

29 High Commission of India, 'Connectivity', op cit

30 Author's interview with Secretary, Sylhet Chambers of Commerce, Sylhet, May 2018

Check Post on 23 July 2020 morning. The Indo-Bangladesh Coastal Shipment agreement signed in 2018 led to the cargo movement on the first trial container ship from Kolkata on July 16. This cargo destined for Agartala travelled to Chattogram Port in Bangladesh to then be transported in trucks across Bangladesh to Agartala. The consignment of the trial movement included two container ships carrying TMT steel bars destined for West Tripura district and two containers carrying pulses destined for Karimganj, Assam.[31]

However, in recent times, there has been substantial progress in this sector. This coastal trans-shipment will complement the recent inland water protocol agreement signed between India Bangladesh on 20 May 2020 that was followed up by Tripura initiating the inland water Protocol route from the lower segment on the Gomati River between Sonamura (Siphajila, Tripura,) and Daudkandi (Comilla, Bangladesh). This route between Ashuganj river port in eastern Bangladesh and Sonamura in Sipahijala district of Tripura through rivers Gomati and Meghna will facilitate cargo movement between Tripura and Bangladesh through a short distance of 60 km.

Small boats and ferries capable of carrying 50 tonnes of goods are expected to run through this route as soon as the temporary jetty is ready within the next 3-4 months. This is certainly significant progress for bilateral trade, especially between Bangladesh and India's Northeast. Thus coastal and inland water transport along with road and railway will enable cost-effective

31 Tripura received the first trans-shipment cargo under India-Bangladesh Coastal Agreement, 2018, *Northeast Today*, 23 July 2020 at https://www.northeasttoday.in/2020/07/23/tripura-received-the-first-transshipment-cargo-under-india-bangladesh-costal-agreement-2018/

cargo movement, hopefully spurring robust bilateral and regional trade in the days ahead. The Northeast region along with West Bengal will in days ahead see cross-border transportations with the neighbours Bangladesh, Nepal and Bhutan.[32]

Additionally, India has invited Bangladesh to use its east coast ports—including Kolkata—for third country exim (export-import) cargo. The move has potential to reduce the coastal shipping rates between the two nations. India is discussing the possibility of giving Bangladesh access to the west coast ports off JNPT or Mundra, which can receive large mother vessels and are located a little over 2,000 km away from Dhaka.[33] The joint statement issued post the meeting with Prime Minister of Bangladesh Sheikh Hasina on 5 October 2019, also agreed to collect data for six transboundary rivers that originate in India's Tripura state—i.e. Manu, Muhuri, Khowai, Gumti, Dharla and Dudhkum—and to finalise an interim draft of a water sharing agreement on the Feni River. These are interlinked economically in areas like agricultural markets, fisheries and rubber trade.[34] In this same meeting (October 2019) Bangladesh had agreed

32 Sreeradha Datta, Is South Asia ready to develop a robust Regional Value Chain? *VIF, 23 July 2020 at* https://www.vifindia.org/article/2020/july/27/is-south-asia-ready-to-develop-a-robust-regional-value-chain

33 Pratim Ranjan Bose, 'Delhi mulls giving access to Dhaka to ports on west coast', *BusinessLine*, 19 July 2019 at https://www.thehindubusinessline.com/economy/logistics/delhi-mulls-giving-bangladesh-access-to-ports-on-west-coast/article28593841.ece Accessed 15 April 2020 India is building three ports as part of a strategy to attract trans-shipment traffic from Colombo or Klang. Among them is the proposed $4 bn Vizhinjam port by Adani Group. As construction of the three ports will take time, the Indian government is urging neighbouring countries to use the deep-draft port facilities on the west coast as part of plans to improve the country's attractiveness as a trans-shipment hub

34 High Commission of India, Brief on Bilateral Relations. HCI Dhaka, Accessed 15 April 2020

upon Indian withdrawal of 1.82 cubic feet per second (cusec) of water from the Feni river for a drinking water supply scheme for Sabroom town in Tripura.

There are more possibilities for greater utilisation of water resources. Journalist Pratim Ranjan Bose also suggests that ports such as Dhamra or Paradip can serve south-eastern Bangladesh better, if India provides the rail-connected trans-shipment facility. For example, India recently granted Nepal access to Vizag seaport for third-country imports as an efficient alternative to Kolkata river port. Both are controlled by the Government. However, the trade is barely benefited as costlier rail freight erodes the advantage of efficient port handling at Vizag.[35] Clearly, railway networks are equally important links to complete the trade routes and they have also received greater salience in the past few years.

Indeed, there has been disappointment about the low cargo movement and poor fees earned. Bangladesh recorded low earning of Tk 17,81,184 as trans-shipment fees for 9,277 tonne of cargos in fiscal year 2018-19 and Tk 4,66,339 for trans-shipment of 2,270 tonnes of goods in 2017-18. This was lower than the past two batches of cargo sent by India—a 7,297-tonne power plant in 2010-11 and 19,537 tonnes of rice in 2014-15 trans-shipped on the same route.[36] The report also pointed out that lack of cargo movement can be attributed to the 'long turnaround time ranging from 21 to 28 days, poor port facilities, transit-related procedural hassles and road and

---

35 Pratim Ranjan Bose, 'Time and Trade Wait for No One', *BusinessLine*, 3 April 2017

36 Shakhawat Hossain, 'Transshipment: Bangladesh gains little from India', *New Age*, 5 September 2019 http://www.newagebd.net/article/83610/transshipment-bangladesh-gains-little-from-india, Accessed 15 April 2020

rail transport through the Siliguri corridor as reasons for the limited use of the trans-shipment facility'.

Railways

Bilateral railway connections are also being revived and more routes are being planned. Indeed, of the sixteen projects that are included in the $800 million Line of Credit (LoC) to Bangladesh sanctioned by the Indian Government in 2010, thirteen are railway projects involving $687.4 million.[37] Similarly, Bangladesh Railway Minister Mujibul Haque Mujib during his November 2017 visit to Agartala announced a decision to restore twelve railway lines between India and Bangladesh that existed in the past.[38]

Prior to Partition of the sub-continent, the states of Assam and Tripura were connected to Bangladesh through rail lines that included Belonia-Feni, Karimganj-Chattogram, Mahishasan-Chattogram, Khowai-Akhaura via Balla and Amarpur to Bhairab Bazar. While West Bengal enjoys four operational inter-country railway links, with western Bangladesh—Petrapole-Benapole, Gede-Darshana, Radhikapur-Biral and Singhabad-Rohanpur—the NE has been able to establish one railway line between Akhaura (Bangladesh) and Agartala, Tripura (India).[39]

---

37 Booking of return tickets on Maitree Express likely soon, *Economic Times*, 18 September 2013 at https://economictimes.indiatimes.com/industry/transportation/railways/booking-of-return-tickets-in-maitree-express-likely-soon/articleshow/22719272.cms?from=mdr, Accessed 15 April 2020

38 High Commission of India, 'Connectivity', HCI, Dhaka at https://www.hcidhaka.gov.in/pages?id, Accessed 15 April 2020

39 Internal links, the 115-km Agartala-Sabroom railway line passes through four of the eight districts of Tripura -West Tripura, Sepahijala, Gomati and South Tripura. As of now, the 23.32-km Garjee-Belonia section, built at a cost of Rs 400 crore has been completed. It is part of the Rs 3,407-crore national railway project aiming to link southern Tripura's last border town (Sabroom), just 72 km from Chattogram port

The 15.054 km-long railway line, with a budget of Rs 972 crore, would have 5.46 km railway track on the Indian side with 6.57 km railway line on the Bangladeshi side. It was scheduled to be completed by 2020 after missing its 2018 deadline. This route will reduce journey time to ten hours from the present 31 hours between Agartala and Kolkata, with distance reduced to 550 km through this route. Thus, goods from Tripura which currently take the 1,645 km route to Kolkata Port through the 'Chicken's Neck' would travel only 400 km by crossing Bangladesh to reach Kolkata.

More importantly, this will provide a shorter route through Dhaka instead of Guwahati and will help in freight movement from the NE state, while goods from Chattogram port will reach Agartala quicker. Furthermore, the proposed railway station would be just 75 km from Chattogram Port and Akhaura is linked to the Dhaka-Chattogram rail route. The total project cost of Rs 972.52 crore is being borne by the Government of India with the Indian side being funded by the Ministry of Development of North Eastern Region (DoNER), while the MEA is financing it for the Bangladesh side. The higher cost is attributed to lavish planning on cargo and passenger terminals and high land acquisition costs in Tripura. To avoid land acquisition, the rail lines will pass through a 3.1-km viaduct.[40] Not only that, since there exists a functional ICP at Agartala with another railway custom facility, the viability has been questioned.[41] The inauguration of the commencement of work for the Agartala-Akhaura railway project was done in September

40 Pratim Ranjan Bose, Tripura's 972 cr railway line on wrong track, *BusinessLine,* 17 June 2018

41 Pratim Ranjan Bose, ibid

2018. This project was conceptualised in the year 2010 and then both sides signed a Memorandum of Understanding (MoU) on a couple of issues, including the railway project, in 2013.[42] This is now rescheduled for completion in 2021.

The second railway line proposed is the Belonia-Chattogram line[43] in south Tripura, now connected with Agartala through a 98-km broad gauge track Belonia-Sabroom via Jolaibari. Belonia will be connected to Feni, which will have the Maitraee Setu. This is under construction, having missed the initial deadline of June 2018.

India is building road and railway tracks that would provide direct access to Chattogram Port, thereby enabling the passage of goods and heavy machinery for the land-locked region. The port is 75 km from Sabroom. Belonia-Feni railway track was commissioned in 1929. There are eight railway stations on the Belonia-Feni route: Bondhua, Daulatpur, Anandapur, Pirbox, Munshir Haat, Notun Munshir Haat, Fulgazi, Parshuram and Belonia. Part of the Agartala-Sabroom route section, the Garjee-Belonia 23.3-km railway track connecting a remote corner of Tripura close to the Bangladesh border was inaugurated in February 2019.

In September 2018, India and Bangladesh also decided to revamp the Chilahati-Haldibari rail connectivity which would

42 Devangana Nag, 'Agartala-Akhaura railway project kicks off! This Indo-Bangla rail link will be an infra boost at the border, *Financial Express* , 11 September 2018 at https://www.financialexpress.com/infrastructure/railways/agartala-akhaura-railway-project-kicks-off-this-indo-bangla-rail-link-will-be-an-infra-boost-at-the-border/1309426/, Accessed 15 April 2020

43 Shilajit Kar Bhowmick, Bridge link to Chittagong transforms Tripura's Sabroom' *The Telegraph,* 16 February 2019 at https://www.telegraphindia.com/states/north-east/maitree-bridge-link-to-chittagong-could-transform-tripura-s-sabroom/cid/1684623, Accessed 15 April 2019

facilitate plying of freight and passenger trains from Bangladesh to Darjeeling via Siliguri. Bangladesh has undertaken a project to reconstruct over 7 km of rail track in bordering Chilahati district to connect Haldibari on Indian side with government financing. According to reports, Bangladesh government will spend Tk 80 crore for the rail project, while the Indian government will reconstruct 3 km rail track in its part to revive the British-era rail connectivity which was closed after the 1965 war. The entire project is expected to be completed by 2021. This rail route will provide land-locked NE states of India and Himalayan countries like Nepal and Bhutan direct access to the Mongla port in Khulna, which is the second busiest seaport in Bangladesh. [44]

India's assistance to build the second Bhairab Bridge and Titas Bridge will facilitate train movement between the main Chattogram-Dhaka trunk rail line. The Bhairab railway bridge will connect Ashuganj in Brahmanbaria district, on the border with Tripura. Bangladesh's nearly 1-km-long Bhairab Railway Bridge was built over the Meghna river at a cost of nearly \$75m, while the \$25m Titas bridge was constructed over the Titas river in the country's eastern region. It was also decided Bangladesh would be allowed to use the Rohanpur-Singaband broad gauge rail link for transit to Nepal. Towards this end, Bangladesh has plans to convert the Radhikapur-Birol line into broad gauge.

The two sides have also recently decided to facilitate plying of freight and passenger trains from Bangladesh to Darjeeling via Siliguri which was in operation earlier. Bangladesh Railway

44 'Project taken for direct train link with Darjeeling', *The Independent,* 18 September 2018, http://www.theindependentbd.com/post/166881, Accessed 15 April 2019

has taken a fresh project to construct over 7 km of new rail track in bordering Chilahati in Nilphamari district to connect Haldibari on the Indian side.[45]

West Bengal has two inter-country passenger trains. Maitree Express runs four days a week between Kolkata and Dhaka, and Bandhan Express operates between Kolkata in India and Khulna in Bangladesh. Two more cross-border rail routes through West Bengal, namely, Burimari to Changrabandha and Banglabandha to Siliguri, still remain non-operational.[46] It is now being proposed that the frequency be increased.

Out of railways routes in both India and Bangladesh established during the British times, at present there are four operational inter-country railway links and two more are proposed to be reopened. One new rail link between Akhaura (Bangladesh) and Agartala (India) is proposed to be built.

Besides, every February, a pilgrim special train is run from Rajbari (Bangladesh) to Midnapore (India) for pilgrims to attend the Urs Sharif at Midnapore. Anjuman-e-Quaderia, Bangladesh organises this special train.[47]

The four operational routes are:

- Gede (India)-Darsana (Bangladesh)
- Petrapol (India)-Benapol (Bangladesh)
- Singhabad (India)-Rohanpur (Bangladesh)

---

45 Earlier in the Inter-Governmental Railway Meeting (IGRM) held in New Delhi on 25-27 May 2015, both the governments have also decided to reopen the important Chilahati-Haldibari railway interchange.

46 Rupak Bhattacharya, 'Railway connectivity: Taking India-Bangladesh ties to new heights', *Northeast Now*, 13 December 2018 at https://nenow.in/neighbour/bangladesh/railway-connectivity-taking-india-bangladesh-ties-new-heights.html, Accessed 15 April 2020

47 HCI, Railway, Dhaka at https://www.hcidhaka.gov.in/

- Radhikapur (India)-Birol (Bangladesh).[48]

The operation of freight trains between the two countries is regulated by the Fundamental and Subsidiary Rules. Wagons of Indian Railways are used for freight traffic. About 2 mmt of cargo is moved by rail per annum, 99 per cent of the cargo moved by rail being Bangladesh imports from India. The major commodities are gypsum, stone, de-oiled cake, onions, sugar, maize and food grain.[49]

The trial run of the Kolkata-Dhaka container train through Sealdah, Naihati, Ranaghat and Gede in India and Darsana and Ishurdi in Bangladesh was conducted on 3 April 2018. Businessmen of the two countries had long been demanding container trains to make transportation of goods cheaper, faster and safer. Container trains are generally used to ferry machine parts, chemicals, automobiles and consumer durables. The road connections have been increased too. The first cross border train service for consumer goods has also been started recently in July 2020.

Upcoming Railway projects include:

1. Agartala-Akahaura 15.061 km railway line being built at a cost of Rs 967.85 crore.[50] India's Ministry of DoNER will be building 5 km and Bangladesh portion (10 km) was to be funded by Ministry of External Affairs.[51] This

48 http://loksabhaph.nic.in/Questions/QResult15.aspx?qref=63615&lsno=16, Accessed 15 April 2020

49 HCI, op cit

50 Lok Sabha Unstarred Question 2966, 16 Dec 2015 at http://loksabhaph.nic.in/Questions/QResult15.aspx?qref=27284&lsno=16

51 Lok Sabha Unstarred Question 2966, 16 Dec 2015 at http://loksabhaph.nic.in/Questions/QResult15.aspx?qref=27284&lsno=16, A, Accessed 15 April 2020

was scheduled to be operational by 2020.

2. Agartala-Sabroom (115 km) being built at cost of Rs 1,141.75 crore. The 38-km single broad gauge rail line between Belonia and Sabroom, last leg of 110-km Agartala-Sabroom railway line, completed its trial in August 2019.
3. Haldibari-Chilahati: Indian Railways sanctioned an amount of Rs 11 crore in addition to Rs 31 crore for Haldibari. The Bangladesh railway has reportedly sanctioned Rs 80.17 crore in order to develop infrastructure, including fresh rail tracks along 7.5 km on this section.[52] Nearly 95 per cent of the line was completed by January 2020.
4. India is also repairing the Kulaura-Shahbazpur section of Bangladesh Railways.[53]
5. While railway lines are in use now, the road connections remain but were always underutilised for a variety of reasons including rules and adverse conditions. However, a breakthrough has been possible with the first cross-border train movement of 50 containers of fast moving consumer goods and fabrics in July 2020. Earlier in the same month, for the first time a special parcel train transported dry chillies from Andhra

52 Devanjana Nag, 'Indian Railways to revive Siliguri-Sealdah route via Bangladesh? Train travel time to reduce to 7 hours', 11 Dec 2018 Financial Express, at https://www.financialexpress.com/infrastructure/railways/indian-railways-to-revive-siliguri-sealdah-route-via-bangladesh-train-travel-time-to-reduce-to-7-hours/1410499/, Accessed 15 April 2020

53 Tripura to supply additional 60 mw to Bangladesh, *Business Standard*, 4 March 2017 at https://www.business-standard.com/article/news-ians/tripura-to-supply-additional-60-mw-to-bangladesh-117030400306_1.html

Pradesh to Benapole in Bangladesh. Early August 2020, Bangladesh also received 10 railway broad gauge diesel locomotives from India. Given their competitive rates, trains will assume a larger role in Indo-Bangladeshi cargo and passenger movement too.

Roads

The Indo-Bangladesh border saw 85.64 km of roads being constructed during 2015-19. At the same time, road transport between the two neighbours improved during the same period. A trial run in November 2017 with a cargo vehicle carrying a car and some goods made the first successful trial run from Kolkata to Agartala through Bangladesh, reviving a route shut since Independence, and cutting the travel distance by a thousand kilometres. This is now in operation and has been effective towards reviving the truncated transportation that was so effective in the pre-1965 period. The operational bus services in the region include:

1. Dhaka-Kolkata Direct Bus Service operates six days a week.
2. Dhaka-Agartala Direct Bus Service operates six days a week.
3. Kolkata-Dhaka-Agartala Direct Bus Service operates six days a week.
4. Dhaka-Shillong-Guwahati direct bus service operates once a week. [54]

54 Details of bus services between India and Bangladesh, HCI, Dhaka at https://www.hcidhaka.gov.in/bus_services, accessed 15 April 2020.

India has commenced work on Maitree Setu (bridge) being built over Feni river, estimated at Rs 73-crore, which divides India and Bangladesh on the southernmost tip of Tripura. It is expected to transform Sabroom town into the largest transit hub in NER. This 150-metre bridge will connect Sabroom to Ramgarh in Bangladesh. Access to Chattogram Port will become easier. Linked to the transport linkages, bilateral energy trade has been one of the most important takeaways between the two neighbours.

Apart from several cross-border linkages both the neighbours are developing together, Bangladesh's development of the Khulna-Dhaka-Sylhet Economic Corridor and the Banglabandha-Dhaka-Chattogram-Cox Bazar Economic Corridor will promote industrial development in the region. This would also have an impact on the economy in India's NER. Closely linked to the issue of economy and infrastructure is the energy collaboration made possible between the two neighbours.

Energy

The agreement to facilitate the movement of ODC for construction of a power plant in Tripura through Ashugunj Port, as mentioned earlier, led to Bangladesh receiving its first 250 mw of power supply in 2013.

Apart from this, India and Bangladesh have been able to initiate a process of exchange of energy. In areas close to Bangladesh where India has surplus, it can send that power to Bangladesh while India will draw similar amount from Bangladesh in areas in India which suffer a deficit. In accordance with this, India and Bangladesh signed a deal for 35 years. Bangladesh Power Development Board (BPDB) will buy 500 mw power from different power plants of India and India will import it through the Power Grid Corporation of India (PGCI) regional transmission system. Energy cooperation benefits both countries and they were quick to get off to a great start. Tripura was in the forefront of this energy cooperation and through the Tripura Monarchak power project of North Eastern Electric Power Corporation Ltd is planning to increase its supply of 68 mw to 101 mw shortly.

Both sides further welcomed the steps being taken to augment supply of power through the Bheramara-Behrampur grid inter-connection from 500 mw to 1,000 mw. An agreement was signed between Numaligarh Refinery Ltd (NRL) and Bangladesh Petroleum Corporation (BPC) for construction of a pipeline from Siliguri to Parbatipur for supply of high-speed diesel to Bangladesh.[55]

India and Bangladesh also signed an agreement for peaceful uses of nuclear energy. Although there were several domestic concerns about the location of the nuclear power plant among Bangladesh's social activists, India has been able to make some progress in starting construction. Several other projects have been initiated, including the Maitre Super Thermal Power Project at Rampal, Bagerhat by Bangladesh-India Friendship Power Plant Company, which is also progressing well. Under this project, 1,320 mw power will be produced. Alongside, a solar power project at Rampal in two blocks is also under progress with a capacity of about 180 mw.

Subsequently, in 2016, Indian Oil Corporation Limited (IOCL) and Bangladesh Petroleum Corporation (BPC) agreed

55 MEA, Joint Declaration between Bangladesh and India during Visit of Prime Minister of India to Bangladesh- Notun Projonmo–Nayi Disha at https://mea.gov.in/bilateral-documents.htm?dtl/25346/Joint_ 7 June 2015, Accessed 15 April 2020

to set up an LPG terminal in Chattogram. This would make it possible not only for Bangladesh to receive gas but facilitate supply of liquefied petroleum gas (LPG) to NE states, including Tripura, thereby benefitting both the countries. Thus private enterprises like Adani and Reliance Groups have been engaged in bilateral cooperation in energy trade, a robust engagement that has been very beneficial to the two neighbours. [56]

Indo-Bangladesh Energy Projects

- Tripura Monarchak Power Project, managed by NEEPCO, supplies 160 mw power to Bangladesh since March 2017.
- Bheramara-Behrampur Grid: First cross-border interconnection between India and Bangladesh of 125-km transmission line, built at a cost of $158.60 million (Asian Development Bank).[57] This supplies 500 mw to Bangladesh.
- India and Bangladesh had formed a company—Bangladesh-India Friendship Power Company Ltd—to set up a coal-fired 1,320 mw (660X2 mw) capacity power plant at Rampal in the country's south-eastern coastal area.[58]

56 For details see, Joint Statement: India-Bangladesh Joint Statement during the State Visit of Prime Minister of Bangladesh to India 8 April 2017, at https://mea.gov.in/bilateral-documents.htm?dtl/28362/india++bangladesh+joint+statement+during+the+state+visit+of+prime+minister+of+bangladesh+to+india+april+8+2017, Accessed 15 April 2020

57 ADB, 'Bangladesh-India Electrical Grid Interconnection Project', https://www.adb.org/projects/44192-013/main#project-pds, Accessed 15 April 2020

58 'Tripura to supply additional 60 mw to Bangladesh', *Business Standard*, op cit

- The 130-km Bangladesh-India Friendship Pipeline will run from Siliguri to Parbatipur in Bangladesh. It will provide fuel from Assam's Numaligarh oil refinery to Bangladesh. The 125-km stretch of the pipeline is in Bangladesh, while the remaining 5-km stretch will be in India. India will provide Rs 303 crore funding while Bangladesh Petroleum Corporation (Bapex) will provide Tk 150 crore.[59]

Bangladesh India Friendship Power Company is building a plant with capacity of 1,320 mw at Rampal in Bagerhat district of Khulna division, Bangladesh. The cost of $1.49 billion is financed by India's Exim Bank.[60] This joint venture is also constructing an imported coal-based 2x660 mw Maitree Super Thermal Power Project.

Although delays in completion of projects have resulted in rise of building costs and other issues, each government has expressed its desire to complete the project and initiate a sub-regional trade agreement. While energy holds immense potential for regional development, the issue of common rivers can also be viewed through a similar perspective. India and Myanmar also share energy trade.

---

59 'PM Modi, Sheikh Hasina inaugurate India-Bangladesh oil pipeline construction', *India Today*, 19 Sep. 2018 at https://www.indiatoday.in/india/story/pm-modi-sheikh-hasina-inaugurate-india-bangladesh-oil-pipeline-construction-1343280-2018-09-19, Accessed 15 April 2020

60 Press Release, 'BIFPCL Signs Contract Agreement for Main Plant EPC (Turnkey) Package of 2x660 mw Maitree Super Thermal Power Project at Bangladesh', 14 July 2016 at, https://www.ntpc.co.in/en/media/press-releases/details/bifpcl-signs-contract-agreement-main-plant-epc-turnkey-package-2x660-mw-maitree-super-thermal-power, Accessed 15 April 2020

Myanmar

India shares a 1,600-km border with Myanmar along four of its NE states—Arunachal Pradesh, Nagaland, Manipur and Mizoram—as well as a maritime boundary in the Bay of Bengal. Indo-Myanmar relations have been in an upward trajectory. Bilateral trade rose from $12 million in the early eighties to $100 million in 2000 to reach $2.18 billion in 2016-17 but declined to $1.6 billion in 2017-18. This drop was attributed mainly to imposition of quantitative restrictions by India on import of beans and pulses. India is the fifth largest trading partner of Myanmar.[61]

Energy

To recall briefly, the proposed bilateral 1,200 mw Tamanthi hydro-electric power plant and 642 mw Shwezaye project on the Chindwin River, the largest tributary of the Irrawaddy river, Myanmar's key commercial waterway, stands cancelled. While Myanmar has hydro-electric power potential of 39,720 mw and an installed capacity of 747 mw, it also has the world's tenth largest natural gas reserves, estimated at over 90 trillion cubic feet in nineteen onshore and three major offshore fields. Myanmar has natural gas reserves of 89.722 trillion cubic feet (tcf), of which 18.012 tcf are proven recoverable reserves, or gas that can be easily extracted and tapped.[62]

India has an investment of $743.642 million by twenty-six Indian enterprises, mostly in the energy (oil and gas) sector in

---

61 India-Myanmar Bilateral Relations, Jan 2019, at https://mea.gov.in/Portal/ForeignRelation/India_Myanmar_Bilateral_Brief_Website_jan_2019.pdf Accessed 15 April 2020

62 'Myanmar Open for Business' at www.hfw.com/publications/client.../myanmar-open-for-business) Accessed 19 Feb 2013.

Myanmar. With Myanmar, the Numaligarh refinery in Assam is exploring commercial supplies of diesel and also exploring options to build diesel storage and distribution sector in Myanmar. The Indian Oil Company Ltd is also working with Myanmar companies in setting up LPG storage facilities and Petronet LNG Ltd (PLL) is working on setting up an LNG terminal there. Hydrocarbon Vision 2030 for North East India envisages a natural gas pipeline from Numaligarh towards Sittwe (in Myanmar) in different phases. It is hoped that this gas pipeline will lead to possibilities of gas exchange and grid connectivity.[63]

Currently, ONGC Videsh Ltd (OVL) and GAIL have invested in gas producing blocks in Myanmar. OVL also has stakes in exploratory blocks in Myanmar. Indian companies IOCL, NRL and HPCL are exporting petroleum products, lubricants and paraffin wax to Myanmar. The hydrocarbon engagement between the two sides has been steadily growing. Indian PSU companies have invested over $1 billion in the upstream and midstream sectors in Myanmar.[64] India has also shown interest to participate in midstream and downstream sectors in Myanmar, including setting up a refinery, storage, distribution and marketing of petroleum products in Myanmar, as well as extending proposals to assist Myanmar in training and capacity building in hydrocarbon sector.[65]

---

63 VIF/CII report, 'Assessing India's Connectivity with Its Neighbourhood', 2018 https://www.vifindia.org/sites/default/files/Assessing-India-s-Connectivity-With-its-Neighborhood.pdf Accessed on 15 April 2020

64 PIB, Shri Dharmendra Pradhan meets H.E. Union Minister for Construction, Electricity and Energy of Myanmar Oct 4 2018 at http://pib.nic.in/newsite/PrintRelease.aspx?relid=183948, Accessed 15 April 2020

65 PIB, ibid

Myanmar is considering opening up bids for its oil and gas blocks. The possibilities remain. At the moment, bilateral trade figures fall far below the potential that was expected. Several studies point towards potential for greater robust economic ties between these neighbours. Indeed, regional transport corridors have been argued to be a primary determinant of greater economic linkages. Improved regional connectivity facilitates the flow of goods and services across borders, which enables countries to benefit from a better reallocation of resources. Further, transportation networks linking neighbouring countries enlarge market size and help national economies to grow.[66]

India has extended development assistance to Myanmar on generous terms and our assistance portfolio is now over $1.75 billion. The bulk of the assistance is grant-funded. Projects include the Kaladan Multi-modal Transit Transport Project; the Trilateral Highway Project, which is an East-West corridor connecting our Northeast with Myanmar and Thailand: the Rih-Tiddim road.[67] In 2001, India built the 160-km Moreh-Tamu-Kalemyo-Kalewa (TKK) Friendship Road in Myanmar at a cost of Rs 90 crore.

India signed an MoU for construction of Rih-Tiddim road in December 2012, which would provide connectivity from Zokhawthar in Mizoram to Tedim in Myanmar. Zokhawthar

---

66 Biswa N Bhattacharyay and Prabir De, 'Restoring the Asian Silk Route: Toward an Integrated Asia,' *ADBI Working Paper Series*, No. 140 June 2009, Asian Development Bank Institute, 2009 ,Japan, Accessed 15 April 2020

67 India-Myanmar Bilateral Relations Jan 2019, at https://mea.gov.in/Portal/ForeignRelation/India_Myanmar_Bilateral_Brief_Website_jan_2019.pdf, Accessed 15 April 2020

is 225 km from Aizawl, capital of Mizoram. The Aizawl-Zokhawthar stretch is largely double-lane through highly mountainous terrain. India allocated $60 million for the project in 2012 but it was only on 11 May 2018 that the two sides signed the Land Border Crossing Agreement between India and Myanmar. This also ensured the simultaneous opening of international entry-exit checkpoints at the Tamu-Moreh and the Rihkhawdar-Zokhawthar border.

India and Myanmar also signed an MoU that would facilitate the respective private operators to launch a coordinated bus service between Imphal and Mandalay by 7 April 2020 but the Covid pandemic led to a lockdown.[68] A weekly bus service has begun operation.

Under the Border Region Development MoU, Government of India is extending $5 million micro development assistance every year for five years for projects on India-Myanmar border. Under the first year project plan, twenty-one schools, seventeen health centres and eight bridges are being built in Chin state and Naga Self Administered Zone of Myanmar. The first year projects are on the verge of completion and Government of Myanmar is in the process of selecting contractors to execute the second year projects. [69]

Although India inaugurated the Land Border Crossing between the two countries at Zokhawthar in August 2018

68 PIB, 'India-Myanmar Joint Statement during the State Visit of the President of Myanmar to India (February 26-29, 2020)' , 27-February-2020 at https://pib.gov.in/newsite/PrintRelease.aspx?relid=199620

69 Indian Embassy, 'India Myanmar Development Cooperation' Indian Embassy, Yangon_Accessed 15 April 2020

and has opened an immigration checkpost in Mizoram along the border with Myanmar, it has not reported any major cross border trade. Goods from Myanmar move from Rih border to Zokhawthar and then they are transported to Champhai. Illegal goods tend to dominate this border trade. Urea, used for agricultural purposes and also for the manufacture of plastics, is a one of the most common illegal commodities sent to Myanmar. Items being smuggled into India include areca nuts from Thailand, Indonesia and Malaysia and black pepper.[70] A free movement regime has been proposed of upto 16 km without valid documents.

There is also a proposal to start the bus service between Mizoram and Tahan township in Myanmar, given the large number of Mizos residing in that area.

Kaladan Multi-Modal Transit Transport Project (KMMTTP)

This project which is now scheduled to be inaugurated in 2024 by the two sides was initiated in 2008 at an estimated cost of Rs 535.91 crore. It comprises of three sectors: an inland waterway, a port and road network connecting the ports. It included the following:

(i) Construction of an integrated port and IWT terminal at Sittwe, including dredging;
(ii) Development of navigational channel along river KMTTC from Sittwe to Paletwa (158 km);

70 Sadiq Naqvi, 'Assam Rifles crack down on illegal trade on Indo-Myanmar border', *Hindustan Times*, 25 Sep 2019 at https://www.hindustantimes.com/india-news/assam-rifles-crack-down-on-illegal-trade-on-indo-myanmar-border/story-H5YuKdPHM5l983cNVw723I.html, Accessed 15 April 2020

(iii) Construction of an IWT-Highway trans-shipment terminal at Paletwa;

(iv) Construction of six IWT barges (each with a capacity of 300 tonnes) for transportation of cargo between Sittwe and Paletwa; and

(v) Building a highway (109 km) from Paletwa to the India-Myanmar border (Zorinpui) in Mizoram. Then one from Sittwe Port to Kaletwa (225 km) along the Kaladan River and thereafter a roadway from Kaletwa to the India-Myanmar border (62 km).

The framework agreement and two protocols (Protocol on Transit and Transport and Protocol on Maintenance) were signed by India and Myanmar on 2 April 2008. Given the delays, in 2015, the revised cost estimate (RCE) stood at Rs 2,904.04 crore.[71]

Under this project, loaded freight ships will leave Kolkata port and dock at Sittwe, a port in Myanmar's Rakhine province. There, the goods will be loaded on barges that will transport them upstream for 15 km to the Kaladan river to Paletwa. From Paletwa to Zorinpui on the Mizoram border, and further inland into the Northeast, the goods will be transported by road through a 10-km distance. From there, goods will move via road to Lawngtlai in Mizoram which will connect to NH-54. This road will need to be built to connect with the road that is completed connecting Sittwe port and Paletwa. While

71 PIB, Implementation of the KMMTTP in Myanmar at the Revised Cost Estimate of Rs 2,904.04 Crore, 14 Oct 2015 at (http://pib.nic.in/newsite/PrintRelease.aspx?relid=128699, Accessed 15 April 2020

Stretch	Mode	Distance
Kolkata-Sittwe port in Myanmar	Shipping	539 km
Sittwe to Paletwa	Inland Water Transport	158 km
Paletwa to Indo-Myanmar Border	Road	110 km
Border to NH-54 Lawngtlai	Road	100km

the dredging of the Kaladan, the construction of the unloading and loading terminals at Sittwe port and Paletwa have been completed, and seven barges readied and handed over to the Myanmar government, the road remains a work in progress. The ₹1,600-crore road project that passes through dense forests and hilly areas was unable to start on time as the contractor had to wait till January 2018 for the requisite clearances from the Myanmar government to start ground work.[72]

There was a delay in the 60-km stretch from Paletwa due to local political unrest in the Chin state of Myanmar bordering south Mizoram, after which work was resumed. In the absence of road connectivity, it is imperative to carry heavy equipment by barges from Sittwe to Paletwa. But low end-season draft in Kaladan river made it impossible, as deployment of machines becomes problematic, causing delays. The contractor also did not receive the due clearance to import some spares on an urgent basis from India.[73]

72 Pratim Ranjan Bose, 'India starts construction of ₹1,600-cr Mizoram-Myanmar Kaladan', *BusinessLine,* 17 April 2018 https://www.thehindubusinessline.com/news/india-starts-construction-of-1600-cr-mizoram-myanmar-kaladan-road/article23577107.ece Accessed 15 April 2020

73 Pratim Bose, ibid

Also, ethnic conflicts among the tribes over scarce economic resources and limited opportunities continue to flare from time to time. The Arakan Army and the Myanmar Army have been in constant strife and in Manipur, the border Moreh is susceptible to such conflicts, specially over the struggle to dominate the Moreh market.[74]

In sum, while plans have been made, delays have been routine. For instance, the Rih-Tiddim MoU was signed in 2012 and as per schedule the detailed project report was to be prepared in 2014. The Rih-Tiddim road (60 km, estimated to be $150 million in the initial planning stage) will connect Zokhawthar in Mizoram to Monywa onwards to Mandalay. Right now a roughly patched up 4.5-km road stretch can use used only during dry season.

Projects worth ₹31,000 crore are under implementation and schemes worth another ₹1,33,000 crore are to be awarded for connectivity between India and Myanmar.[75] This apart, the 1,360-km long India-Myanmar-Thailand Trilateral Highway involving the three neighbours has also been initiated. This route is designed to connect Moreh in Manipur to Mae Sot in the Tak province of Thailand via Myanmar. This would have two border crossings (India-Myanmar and Myanmar-Thailand), four customs checkpoints, three international time zones, three customs Electronic Data Interchange

74 'Economic Potential of Northeast India: An Asset or Threat?' *IDSA Comments,* https://idsa.in/idsacomments/EconomicPotentialofNortheastIndiaAnAssetorThreat_shivanandah_120511, Accessed 15 April 2020

75 Pratim Ranjan Bose, 'Patchy pace of North-East highway projects', *BusinessLine,* 10 June 2018 at https://www.thehindubusinessline.com/news/patchy-pace-of-north-east-highway-projects/article24129551.ece, Accessed 15 April 2020

(EDI) systems, two different vehicle-driving standards, and three different motor vehicle laws. However, there are several challenges over convergence in standards and procedures along the corridor.[76] India is undertaking construction of two sections of the Trilateral Highway in Myanmar namely, the 120.74-km Kalewa-Yargyi road section, and building of 69 bridges along with the approach road on the 149.70 km Tamu-Kyigone-Kalewa (TKK) road section. The Kalewa-Yargyi section of the Trilateral Highway is expected to be completed by 2021.

Both these sections were awarded on Engineering, Procurement and Construction mode in May 2018 for Kalewa-Yagyi section and November 2017 for the TKK section. The scheduled time for completion of both the projects is three years from the date of commencement at the project site by the executing agency. But as yet there has been no progress, so the Mumbai-based contractor was cancelled and the project remains at a standstill. Given the presence of the Karen National Union and the Chin National Liberation Front, there have been apprehensions too, especially over the rampant narcotics business.

On completion, the project will help connect Mizoram with the Sittwe Port in Rakhine state of Myanmar.[77] Apart from rising costs, this project has met with a few roadblocks, the political strife within Myanmar being one of them. The two sides signed an MoU on 22 October 2018 for operationalisation of the Port at Sittwe, but the conflict between the Myanmar military, known as the Tatmadaw and the Arakan Army continues. The

76 Prabir De, Sunetra Ghatak, Durairaj Kumaraswamy, 'Assessing Economic Impacts of Connectivity Corridors in North East India, An Empirical Investigation', *EPW* Vol. 54, Issue No. 11, 16 Mar, 2019

77 Pratim Ranjan Bose, 'India starts construction...' op cit

capture of five officials including two Indian officials working at the port by the Arakan Army has not been conducive to smooth running of an already much beleaguered project. More importantly, how much commerce is this geography likely to generate to make this project commercially viable?

The KMMTTP, once completed, will create a shorter and cheaper supply route by halving the route from 1,880 km via 'Chicken's neck' to 950 km. But essentially this route was created to circumvent Bangladesh at a time when India and Bangladesh were going through during a difficult phase in relations. Now, with the deepening engagement with Bangladesh that will allow NER to access closer ports, the ground situation will change substantially. India will be able to access the Chattogram port in a short while directly from Tripura and eastern India, thus putting a question mark over the potential cargo movement through this region. Some have argued that the KMMTTP project, once completed, can share the eastern India traffic and it would be viable for sending cargo meant for Singapore and other posts in South East Asia.[78]

India is also extending the highway by 90 km to Zorinpui on Myanmar border to connect to Rakhine state. From Zorinpui, a 1090-km road will connect Paletwa inland river terminal on Kaladan river in Myanmar. This is connected to Sittwe port at the Kaladan river.[79]

---

78 Author's discussion with Col Jaideep Chanda, an expert on Myanmar who follows this project closely. 30 March 2020.

79 Pratim Ranjan Bose, 'Rs 7,500 crore road neywork to boost North-East Economy', *BusinessLine, 24* Feb 2017 https://www.thehindubusinessline.com/news/national/7500crore-road-network-to-boost-northeast-economy/article9559199.ece, Accessed 15 April 2020

Nepal-Bhutan Transport Linkages

These two Himalayan neighbours have tenuous links with NER but given their location, their cargo movement traverses the NE. Trade with India is mostly conducted through Kathmandu, Biratnagar, Birganj and Nepalganj. Significantly, the first three towns cover the trade between Nepal and Bihar. Much of the trade with West Bengal in India also passes through Biratnagar, an industrial town in southeast Nepal.

In recent years, India has been assisting Nepal in development of border infrastructure through upgradation of roads in the Terai areas; development of cross-border rail links at Jogbani-Biratnagar, Jaynagar-Bardibas; and establishment of Integrated Check Posts at Birgunj, Biratnagar, Bhairahawa and Nepalgunj.[80] Similarly, for Bhutan (linked to India through the Siliguri corridor in West Bengal adjacent to NER) much of the trade is linked to this region. Both these two landlocked states have gained tremendously with India agreeing to allow transit trade through India without too many conditions. Since 2010, India has gradually embraced regionalism which indeed has strengthened its bilateral relations with the neighbours.

Notwithstanding the above, there is no progress on the proposed 30-km rail link to Bhutan. Nepal imports third-country products through the Kolkata port, which lies barely 700 km from Birgunj. And, the freight train takes a minimum of three days to cross this distance due to poor track capacity in north Bihar.[81] Once the rail and port facilities are operational, Assam could

80 MEA, 'India–Nepal Relations', https://mea.gov.in/Portal/ForeignRelation/India-Nepal_bilateral_brief_02.11.2018.pdf Accessed 15 April 2020

81 Pratim Ranjan Bose, '*Time and Trade Wait for No One*', *BusinessLine*, 3 April 2017

become a trade and investment hub of the region, connecting it with Nepal, Bhutan, Bangladesh and Myanmar also.

The Regional Landscape

India's Act East Policy as well as its outreach to the immediate neighbourhood goes beyond bilateral projects. These projects are being planned to dovetail the regional transport systems that will connect many NE locations with the adjacent region to create a cobweb network, thereby transforming the underdeveloped border regions.

One of the first moves towards this regionalism was signaled in 2010 when India agreed to facilitate Bangladesh's trade with Nepal and Bhutan. India initiated steps towards improving border trade and connectivity by agreeing to prolonged demands of Nepal and Bhutan for direct land trade links with Bangladesh through India. In the past, both India and Bangladesh had used transit rights as bargaining chips for larger political concessions from the other.[82] As landlocked countries, the Himalayan states are heavily dependent upon India for their economy. Nepal uses Kolkata and Haldia ports for its overseas trade. Nepal and Bangladesh are separated by a mere 27-km stretch, Siliguri Corridor, in West Bengal.

The following measures were undertaken to further cross-border trade:

- India and Bangladesh agreed to trucks carrying goods from Nepal and Bhutan enter 200 metres into Zero

---

82 Prabhu Ghate, 'South Asia: Towards Greater Connectivity? *Economic Times,* 8 Nov 2010

Point at Banglabandh Phulbari Land Custom Station.

- Bangladesh would be allowed to use the Rohanpur-Singaband broad gauge rail link for transit to Nepal. Towards this end, Bangladesh planned to convert the Radhikapur-Birol line into broad gauge.
- Bangladesh agreed to Nepal and Bhutan accessing its Mongla and Chattogram ports, and further Bangladesh offered a 50 per cent fee discount for the use of Mongla port. But it needs to be remembered that the port at Chattogram in the southeast suffers from low draft and congestion. The deep-sea port will take a long time to come. Also, there are road and rail logistics gaps to be mitigated.[83]

In the past, while providing transit routes to Nepal and Bhutan, India had been reluctant to expand these facilities to their extra-regional trade. As part of its new desire to expand intra-regional trade cooperation, it agreed to expand trade routes for Bangladesh's trade with the Himalayan states. Citing security concerns, India did not allow the route for third-country trade. Earlier, Nepalese trucks were allowed only on specific routes and the Indian trucks which entered Nepal would have to depart within 72 hours.

Since Nepal currently imports raw material for its handicrafts industry, Bangladesh's cotton, chemicals and processing equipment would have been cheaper. Similarly, Bangladesh's producers of packed foods were keen to import cheaper and high-quality grains, lentils and fruits from Nepal.

83 Pratim Ranjan Bose, 'Time and Trade…', op cit

In fact, three-fourths of Nepali exports continue to exit Nepal through the Birgunj border and on to Kolkata port.

Apart from road connectivity, India is also upgrading the railway projects connecting Nepal with Bangladesh through the Birgong-Rauxul-Katihar-Singhabad line and the Partbatipur-Birol-Radhikapur-Jugabani-Biratnagar line. The railway link through Rohanpur (Bangladesh)-Singhabad (India), Kathihar-Raxaul (Nepal) to Birgonj in Nepal is within 1,000 km from Khulna in Bangladesh.

Similarly Modi and Nepal Prime Minister Sher Bahadur Deuba had in 2017 agreed to improve the infrastructure between them which would also benefit its trade route and connectivity with Bangladesh. The agreements included:

- Transit between Nepal and Bangladesh through Kakarbitta-Banglabandh corridor.
- Rail transport to/from Vishakhapatnam,
- Rail transit facility through Singhabad in India for Nepal's trade with and through Bangladesh.

The regional transport cobweb is emerging and the recent decision between Bangladesh and Nepal that would enable Nepal access to Bangladeshi Saidpur airport as well as Chittagong and Mongla seaports will ease the cargo movement in the sub-region further.

Regional Infrastructural Development

These agreements and connectivity corridors need to be viewed within the wider context of transport infrastructure that is taking place at both domestic and regional levels. For instance, regional initiatives such as SAARC and the South Asia Sub-regional Economic Cooperation (SASEC) initiative involving Bangladesh, Bhutan, India and Nepal have been simultaneously working on improvement of cross-border vehicular operation and other cross-border issues. Likewise, under the Bay of Bengal Initiative for Multi-Sectoral Technical and Economic Cooperation (BIMSTEC), a regional level BIMSTEC Transport Infrastructure and Logistic Study was completed in 2008. The implementation of BIMSTEC Trilateral Highway linking India-Myanmar-Thailand has also been undertaken by the member countries since 2005 for improving connectivity in the sub-region. But progress on all these fronts has been slow. Also while regional integration has been much discussed, Nepal, Bhutan and Bangladesh are not included as partners in India's Act East Policy, excluding them from using the India-Myanmar-Thailand trilateral highway for the import and export of goods and services'.[84]

The development map of NER can be transformed, but existing protocol hampers regional integration. Indeed, the ADB-supported Asian Highway and Asian Railway projects overlap with some of the bilateral routes designated by India and Bangladesh. Within India, the ADB has supported several projects with significant sub-regional implications. These include:

- The West Bengal Corridor Development Project; a north-south road corridor from Raiganji near Siliguri to Barasat, the north of Kolkata with links to border points in Bangladesh;

84 Sujan Ghosh, 'Is the Indian Government Impeding Infrastructure Development in the Northeast', *EPW, Vol 54, Issue 17, 27 Apr 2019*

- Nepal's East West Highway, which links to India and Bangladesh through Kakarbita.

Bangladesh, Nepal and Bhutan are also part of the proposed Trans-Asian Railway network and Bangladesh is also upgrading rail routes for facilitating trade between India, Nepal and Bhutan. The 10-km Rohanpur-Singhabad link will connect Chapai Nawabganj in northern Bangladesh with West Bengal's Malda district. Bangladesh Railway plans to use this link as a transit route in the rail link between Nepal and Mongla seaport in Bagerhat district. The broad gauge Rohanpur-Singabad railway links connected upto the Indian border near Birgunj and Biratnagar—the financial hubs of Nepal—have paramount significance from the administrative point of view.

BBIN MVA Initiative

India and Bangladesh in December 2019 have taken a significant stride in trans-shipment trade. After years of discussion and negotiations, the first land and air trans-shipment with cargo weighing 4.41 tonne from Bangladesh moved through the Benapole land border into India through the Petrapole border to head towards Kolkata airport for air freight to Europe. GPS-enabled trucks move across the border, allowing officials from both India and Bangladesh to monitor progress. This form of cargo movement was also possible due to the signing of the BBIN agreement in 2016 that seeks to enable seamless trade movement among the four neighbours. Although BBIN has only had a trial run and is yet to be fully functional, the opportunities for all to reorganise their trade and transport systems are immense.[85] While various road and rail trips are at various stages of planning and implementation, BBIN have embarked on a MVA for seamless movement of personal as well as passenger vehicles and cargo through the four states. The BBIN Agreement consisting of 17 articles signed in June 2015 in Thimphu would enable vehicles to enter any of the four nations, replacing the earlier system of trans-shipment of goods from one country's truck to another's at the border. As per estimates, the BBIN corridor will lead to increase in the flow of goods across borders, thereby giving these four countries opportunities to expand their consumer base internationally.[86] NER has trade potential of anywhere from Rs 180,000 crore to Rs 350,000 crore.[87]

Under BBIN MVA, seamless movement would be possible through online permits and electronic tracking of vehicles. The vehicles would be fitted with an electronic seal with alerts linked to ensure misuse of the containers. While the BBIN friendship motor rally initiated the trial runs for cross-border movement, India had already undertaken cargo trial runs from Dhaka to Delhi in August 2016 for smoothening the implementation process. The implementation of the agreement is expected to improve the value chain in sub-regional trade. To overcome the immediate issue, Bhutan has suggested that the other three countries go ahead with the agreement and as per Indian official

---

85 Sreeradha Datta, 'Bangladesh: Leveraging its Locational Advantage', *VIF Commentary*. 11 Jan 2019 at https://www.vifindia.org/2019/january/11/bangladesh-leveraging-its-locational-advantage, Accesses 15 April 2020

86 FICCI & AT Kearney Report 'Connectivity-led development of Northeast India through BBIN corridor', p71

87 FICCI & PWC Report 'Gateway to the ASEAN: India's North East Frontier', p13

statement 'Bangladesh, India, and Nepal have already ratified the MVA and have agreed to start implementation of the MVA among the three signatory countries, with Bhutan joining after it ratifies the Agreement'. Bhutan's environmental issues as well as their truckers lobby has held them back from joining the transport agreement for now, hopefully the issues will be sorted out at a later date. The 72-km Nepal-Bangladesh highway will start from Mechinagar and enter Bengal at Panitanki, near Siliguri's Bagdogra. It will then lead to Fulbari near the Bangla border and end at Banglabandha in the neighbouring country. In the initial stretch, an existing two-lane bridge on Mechi near the Nepal border will be widened to four lanes.

As it stands now India, Bangladesh and Nepal have agreed on the text of the passenger protocol, the document detailing procedures for cross-border movement of cargo vehicles along scheduled routes before finalising the protocol for cargo vehicular movement. But there are several issues in the sectors of trade facilitation, development of economic corridors, national security and strategy for land and seaport connectivity, for greater regional integration.[88] Alongside the land connectivity projects underway, the neighbours are also examining the possibility of using inland waterways as an alternative mode of transport connectivity. Indeed BBIN sub-grouping was expected to be the gateway to South East and East Asia and is also being seen as a viable sub-regional sector within the BIMSTEC regional organisation.

A fully functional transport route will also have to factor in the existing domestic logistical bottlenecks in India which need

88 Report, 'Advancing the BBIN Sub-regional Cooperation' Vol. 2, Issue 8, *Delhi Policy Group*, 2017.

to be resolved and integrated with the growing connectivity infrastructure that is being planned with the neighbourhood. It has been pointed out India needs to give a systemic push for conversion of non-containerised road cargo to containerised rail cargo for regional trade.[89] A recently submitted study mapped a total of 476 freight-carrying routes in the region. Of the total, 90 routes will be connected to all NE capitals and contribute 80 per cent of the total freight flow in the region.[90] But operability remains a question as yet. Interestingly, a CUTS policy brief points out that the sub-optimal conditions of road will hardly facilitate the planned BBIN seamless traffic movement.[91]

Some international projects will supplement Indian transport projects. It is proposed that a rail track will connect NE India to Myanmar through the 81,000-km-long Trans-Asian Railway Network (TARN). This 118-km railway track would be laid between Manipur's capital Imphal and border towns Moreh and Tamu in western Myanmar.[92]

As part of TARN, another 257-km railway route from north Tripura's Jawahar Nagar railway station to northern Mizoram's Kolashib and Myanmar's Darlon has been proposed.[93] Of particular importance is the proposal of an Istanbul to Dhaka rail route, also known as the ITI-DKD rail corridor. India

---

89 Pratim Ranjan Bose, 'Time and Trade… ' op cit

90 FICCI & AT Kearney Report, 'Connectivity-led development…' op cit

91 'A Bridge Across Forever, Bridging Infrastructural Gaps in Bangladesh for Improved Regional Connectivity', *CUTS Policy Brief* on Connectivity, March 2019

92 Sujit Chakrabarty, 'India's northeast to be linked to Trans-Asian Railway Network, *Business Standard, September 16 2013.* https://www.business-standard.com/article/news-ians/india-s-northeast-to-be-linked-to-trans-asian-railway-network-113091600475_1.html, Accessed 15 April 2020

93 Sujit Chakrabarty, ibid

hosts an important segment of this rail route.[94] For the Trans-Asian railway from Delhi to Hanoi to be actualised, India and Myanmar railway systems have to be connected and synchronised. While India is building the Assam-Manipur rail link (scheduled for December 2020) there is no plan as yet to take the railway beyond Imphal or the Moreh border.[95] The feasibility of connecting Moreh to the Myanmar rail network at Kalay was assessed as well as the prospects of connecting southern Myanmar to Thailand.[96]

Similarly, apart from building transport systems to connect with India's borders, the Padma Bridge project in Bangladesh will connect the east part with the rest of Bangladesh and will play an important role in the context of regional connectivity with India, Nepal and Bhutan. The plan emphasises Bangladesh's participation in global and regional transport connectivity initiatives to develop land routes between South Asia and East Asia through Bangladesh under the Asian Highway Project being implemented by UNESCAP.[97]

The regional network would be strengthened with Bangladesh Railway reconstructing the 9-km rail network from Chilahati, Nilphamari to the Indian border, at cost of Tk 781.29 million. India will reconstruct the 3-km track from

94 Two-day meeting on "Strengthening Railway Transport Connectivity in South and South West Asia' PIB, 15 March2018 at http://pib.nic.in/newsite/PrintRelease.aspx?relid=159276

95 Subhir Bhaumik, 'Delhi uncertain over Trans-Asian railway', *Look East*, 28 June 2016, https://lookeast.in/delhi-uncertain-over-trans-asian-railway-plans/, Accessed 15 April 2020

96 Report, 'Assessing India's Connectivity with its Neighborhood' *VIF-CII*, 2018

97 Mustafizur Rahman, Khondaker Golam Moazzem *et al*, 'Bangladesh: Perspectives on Deepening cross-border Link' in Michael G. Plummer Peter J. Morgan Ganeshan Wignaraja Ed. *Connecting Asia*, Edward Elgar Publishing, UK, 2016, p325.

Haldibari to the Bangladesh border. Once the railway line is rebuilt, Nepal and Bhutan would be allowed to utilise the route for transporting their products through the Mongla sea port for the foreign trade of those countries.[98] Radhikapur-Biral and Singhabad-Rohanpur are also notified for use of Nepalese transit traffic.

The Mekong-Ganga Cooperation and Kunming Initiative have been undertaken by India and China to engage with ASEAN countries through cooperation in tourism, culture and education. The signatories were India, Thailand, Vietnam, Cambodia, Laos and Myanmar. These countries agreed to undertake joint transportation projects including the trans-Asian highway. In the latest 11th Mekong Ganga Cooperation Senior Officials' Meeting (11th MGC SOM on 9 July 2019) it was noted that a total of twenty-four projects have been completed so far, including fifteen in Cambodia and nine in Vietnam at a cost of $1.2 million, generating significant positive impact among beneficiary communities. In addition, currently one project in Cambodia and three projects in Lao PDR are under implementation.[99]

Under the Mekong initiative, directly connecting Assam with Vietnam is a real possibility. Asian Highway (AH-48), which would be connecting Phuentsholing in Bhutan to Indo-

---

98 Deepshikha Sikarwar, 'Modi govt to change customs duty architecture to boost trade, ease of doing business', *Economic Times*, 3 December 2018, at https://energy.economictimes.indiatimes.com/news/power/modi-govt-to-change-customs-duty-architecture-to-boost-trade-ease-of-doing-business/66914087, Accessed 15 April 2020

99 Press Note, 11th Mekong Ganga Cooperation Senior Officials' Meeting, Ministry of External Affairs, 9 July 2019 at https://www.mea.gov.in/press-releases.htm?dtl/31560/11th+Mekong+Ganga+Cooperation+Senior+Officials+Meeting, Accessed 15 April 2020

Bangladesh border point at Changrabandha in Cooch Behar, West Bengal via Dooars, which is being built in full swing. It should act as a major boost to further cooperation with Bangladesh.[100]

Regional transportation recorded a success in a first-of-its-kind multi-modal cargo movement amongst India, Bhutan and Bangladesh. The trucks travelled with stone aggregates from Phuentsholing to IWAI's Dhubri jetty in Assam, a distance of 160 km. The Indian ship with stone aggregates sailed from Dhubri over the river Brahmaputra and arrived at Bangladesh port of Narayanganj on 16 July 2019. This is the first time an Indian waterway is being used as a channel for transport of cargo between the two countries, using India for transit. Prior to this, Bhutan has been exporting significant quantity of stone aggregates to Bangladesh through the land route. The ship carried 1,000 mt of stones–over 50 trucks would be required to transport the same cargo by road.[101] Notwithstanding this incremental progress, the ground reality as yet does not point to any significant changes that would alter the regional landscape. Evidently, the big picture is yet to emerge despite the rhetoric of a strengthened outreach, the capacity to extend regional connectivity and infrastructure building has been insufficient. The suggestion that 'the Modi government too appears to have laid more emphasis in its official statements, with very little to

---

100 Report, Act East Policy Tripura, Government of Tripura, 2014 https://planning.tripura.gov.in/sites/default/files/Tripura_Act per cent20East per cent20Policy per cent20 per cent28Modified per cent29.pdf p4. Accessed 15 April 2020

101 'First Cargo Ship from Bhutan arrives in Bangladesh via India', *Economic Times,* 18 July 2019

show on the ground' may not be very misplaced as the work in progress seems rather prolonged.[102]

India has also turned its attention to improving the regional trade, especially energy. Although the earlier chapter on energy delineate much of the energy potential within NER, the regional scope is outlined here.

Regional Energy Trade

Although the BBIN MVA has been delayed, the idea of this sub-regional process, as seen earlier, has led to sub-regional cargo movement. Similarly, the idea of developing an energy grid is receiving greater traction and is also being discussed at various levels. India is also preparing a draft agreement for regional energy trade. Apparently, a more tangible initiative of energy trade seems in the offing amongst India, Nepal and Bangladesh. Currently, India buys 1,450 mw from Bhutan and sells 60 mw to Nepal. But Nepal still experiences severe shortage of around 550 mw. The recently inaugurated 69-km Indo-Nepal pipeline, from Bihar's oil refinery Motihari to Amlekhgunj will significantly reduce the transaction costs.

At present, Bangladesh and India share a robust energy trade. The 600 mw of electricity export that began in 2013 is cheaper than all the other options, including generation from coal, for Bangladesh. The two neighbours are also looking for another 500 mw through the Behrampur-Bheramara inter-connection, which is under construction. The 1,320 mw Maitree Thermal Power Project, a joint venture of NTPC and the Bangladesh

102 Rajeswari Pillai Rajagopalan, 'Minding the Gaps in India's Act East Policy', *The Diplomat,* 17 Sep 2018 at https://thediplomat.com/2018/09/minding-the-gaps-in-indias-act-east-policy/

Power Development Board, is under development (IRADE Report 2017). Bangladesh has signed an agreement with India to import additional 160 mw from Tripura.

Bangladesh has also shown interest in signing a mutual Power Trade Agreement with Nepal and has proposed to invest $1 billion in Nepal's hydropower sector. Bangladesh had expressed its willingness to facilitate this cross- border energy trade between Bangladesh and Nepal. This commitment was in fact reiterated by the Bangladesh ambassador in Nepal Mashfee Binte Shams recently: 'India is positive and has agreed to allow transmission of electricity to Bangladesh from Nepal. We are ready to import electricity from Nepal after meeting Nepal's requirements as much as Nepal can export to us.'

An Indian company has already signed an agreement with the Nepal government to build the 900-mw Upper Karnali project in western Nepal and is in the final stages of acquiring permission for constructing the 600-mw Upper Marsyangdi-II project in central Nepal. Bangladesh will import 200 mw from the Upper Marsyangdi-II project and the remaining 300 mw will be imported from Upper Karnali. Bangladesh has been making several proposals to Nepal for purchase of electricity and India will provide the transmission lines needed to cross over through India.[103] This was possible due to the 2018 tripartite arrangement in cross-border trading of electricity, paving the way for Nepal to export surplus electricity to Bangladesh via Indian transmission lines.

103 'GMR India to sell 500 mw power to Bangladesh from Nepal', *Nepal Energy Forum*, 14 August 2018, at http://www.nepalenergyforum.com/gmr-india-to-sell-500-mw-power-to-bangladesh-from-nepal/

While political differences had for long prevented energy trade between India and Nepal, the bilateral Bangladesh-Nepal energy trade will allow the process to start. Maybe with improvement of political ties, India and Nepal will be able to embark on similar cooperation. Thus, a cooperative framework amongst three neighbours is leading to a distinct sub-regional momentum developing in this region, as with Bhutan too.

Although the neighbours seem to be moving on a positive track, the issue of human trafficking along the same corridors has been an issue that remains unresolved. While all the governments recognise the problem, the entrenched nexus and network of human traffickers has been difficult to break. Similarly, the issue of drug trafficking is rather critical. Since the late 1990s, the Indian route for drugs from Myanmar has expanded further, flooding the NER. A significant number of youth residing in the Indian states bordering Myanmar—Mizoram, Manipur and Nagaland—fall prey to this addiction of drugs, heroin as well as opium. Despite the joint efforts, drug trafficking and money-laundering transactions continue unabated.[104] The growing wide cross-section of cooperation taking place amongst the neighbours may finally find ways to address this malaise that is freely moving across the borders in the region. Only joint action will provide a firm resolution of this prolonged problem.

Conclusion

Building roads, highways, railways and airports are essential to connecting NER with the mainland. There is no doubt

104 'In a vicious circle', *Frontline,* Vol 19, Issue 15, July-Aug 2002

about the progress that has been made vis-à-vis infrastructural development in the region but that cannot be enough to make NER a partner in the Act East Policy. The region and the Centre's aspirations need to coincide for the full optimisation of potential.

Evidently, the plan for creating a network of transportation corridors is facing a number of problems on the ground. They range from incomplete planning to lack of synchronisation of the hardware and software linkages. Also, it has been seen that many of the Land Customs Stations are underutilised and there is (specially on the Indo-Bangladesh border) no attempt to coordinate the planning or understand the ground realities. More importantly, while the road networks have improved their pathetic quality certainly leaves a lot to be desired. Unfortunately in India, the lack of checks and quality control continue to hamper smooth functioning of most spheres, more so physical road networks. While India works on building and creating transport corridors which are envisaged to become economic corridors eventually, providing greater economic benefit to the region, it is useful to understand how the present economy in NER can support the transport/economic corridors.

The CUTS policy brief points out that the sub-optimal conditions of road will hardly facilitate the planned BBIN seamless traffic movement.[105] As this report points out, the cross-border facilities lack testing laboratories and inadequate warehouses, cold storage facilities and parking areas, the cross-border trade will never reach the expected potentials. Without

105 'A Bridge Across Forever', CUTS Policy Brief on Connectivity, 20 March 2019, Jaipur.

a doubt, physical LCSs are necessary for cross-border trade facilities but without the last mile connection, much of the investment in personnel and finance will not yield the expected results. Often in a rush to tick the box some projects are officially completed without ensuring a fully functional system is in place.

Undoubtedly, the improved transport systems will bring NE close to India and vice versa. The knowledge and perception gap that exists between mainland India and NE region will be bridged steadily, while exposure to the other way of living will be beneficial and open up another world for all. But all the developmental projects from transport corridors to economic schemes will take a decade to fall in place before the region begins to reap the corresponding dividends. In the meantime, ground conditions need to be prepared for the region to be able to adapt to the changing circumstances.

Transforming the Border Economy[1]

Our Vision is of Act East and Act Fast
—Narendra Modi, 4 January 2019

BORDERS HAVE a special significance for the Northeast region. While it shares over 5,000 km international border with neighbouring countries, NE states' borders with the rest of India are very narrow and limited. Thus, the borders have distinctly reflected NER development, its trade and commerce and inevitably its livelihood. More importantly, they have also influenced people's perceptions about their individual identity and Indianness. Evidently, the borders have assumed a new significance in India's quest for deepening engagement but also repositioning India with its immediate neighbours.

---

1 A few sections are a revised version of an earlier publication. Sreeradha Datta, 'The Changing Narrative: India's Northeastern Borders with Bangladesh and Myanmar', AsCon-Monograph Series, Asian Confluence, April 2017 Delhi,

This chapter very briefly examines how the perceptions of borders is varied and also how they have evolved over time. It will also attempt to understand the changing nature of India's ties with its eastern neighbours, Bangladesh and Myanmar. Nepal and Bhutan's cross-border terrain in the Northeast does not share similar landscapes, thus these countries are not in focus in this chapter—but the cross-border community has possibilities on all these borders too.

This chapter will also examine the possibilities of going beyond the nationalist construct. In the Indian context, borders essentially outline the physical contours of any modern nation-state and have largely been left out of the developmental programmes undertaken in the mainland.

The next section will highlight some of the studies on our borders and how the expanding scope has impacted upon the more comprehensive understanding of borders and their functions. It will examine the mechanism and tools that could be made available for the locals—not only those affected by the large connectivity project but also those who are in a position to make a difference on the ground by creating narratives and sub-narratives for ground-level value addition to trans-boundary connectivity.

Understanding Borderlands

Borders necessarily are a core, constitutive element of international order but with an element of inherent dynamism. International relations literature has thus given way to new approaches to understanding its evolving character, from one that is a purely geographic line to that of a more encompassing interdisciplinary concept. While the basic understanding of borders is that of a barrier, the narrative surrounding borders is increasingly widening to include a functional space moving far beyond the physical territorial marker they provides for modern nation-states.

Depending upon the nature of the polity, borders assume varying salience and relevance. Borders are perceived as rigid lines where the state is the most important subject, and borders function as the line for inviolability of its sovereignty and national interest, while others develop broader utility as gateways to international markets and greater outreach beyond its own boundaries. Borders, while remaining connected with territorial and sovereignty identification, actually include a much broader functional scope as zones of cooperation.

Borders and nation-states have an intrinsic relationship: both mirror the nature and function of each other. Over the years, while being the cornerstone in the understanding of nation-state, borders have also periodically evolved, reflecting both the nature of the government and society within the structured context. Given the evolving and complex nature of borders, it has been a focus of study for an array of scholars belonging to the disciplines of international relations, sociology, anthropology and of course history. They identified the crucial role of borderland communities as organised polities within the larger institutional architecture of their state of belonging and have underlined the importance of local culture. Political geographers Anssi Paasi and David Newman contended that borders may be institutions but their very functions may be challenged; economists generally disagree with all other social scientists, pointing to the limiting and restrictive role that borders play in trade and flows of goods and people.

Since the last three decades, new approaches are evident in the professional literature, examining it through the lens of a purely geographic one to interdisciplinary one.[1] Through the international relations perspective, states and borders are dynamic and changing with differing situations and circumstances.[2]

As elsewhere, borders have also assumed a criticality in the Indian subcontinent. The history of Partition and its subsequent trajectory had a sobering effect, especially in India, and contributed towards shaping the perspective of its borders. Both the troubled memories of communal tension and hastily drawn up borders just before Partition have dominated the Indian narrative on the border and the corresponding inability to overcome the consequences and a number of conflicts at the borders have largely influenced the Indian perspective of its borders. Given the uneven bilateral ties in the neighbourhood, India realised the necessity of ensuring strict border security protocol and its inviolability.

For long years, this situation remained nearly the same. Despite the passage of time, developments in the neighbourhood have not been conducive to changing the status quo in the bordering areas significantly. Given the prevailing tension across the western border that India shares with Pakistan, border engagement has remained confined to limited activity and photo ops. Despite cross-cultural links, the relentless security transgression from across India's western border has essentially ensured the continued rigidity of the borders.

1 Emmanuel Brunet-Jailly, 'Theorizing Borders: An Interdisciplinary Perspective', *Geopolitics*, 10:4, 2005

2 Beatrix Haselsberger, 'Decoding borders. Appreciating border impacts on space and people', *Planning Theory & Practice*, 15:4, 2014

The socio-political environment on India's borders with Bangladesh and Myanmar both have undergone changes and have possibly set the tone for a new discourse that encompasses not only improved state to state bilateral ties but will also increase the local and regional cooperation. Involving and engaging the border population to take bilateral relations forward is not only a distinct possibility but also a need of the hour.

India's Neighbourhood First and the refocused Act East Policy both significantly impact upon the borders and are giving way to a new discourse of a cross-border cooperative framework in both philosophical and actual physical terms. Evolving situations have made the borders become 'central to the nationalist agenda and the development of nation-states and have been identified such boundaries as institutional constructs.'[3] Given the present momentum of India enhancing cross-border structures, the borders are assuming salience in the new construct that the government is attempting to develop.

The previous chapters have illustrated that while cross-border infrastructure and transport corridors are being created, the ground situation in NER as yet will stop short of making the NE a serious stakeholder in the economic corridors, other than providing physical connectivity. The present NE economy does not support any significant scope for it to become producer and exporter of any substantial quantity of goods, nor can it offer very large markets. Also, the border trade as yet is low and even at trading points which record a substantial level, the

---

3 Emmanuel Brunet-Jailly, 'The State of Borders and Borderlands Studies 2009: A Historical View', *Journal of Borderlands Studies*, Eurasia Border Review 1 (1), 1-15, 2010 pp1-14.p 3 at src-h.slav.hokudai.ac.jp/publictn/eurasia_border_review/no1/01_Brunet.pd

commodities are not peculiar to the state it crosses. Border trade has often bypassed the local geography. Transport corridors once fully implemented will become economic corridors and provide new opportunities to the regions they traverse through.

While cross-border facilities have improved over time, apart from a few pockets, there is no upward momentum in the trade commerce. As is evident from some of the ICPs built, they fall short of full functionality given the invariable issue of the 'last mile' connect in India. At times, the cargo terminal is not completed, quarantine facilities for commodities do not exist, banking services are not functional. For a variety of reasons, the much talked about potential of NER is yet to be realised. Certainly, once the physical connectivity infrastructure is ready and investments are substantial, there will be significant transformation of the economy and commercial activities. But not yet. In fact, at present much of this is at speculative and proposed levels.

It is being proposed here to make NE states real stakeholders through increasing the cross-border linkages. This can have an immediate effect in the short or middle term. With the political narrative about NER being the gateway growing, the ground conditions ought to be readied for the eventuality. The hype of potential is often misplaced and misinterpreted. The region, known for its volatility and sensitivity, will not be happy to see the dividends accruing from the economic corridors bypass the locals. Their reaction and responses to the projects that have claimed their land and altered the landscape may not be very welcoming nor forthcoming. While the other necessary conditions develop for the region to increase production and manufacturing to compete with the rest of the country, the low hanging fruits towards opening up the border zones for common community development is feasible and can open up further avenues of cooperation between India and its neighbours. The cross-border activities factor in local aspirations and local requirements and necessities. Social inclusion is imperative for the region that, for long, has struggled for its own identity and rights and is now is trying to overturn their geographical disadvantage and build a viable ecosystem.

Historical Perspective

Given the history of the sub-continent, India and its South Asian neighbours viewed its borders as a reflection of its sovereignty. They perceived borders as one-dimensional, with a core function that was borne out of security considerations. That the borders could also contribute and develop as spaces for connectivity and mutual development was an idea that found appeal much later. Borders essentially are viewed through the security prism and are a 'territorial' line linked to defence management. They primarily assume the role of barriers that need to be safeguarded through positioning of troops, walls, posts and wires rather than as windows of opportunity and possibility. Ironically, this region was once a source of continuous cross-border flows of people and goods, myths and legends, poetry and religion. Unfortunately, the twentieth century experience in South Asia has not been conducive to perceiving borderlands as 'ways of conceptualising social space and local identity, and the roles these have played in promoting or thwarting the development of modern states.'[4]

---

4 Michiel Baud & Willem van Schendel, "Toward a Comparative History of Borderlands", *Journal of World History*, Vol. 8, No. 2, Fall 1997

With Partition of the sub-continent, borders in South Asia took on an identity that was both sensitive and critical and defined the contours of the new nation-states. In India the borders, viewed through the security prism, were a constant source of attention of academia and policy makers. Over seven decades, attention has centred on keeping the borders safe and ensuring their inviolability. Borders' sole attribute to protect and guard was the dominant narrative for the administration, political leaders and civil society. Ironically, this truism did not lead to making our borders impregnable. Half-hearted attempts at security measures allowed for continuing cross-border movement at several points without much attempt to bring about improvement in local ground conditions. For the border population, more often than not, it has been about prolonged hardship and constant struggle with the difficult geographical realities as well as dealing with security apparatus.

Before it is attempted to examine the borders India shares with its neighbours and the nature of transformation that is taking place, it is useful to move the discourse from a security paradigm to a cooperative framework and see what the narrative of borders through the international lens has been showing. A theoretical underpinning will be a useful exercise for greater clarity to understanding the border conditions and its possibilities.

Expanding Narrative

Borders have been viewed through various lenses. According to one school of thought, the state has to manage its borders as a fundamental role of making peace and order in its inner and outer environment. The border essentially defines the limits of state sovereignty.[5] Although this school also factors in the functional evolution of borders as propounded by authors like Alina Mingui, borders are generally perceived as being under the control of the state and any cross-border activities are to be necessarily controlled by the state. [6]

The Liberal argument is centred on the universal condition of world politics being globalisation. States are, and always have been, embedded in a domestic and transnational society, which creates incentives for economic, social and cultural interaction across borders. State policy may facilitate or block such interactions.[7] Political scientist Malcolm Anderson writes that globalisation has impacted on the nature and understanding of borders. Increasingly, the sovereign state is losing control due to mobilities it could not contain within its borders.

Three kinds of function of borders have been identified. The first function of borders aims to delimit the territorial sovereignty of a state in order to distinguish what is included and what is excluded. Flowing from this, it is also a tool of separation constituting the second function through which the border can regulate the degree of control, filtering and protection. The third function constitutes its role as an interface. Different aspects are associated with this element such as contact, exchange, collaboration or even confrontation. The functions of separation and interface are always potentially

---

5 Presscot and JRV Prescott, 'Political Frontiers and Boudaries', Unwin Hyman, London, 1987, p80.

6 Anna Moraczewska, 'The Changing Interpretation of Border Functions in International Relations', *Revista Român de Geografie Politic,* Vol XII (2), November 2010, pp329-40

7 Andrew Moravcsik, *Liberal Theories of International Relations: A Primer*, Princeton University, 2010 at www.princeton.edu/~amoravcs/library/primer.doc pp1-16

present and it is the nature and degree of any international border.[8]

That is why social scientists have suggested that the first approach to cross-border region-based integration is to consider the development of economic and social interactions on either side of a border. This focus on exchanges and relationships that link formerly separate social spaces establishes the so-called 'flow approach' and is dominant in economic geography and regional science.[9]

Following this, there can be a distinct correlation with the changing paradigm of the Indo-Bangladeshi and Indo-Myanmar borders under review. The borders with both formal structures and informal patterns often give way to contradictory narratives. Indeed, Partition of the sub-continent caused the severance of the inland water, road and railway communication through East Pakistan/ Bangladesh and access to the Chittagong (now Chattogram) port was lost. The Chinese take-over of Tibet and the virtual closure of borders with Burma/Myanmar added to the isolation of the region. All these factors had an effect on the traditional routes for trade and services. The British encouraged the growth of tea plantations at the cost of other industries in NER.

According to experts, the economic policy for the region must be conceived differently, taking into account its geo-economic and geopolitical predisposition. Economic policy should not be merely a matter of 'quantum variation in monetary allocation'. After an analysis of the state of economies

8 Christophe Sohna, 'Modelling Cross-Border Integration: The Role of Borders as a Resource', *Geopolitic*, Luxembourg, pub.online: 26 Aug 2014, p596

9 Christophe Sohna, Ibid, p590

in the region and the constraints hampering their growth, the report argues in favour of free border trade with Bangladesh, Myanmar and the Tibet region of China. The report has suggested a common economic zone including Bangladesh as the 'ultimate solution' to the economic woes of the Northeast.[10]

It is certainly no secret that the involvement of external powers, especially China, Pakistan, Nepal, Bhutan and Myanmar had complicated the security environment within the Northeast, and Bangladesh was playing host to many insurgent groups from NER. Various opposition parties in Bangladesh led by the Bangladesh Nationalist party (BNP) have argued in favour of treating the anti-India insurgent groups in a soft and relaxed manner. Similarly, many of these groups with cross-border linkages used Myanmar to hide and strike out as well. Internal fissures fuelled by external powers had held back the region for long. Training, funding, arms and safe havens were provided by many of these neighbours.

As discussed in one of the earlier chapters, three distinct shifts in the foreign policy domain finally ushered in a change in India's view of its two immediate neighbours, namely, Bangladesh and Myanmar. This may change the course of the ground situation on the border. Initiation of the Look East Policy and Neighbourhood First coupled with changing bilateral contours; the rapprochement with the Bangladesh and Myanmar; and the need to go beyond bilateral trade and focus are making regionalism and sub-regionalism effective in this region.

10 North Eastern Congress (I) Co-ordination Committee, A Scheme for the Economic Development of North- East, extract from the Report of General Secretaries to the Eighth General Conference (Special) of the North Eastern Congress (I) Co-ordination Committee, Dimapur, June 1993, See PS Datta Ed. *North-East and the Indian State: Paradoxes of a Periphery,* Vikas Publishing House, New Delhi, 1995, Chapter 9.

The government has not only positioned the NE as the gateway to South East Asia and beyond but through multi-pronged efforts of a sustained engagement, developed physical connectivity and encouraged greater investment flows, giving rise to a distinctly upbeat mood about and in the region. A developmental plan consisting of building a network of roads and highways, organising investments fairs, encouraging tourism and building high level of educational institutions was unveiled. Most importantly, establishing connectivity to not only mainland India but also with its immediate neighbours in the East would be the expected outcome.

For long, the security establishment in India had dominated the policy perspective for this region and the borderland and there was no political will to change course. However, with the changing geopolitical environment, several developments in the neighbourhood finally led to recognition of the limits of the policy of keeping the region insulated and infrastructurally deficient, for safeguarding the border zones and the rest of the country from intrusions by aggressive external and extra regional players. India belatedly understood the criticality of improving its border zones and commissioned a large number of highways and other infrastructure development plans in NER, as highlighted in the previous chapters.

Possibilities at the Borders

It is within this context that this chapter focuses on two aspects of bilateral ties: one that falls within the security sector and the other that falls within the people-to-people sector. Both, although distinct, can actually alter the ground situation to capture not only the imagination of the local population on both sides but more important, create the framework for many of the larger initiatives. India has expressed a strong intention to improve the cross-border infrastructure and also alongside undertake measures for greater facilitation of trade and services.

Undoubtedly, India suffers severe contradictions at its borders. The highly securitised systems in the borders in reality are inefficient and not known to have entirely delivered their core purpose. Informal, illegal flows have been the norm rather than the exception at these boundaries. As mentioned earlier, the borders between India and Bangladesh post-1971 became a barrier, with the discontinuation of cross-border movements. The official contact points at the borders were rudimentary and inadequate, at best. This adversely affected a large section of the border population whose lives, for a variety of reasons, were closely intertwined with the lands that now belonged to another state. Till a few years ago, the worst affected were those who were confined within the small pockets of land known as 'enclaves' inside the neighbour's territory. India and Bangladesh preferred to view the border as a 'territorial expression of state sovereignty', determining state control over it.

The Indo-Myanmar borders are no different, criss-crossing five NE states. Consequent to the limiting of the cross-border insurgency movement, the two neighbours have enjoyed amicable ties for nearly two decades. The borders, while enjoying an informal interactive space houses security apparatus, continue to seek the *raison d'etre* of their continued presence on either side of the borders. Access to the mainland has been severely restricted owing to the peculiar circumstances.

While India and its neighbours may have liked to view the borders as a clearly demarcated space with a clearly defined political boundary, the reality was quite the converse. The border complexities were many. The geographical contours of the borders India shares with Bangladesh (4,096.7 km) and Myanmar (1,643 km) made it difficult to draw and maintain boundary lines in the delineated border sections. More importantly, the borders were uneven, overlapping and easily permeable, making them a source of continuous bilateral tension. Ironically, irrespective of the official positions, local cross-border transgressions have been an ongoing phenomenon. Border realities assume national importance only when they influence the state's security-related interest and plainly, very limited thought has been given to improving border management beyond the security paradigm. But the two factors of improvement of local transport systems and with the improved bilateral relations it is possible to create and develop a more imaginative and functional interactive space at the borders.

Globalisation has led to a momentum that has captured the imagination of South Asia too. Today, countries in the region and outside are seeking greater interdependence through a connected infrastructure to obtain greater market access and exploitation of existing natural resource endowments. This has led to re- examination of the borders in India too.

Evidently, the first approach to cross-border region-based integration is to consider the development of economic and social interactions on either side of a border. This focus on exchanges and relationships that link formerly separate social spaces is part of the so-called 'flow approach' and is dominant in economic geography and regional science.[11] With respect to

11 Christophe Sohna, op cit, p590

these borders in the Northeast, two types of activity can be noticed: (1) horizontal relations between similar governments and non-government organisations, which have traditionally been described as governance issues, and (2) vertical relations, which have been understood as intergovernmental relations.[12] While the popular approach has been seeking ethnic overlap cultural similarities as factors for cross-border engagements, it is curious to note that successful attempts at cross-border cooperation in Europe are exceptional on two counts.

First, they did not evolve organically but came into being by decree. They are not those almost-natural frontiers of social communication surrounding populations assimilated into one culture that Karl Deutsch describes in his model of nation-building. Instead, they incorporate various nations, peoples, and groups at different stages of national mobilisation, while leaving out others with similar claims to a European identity.

The second peculiarity of the common European border is that it cuts not between two identities, as is usual with borders, but between a wealthy 'in-group' and an ill-fated 'out-group.'[13]

Borrowing from Chiara Brambillaa's study of identifying different approaches to understanding the changing concept, one that finds resonance in the Indian border regions is the concept of the borderscape that 'highlight the constitutive role that borders in modernity have played in the production of political subjectivity, thereby showing the potential of the

12 Emmanuel Brunet-Jailly, 'The State of Borders and Borderlands Studies 2009: A Historical View and a View from the Journal of Borderlands Studies', *Eurasia Border Review* 1 (1), 2010, pp1-15

13 Alina Mingui, 'Beyond the Borders', *Journal of Democracy*, Vol 15 (1) January 2004, p48-62

borderscape as a space for liberating political imagination from the burden of the territorialist imperative while opening up spaces within which the organisation of new forms of the political and the social become possible'.[14]

The two specific borders with Bangladesh and Myanmar are poised to include much more than what was formally designated as local dynamics. They can bring in spillover activities much beyond what was initially envisaged. India's initiation of border infrastructure development with both Myanmar and Bangladesh assumes greater relevance in the backdrop of the agreements that India and Bangladesh signed in January 2010 to increase regional connectivity as well India's 2005 trade agreements with Myanmar.

States in the region and outside are seeking greater interdependence through a connected infrastructure to obtain greater market access and optimisation of existing natural resource endowments. This necessarily leads to re-examination of the borders in India, especially in the eastern sector. Making NER a stakeholder in cross-border economic activities, apart from providing physical corridors between the two regions of South Asia and South East Asia, is critical for developing socio-economic stability in NE. While the government plans to spend Rs 45,000 crore for the development of the region bordering China, Bhutan, Bangladesh and Myanmar in the days ahead, there is clearly much to be done to improve the conditions at the borders.[15] The possibilities at the borders with Bangladesh and

---

14 Chiara Brambillaa , 'Exploring the Critical Potential of the Borderscapes Concept', *Geopolitics,* 9 May 2014 p15

15 Anil Wadhwa, 'The North East is key for India's ties with Asean', *Live Mint,* 9 March 2018 at https://www.livemint.com/Opinion/o4QSDxyenyvZ0QGwX5mwdL/The-North-East-is-key-for-Indias-ties-with-Asean.html

Myanmar stand unexplored. Flowing from this, political scientist Samir Das points to increasing the scope for border trade.

> Border trade perhaps is the answer—only if we realise that there is a larger moral economy of border trade, the gains of which far outweigh its meagre economic returns. Does not the moral economy of border trade force us to revisit both the dominant discourses of national security and functional integration and see how they mutate and 'dialectically transform' under present conditions?[16]

Indeed, conditions are ripe to examine the ground realities and initiate incremental programmes that provide services to the local population.

Cross-Border Land Trade

Both Bangladesh and Myanmar share land border trade with India. Over the years, the infrastructure has been improved but questions still remain about its efficacy and its operability. Bangladesh shares a 1,880-km-long border with four NE states—Assam (263 km), Meghalaya (443 km), Tripura (856 km), and Mizoram (318 km). Bangladesh's trade with NER was only $50.44 million in exports and $237.5 million in imports in 2009-10. Exports to NER in recent years increased, constituting 16.6% of Bangladesh's total exports to India in 2011. The major exports were readymade garments, cement, pharmaceuticals, ceramic tiles and hosiery. Many of these small-scale, non-traditional items were exported by small and

16 Samir Das, 'Border Economy and the Production of Collective Subjects in India's East' North East *India Quarterly, 70, 4, 2014, pp299–311*

medium operators.[17]

According to Prabir De and Manab Majumdar, official trade between the NER and Bangladesh is primarily concentrated in agricultural commodities, processed foods, minerals and garments. While NER export is dominated by raw materials like coal, limestone, boulders and agri-horticultural products like ginger and citrus fruits, imports from Bangladesh are mostly finished goods such as cement, synthetic fabric, ready-made garments and processed food.[18]

As the study shows, non-tariff barriers remain a block for greater trade between India and Bangladesh. MM Rahman cites examples of Indian customs officials demanding SAFTA/APTA certificates be submitted at the time of shipment, whereas it could earlier be done after shipment. Sanitary and phytosanitary (SPS) and other certifying agencies are situated very far from customs stations, even in other states of India. Getting these certificates takes a long time, and the exporter often has to pay compensation for perishable products.[19]

India and Bangladesh share formal border trade structures. The functional Land Customs Stations include Assam (8), Meghalaya (8) and Tripura (7). Mizoram has one non-functional one.

---

17 Mohammad Masudur Rahman, 'Trade Potential and Economic Cooperation between Bangladesh and Northeast India', in Prabir De Kavita Iyengar ed. *Developing Economic Corridors in South Asia,ADB, Manila 2017.*

18 Prabir De and Manab Majumdar, 'Developing Cross-Border Production Networks between North Eastern Region of India, Bangladesh and Myanmar: A Preliminary Assessment', *RIS, New Delhi, 2014.*

19 Mohammad Masudur Rahman, 'Trade Potential and Economic Cooperation between Bangladesh and Northeast India', in Prabir De & Kavita Iyengar Ed. *Developing Economic Corridors in South Asia, ADB, Manila, 2017*

Of all the LCSs, the most robust trade movement takes place through the Benapole-Petrapole ICP, which handles over 70 per cent of Indo-Bangladesh overland trade. An examination of the traded commodities reveals the low level of commodities from West Bengal.[20] However, this does not create any difficulties as West Bengal has commercial engagement through other ports and railway links and is not sensitive to the issue. In fact, the local mafia on the Indian side control commercial transactions at cross-border points, an ecosystem that is self-sustaining.

De and Majumdar further note that NER-Bangladesh trade mainly flows through Assam, Meghalaya and Tripura. Meghalaya has the highest share in NER-Bangladesh trade volume. The Assam-Bangladesh trade flows mainly through Sutarkandi LCS in south Assam's Barak Valley. As for Meghalaya, the LCSs at Borsora, Dawki and Ghasuapara contribute about 45, 22 and 15 per cent of the total Meghalaya-Bangladesh trade, respectively. As an exception, Tripura mainly imports from Bangladesh. Most of the trade in this state (80 per cent) flows through Agartala LCS, apart from the Srimantapur and Muhurighat LCS.[21]

The India-Myanmar international borders, although delineated (except for that with China) are largely open and allow free movement without visas up to a certain point into each other's territory, especially at Moreh-Tamu border. LCSs have been set up on Mizoram-Myanmar border crossing

20 Pratim Ranjan Bose, 'Connectivity is No Panacea for an Unprepared Northeast India', *Strategic Analysis*, 43:4, 2019, pp335-41

21 Prabir De & Manab Majumdar,' Developing Cross-Border Production Networks between North Eastern Region of India, Bangladesh and Myanmar: A Preliminary Assessment', RIS, New Delhi, 2014.

at Zokhawthar, and Moreh-Tamu at Manipur. Although border crossing points also exist on Borapansury (Mizoram–Bangladesh), and Avangkhu (Nagaland–Myanmar), there are no official trading structures.

Several studies have pointed to the huge potential at the Moreh-Tamu border trade point. But at present, the cross-border buying and selling activity is due to Chinese and Thai goods coming in from Myanmar. Options remain limited given the lack of local productions chains. Similarly, the other border crossing at Rih-Zhokhawthar remains underutilised. The infrastructure is minimal, hardly conducive to providing impetus to trading. A concerted effort is required to provide the population with goods that are in demand, replacing the limited items that are traded at present.

On the Moreh-Tamu side, the flexibility on both sides for people-to-people movement of, has now been extended to 16 km on each side. While people movement has increased, the same does not apply to cross-border trade. As is well known, strong cross-border ethnic linkages have been the source for several of the insurgent movements in India's Northeast. Free movement also led to huge informal trade including smuggling in drugs, weapons and other contraband. The continued traditional headloads of goods moving across the border has been used by some elements to indulge in malpractices. This border was often a security issue but over the years, through various mechanism and presence of Indian security forces, with the support of fifteen battalions of the Assam Rifles deployed in that region, ably supported by the security establishment in Myanmar, many of these insurgent groups have been brought under control and currently there is a ceasefire between three of the Naga groups of National Socialist

State-Wise List of LCSs Handling NER-Bangladesh Trade

State	Sr. No.	LCS in NER	Sr. No	LCS in Bangladesh
	Functional			
	1	Karimganj Streamer Ghat and Ferry Station (Karimganj District)	1	Jakiganj (Sylhet)
	2	Sutarkandi (Karimganj District)	2	Sheola (Sylhet)
	3	Guwahati Steamer Ghat (Kamrup)	3	
ASSAM	4	Dhubri Streamer Ghat (Dhurbi)	4	Rowmati (Mymansing division)
	5	Mankchar (Dhurbi)	5	Natun Bandar (Rongpur)
	Non-Functional			
	6	Mahisashan Rly. Station (Karimganj)	6	Shahbazpur (Sylhet)
	7	Golakganj (Dhurbi)	7	Sonahaat (Rongpur)
	8	Silchar RMS	8	
		Functional		
	1	Borsora (West Khasi Hills)	1	Borsora (Sunamganj)
	2	Bholaganj (East Khasi Hills)	2	Chatak (Sunamganj)
	3	Dawki (Jaintia Hills)	3	Tamabil (Sylhet)
	4	Shellabazar (West Khasi Hills)	4	Sunamganj (Sylhet)
	5	Baghmara (West Khasi Hills)	5	Bijoupur (Mymansing)
MEGHALAYA	6	Dalu (West Garo Hills)	6	Naku Gaon (Mymansing)
	7	Ghasuapara (South Garo Hills)	7	Karoitol (Mymansing)
	8	Mahendraganj (West Garo Hills)	8	Dhannua Kamalpur (Mymansing)
	Non-Functional			
	9	Ryngku (East Khasi Hills)	9	Kalibari (Sonamganj)
	10	Balat (East Khasi Hills)	10	Dolura (Sylhet)

		Non-Functional		
MIZORAM	1	Demagiri (Lunglei)	1	Rangamati (Sylhet)
	Functional			
	1	Agartala (Tripura West)	1	Akhaura (Comilla)
	2	Sarimantapur (Tripura)	2	Bibir Bazaar (Comilla)
	3	Dhalaighat (Dhlai)	3	Kumarghat (Sunamganj)
TRIPURA	4	Khowaighat (Tripura West)	4	Balla (Habibganj)
	5	Manu (Dhalai)	5	Chatlapur (Sylhet)
	6	Muhurighat (Tripura South)	6	Belonia (Feni)
	7	Old Rangabazar (Tripura North)	7	Betul (Faltali) (Sylhet)

Source: Office of the Commissioner of Customs, Shillong, 2018

Council of Nagaland (Neopao Konyak/Kitovi) and the National Socialist Council of Nagaland/Reformation (NSCN/K/Khango till April 2020. With restoration of stability at the borders, the Indian Government decided to give a fillip to the existing cross-border trade, especially at the Moreh-Tamu (Manipur's Chandel district) located in Sagaing in north-west Myanmar.

While there is a designated border point at Zhokhawthar-Rih, it has not generated much traffic in goods. The third border at Lungwa village between Nagaland's Avakhung-Pansat and Myanmar's Somra do not as yet have any formal structures, although it is also proposed for cross-border trade. While several connectivity and infrastructural projects are being developed at these points, the cross-border trade at Moreh-Tamu remains rather low.

The ICP inaugurated in January 2019 at Moreh has not facilitated the border trade as expected, although the number of people moving across stands at 3,056 during 2018-19, marginally higher than past years, but the Indo-Myanmar trade stands at a mere $2.1 billion. Cross-border trade is even more insignificant for barley at $87m (India exported $78 million and imports totalled $9 million during 2018-19). This in fact dipped to $85.8 million in March 2019. As the figures indicate, there is greater demand for Indian buying from across the border at Namphalong market in Tamu, with very little interest among traders to enter Moreh to buy Indian goods.

Where is the problem? Manifold actually.

Firstly, border trade exists but not through formal channels. The items on the formal list have limited demand and this is despite India lowering the tariff to zero for majority of the goods. Items like electronic good, timber, gems and minerals, readymade garments, shoes, slippers and edibles apart from many banned drugs find their way to Indian homes. Thus, third country goods from China, Thailand and Korea are in demand across the Myanmar border into India. Trade 'rules of origin' issues have impeded formalising the ongoing informal trading that takes place. Also, while there is a demand for products required for infrastructure material, like cement from India, there is an inherent reluctance on traders on both sides to operate through the official system. It is also true that some products being traded are not from the formal list. It is possible to examine other products that have a demand in Myanmar like dairy products, construction materials and motor vehicle parts for inclusion in the trade list. It needs to be acknowledged that the illegal sector is so well organised and entrenched, that the transition to formal trade is still facing resistance. But there is also a larger question: whether the agriculture and production centres in Manipur are represented in the border trade items. There is a gap between the border trade and the production facilities in the border region.

Secondly, apparently, ad hoc decisions from India about raising import duty on some of the agro products have stymied the flow of cross-border trade. One such instance was in 2017, when India increased the import duty on betel nut from 4 per cent to 40 per cent. Similar issues have arisen vis-à-vis import of rice and other pulses. In the wake of bumper harvests in India, demand drops and Myanmar farmers are affected. There is a need to address this to ensure the trading basket has continuity.

Thirdly, the banking sector is still a problem. The ban on barter trade which was functional until 2015, allowing for up to $20,000 per transaction, reduced the present border trade transaction drastically. The transition to formal trade has not been easy and due to some issue arising out of the change in the systems, several trading accounts still remain irreconcilable; traders find it difficult to continue with their operations. Despite agreements between the United Bank of India with banks of Myanmar, the problem persists and the inability of the State Bank of India branch at Moreh to handle forex transactions has also been cited as a problem hampering the growth of border trade. Thus, the banks on the Indian side are not yet issuing letters of credit. Many of these issues can only be addressed by the Reserve Bank of India, which is yet to happen, despite many requests.

Fourthly, it has also been pointed out that many of the small and medium businessmen from the border areas on either side do not have the 'capacity to fulfil the criterion and observe the norms'. For the local businessman, the paperwork appears complicated and given the inadequacies in the banking sector, there have been suggestions to introduce convertibility of Indian rupees, as this would boost the existing border trade.

Fifthly, despite the opening of ICPs, they are not fully operational. The goods terminal is not yet functional and the new land bridge which will facilitate the two-way trade is still under construction. Currently, cross-border trade is moving across the Indo-Myanmar Friendship Bridge which is not able to support the potential available, given its limited capacity.

Sixthly, there remains concern over cross-border people's movement. This has increased with the opening of the passenger terminal at the ICP. However, in the wake of security issues at large, India has been asking the Myanmar government to provide identity cards for populations living in the adjoining border areas who can avail the easier visa regime now operational. The fluid domestic environment within Myanmar has impeded this and the momentum of trade and people's movement expected yet remains unfulfilled. India has initiated gratis visas for Myanmar citizens, while Indians still have to pay a steep visa fee to travel to Myanmar.

As of now, while many private initiatives have come forward to support cross-border trade as many of the past practices are holding back the full actualisation of the real potential. Besides the inordinate delays in projects, incomplete and inadequate structures, systems not improvising to address local needs are some of the problems affecting border trade at Moreh. Also, traders on both sides need to work within the formal systems, moving away from the past informal trade practices, to reinforce the formal channels of trade conducive for peace and stability of this border region.

As has been argued by political scientists Das, trading with the nearest neighbour right across the border is meant for catering to the immediate needs of the people on both sides and makes better economic sense than trading with far-off towns and cities on the same side. Border trade is a means of emancipating the border areas from their geographical seclusion and remoteness.[22] Clearly, despite the physical structures often having been put in place, the corresponding soft services required for full implementation do not exist. Undoubtedly, this border region offers tremendous potential that is waiting to be tapped. But policies that reflect the ground realities need to be formulated and implemented.

Arguably, while the border trade holds huge potential, including facilitating buyer and seller interaction, the prevalent flooding of goods made in China and Thailand through this route needs to be addressed. They need to be replaced with local productions chains. Similarly, the other border crossing at Rih-Zhokhawthar remains underutilised. The infrastructure is minimal, hardly conducive to providing impetus to any trading. A concerted effort is required to provide the population with goods that are in demand, replacing the limited items traded at present. The illegal items being traded need to be resolved and local demands needs to be created for local products. Encouraging local investment for local produce and indigenous production is worth examination. This apart, the issue of people's mobility and movement needs a relook. Nagaland

22 Samir Das, 'Border Economy…' op cit, p303

enjoys open borders with Myanmar. The village Longwa with Konyak population overlaps on both sides and continue to enjoy a free flow of social and cultural interaction. Also for Tuensang district of eastern Nagaland, the Khiamniungan people have their brethren across the borders and for long have maintained direct contact. The issue of people's movement has also not received much attention.

That apart, the criterion of tender for choosing the lowest bidder has often been a problem in their capacity to build such infrastructural developments. Many times, they are able unable to even start the project, delivery is delayed and quality remains suspect.

Clearance from local government is delayed due to road or land clearance issues. Also, interior and border areas are unable to attract private sector participation due to lack of lucrative incentive schemes and stringent security rules.[23]

While the above is specific to Moreh-Tamu border, many of these issues are common to the Indo-Bangladesh border to a greater or lesser degree; the border trade in Tripura, Mizoram, Assam and Meghalaya remain low and far below the potential, as per many studies. While structures have been built, ensuring their operability remains an issue.

The lack of consistent, harmonised quality standards across the region is a major deterrent to enhanced trade in the region. This has led to instances of fruit rotting at the borders while some faraway laboratory tests their suitability to be let in, or Bangladeshi Jamdani saris destined for nearby Kolkata, India, first being sent

23 Report, 'Assessing India's Connectivity with Its Neighbourhood: A Retrospect' *VIF*, Dec 2018

to Varanasi, India (almost 700 km away) for testing.

In addition, it has often been alleged that customs officials at times use 'quality assurance' as an excuse to thwart trade.[24]

Changing the narrative

A policy of encouraging local investments for local produce and indigenous production is worth examination. This apart, the issue of people mobility and movement can be treated more positively. The migrant population crossing borders illegally in search of work can be involved in productive activity created through developing programmes at the community level by engaging population with similar economic and social interests and educational levels. It would be relevant to refer to Shibashis Chatterjee's writing while trying to understanding the impact of the cross-border developmental projects underway in the NER.

> The integration of the Indian north east within a dense economic maze stretching from Myanmar to Korea through Bangladesh, Thailand and the new ASEAN states, might ultimately help the marginalised region to transcend the historical tyranny of fixed borders and allow its inhabitants the fullest possible benefits in the process of economic exchanges qua the Look East move. This view interprets the positive dividends of the Look East Policy in terms of investments into community building and soft border exercises. It differs from the second vision in making its communitarian pledges a vital precondition to a successful economic transformation of the north east region. In other words,

24 Amy Warren and Diya Nag, 'Advancing the BBIN Agenda to Promote Sub-Regional Trade, *Asia Weekly Insights and Analysis*, 27 April 2016

> the key to successful economic relations lies in effective community formation.[25]

One of the first successful attempts have been the opening of the border *haats* (market) at the Indo-Bangladeshi borders; (*See Annexure 2*)

At present, the localised border *haats* on the Indo-Bangladeshi borders (two at Tripura and two at Meghalaya) are operational and have gathered momentum, providing direct contact between buyers and sellers. Nine are proposed along the Indo-Myanmar border. The limited opening up is essentially for the local communities living along the border.[26] The vendors selling their products in border *haats* are local residents who live within a 5-km radius. It has been estimated that bilateral trade worth $20 million can take place annually between India and Bangladesh through theses *haats*. These *haats* would facilitate the marketing of some locally produced items among the people living in inaccessible areas of both the countries. In fact, border *haat* is not a new concept—rather, it was re-introduced in 2011 after 40 years in the region.[27] The revival of the past tradition of local markets was indeed welcomed by the local communities. Their lack of access to markets was considered as one of the main reasons for their

---

25 Shibashis Chatterjee, 'Conceptions of Space in India's Look East Policy: Order Cooperation or Community?' *South Asian Survey*, 2007, 14:65, p75

26 Border Haats (localised cross-border market places) are set upon the eastern and northern sides of the India-Bangladesh border, creating better economic environment for the local people.

27 Report, 'Indo-Bangladesh Border Haats reopen after 40 years', *SME Times*, accessed at http://www.smetimes.in/smetimes/in-depth/2011/Jul/26/india-bangladesh-border-haats-reopen-after-40-years7565454.html

impoverishment in the post-1971 period.[28]

The *haats* have seen a very positive response. It was found that distance by itself is not a sufficient deterrent to regular participation on the part of vendees. Thus the stipulation of residence within the proximity of a 5-km radius of the border *haats* should be withdrawn in case of vendees; and also, infrastructural facilities like improvement of roads and approaches to the *haats* and other facilities like washrooms and restrooms needs attention for this to flourish.[29] The cross-border access to local produce and goods has opened up many possibilities. The trade that used to flourish informally has decreased substantially with the establishment of border *haats*.[30]

Thus informal arrangements through which the local population traded goods have now been given formal structure and have generated a specific economic activity, inadvertently opening up avenues for social interaction. The people-to-people connect is rather distinct and needs further nurturing. Although this space is yet to be fully explored, the cultural and social connect is undeniable. The periodicity of these *haats* has led to developing sustained economic opportunities around the borders as well as providing avenues to understanding the common cultural and social ethos. It is argued that the possibility of developing the *haats* into much larger spaces for interaction is real. The people-to-people connect in this space can be given greater salience through a more creative

28 India is keen on setting up 70 new border markets. Tripura has announced that seven new border haats will be established in Tripura, in Bamutia, Hiracherra, Amlighat, Hrisyamukh, Boxnagar, Rasyabari and Akinpur.

29 Report, 'Bordering on Happiness: An Assessment of Socio-Economic Impacts of Bangladesh-India Border Haats', *CUTS, 2019*

30 Ibid

interpretation of existing mechanisms.

As studies have revealed, these *haats* 'have significantly contributed in reducing informal trade along the border areas. At the macro-level, the markets are contributing towards cementing a good economic understanding and cooperation between the two vibrant economies of South Asia. Even as the frontier has divided many families, border *haats* have created a formal mechanism through which exchange of goods take place, enabling the people to reconnect with each other.' [31]

A special outreach and capacity-building programme would be required for building foreign trade capabilities. Trade facilitation programmes to encourage local entrepreneurs to actively participate in foreign trade would build a local buy-in. A strong linkage with mainland manufacturers and traders will be a crucial ingredient for a successful export strategy. Some local value-addition near the border through packaging or assembling facilities could also be established. It is possible to locate regular exchange of trade delegations and buyer-seller meets between neighbouring at these junctures. Certainly, as pointed out by Asish Kundra, pre-identified verticals would serve as a useful enabler to widen the scope of commercial interaction.[32] In fact the small farmers on both sides would benefit from aggregators. Providing a regional platform for regional trade without fear of monopoly is possible. Digital connectivity would be an efficient tool to enabling many

31 Report, 'Border Haats' to boost economy, people's ties: Experts.,' *The News Scroll*, 20 July 2020 at https://www.outlookindia.com/newsscroll/border-haats-to-boost-economy-peoples-ties-experts/1886266

32 Asish Kundra, 'Galvansing the trade via Northeast', *BusinessLine 23 Aug 2018 at* https://www.thehindubusinessline.com/opinion/columns/galvanising-trade-via-the-north-east/article24762267.ece

such limited activities. Local-level administration could be partnering such enterprises.

Border Community Zones

It is not uncommon to see fields and unused land available at borders which are not fully utilised. Border *haat*s, usually held in the open space, have some limited infrastructure available, usually meant for the security agencies. At the initial stages, Border Community Zones can be built with shared resources for common goods, an idea that needs greater exploration. Ranging from cultural interaction during fixed hours, it can include medical facility as that is more often than not available very easily in these border areas. A limited physical space can become the delivery mechanism for many of the needs of the local populace that a peripheral region has been unable to provide for.

By and large, youth from heartland and urban spaces have access to quality education, while children from rural area and border zones are unable to access the same. Indeed, to provide people living on the border zones a better life and greater stakes in creation of wealth and resources, they need to be provided with greater access to opportunities. Border areas in most states in the region are at the same level of development. Poor infrastructural facilities, given limited available resources, impede the opportunities available. But these are the very areas which can be tapped for creation of common physical spaces for nurturing of cultural and natural heritage.

Conceiving Border Community Zones for an outreach to population at the borders can address the huge gaps that remain between the urban and non-urban population in

India, Bangladesh and Myanmar. A shared border community experience can transform the nature of lives on each side. Apart from West Bengal, which shares many common traits with those across the border, Tripura and Assam share a familiar cultural landscape and are easily accessible from villages on the Bangladeshi side. Even the Chakmas residing on either side of Mizoram in Thegamukh and Demagiri, though with limited contact, have much in common. Similarly, the borders Myanmar shares with Manipur, Mizoram, Nagaland and Arunachal are unique not only due to the ethnic overlap but also because the border zones have an environment that is distinct from the mainland for both the neighbours. On the Manipur side, the Tangluk population lives on the Myanmar borders close to the Moreh town, while on the Arunachal side—depending on the terrain—it takes the people 2-12 hours to come to the borders, mainly on foot. While those across Mizoram can reach the borders in an hour, it takes some villagers upto twelve hours. And across Nagaland, villagers from Longkwa, Chen Moho and Chen Loisha take 2-4 hours while from Wangti it takes almost half a day.[33]

Apart from the ethnic overlaps, border economies are similar and population on both sides have limited access to services available in the mainland. In India, the concept of creative economy as an enabler for economic value generation is finding greater acceptability and implementation. NER border zones offer a ready space for creative economy.

33 Walter Fernandez, Tiken Das *et al; Relation Across the Borders: Communities Separated by the Indo-Myanmar Border*, NERC, 2015, Guwahati

Towards a Creative Economy

While the media and entertainment industries have been seen as a core element of the creative economic platform as seen from practices elsewhere, along with the digital economy boom that India is experiencing, it is possible to apply creative economy to the border communities and expansion of border economy. Studies have shown how creative economy has become a powerful transformative force in the world today. This has been instrumental in not only creating income generation but also for job creation and export earnings. More importantly, human creativity and innovation at both the individual and group level are the key drivers of these industries, and have become the true wealth of nations in the twenty-first century.[34] In the context of the NE border regions, the possibility of examining development through this prism may lead to many gains for which the ground situation has the potential.

Indeed, the social and economic environment on both sides of borders are often similar, the livelihood patterns, the available educational opportunities, even cultural practices. This creates an interactive space for building a common knowledge system through interaction and exchange with the local population on each side. This can not only provide basic amenities most required but also de-securitise the border zones to a large extent. The space would be available for prevention and mitigation of changing environmental concerns, new agricultural methods, simple vocational training and issues that are common and

34 Amlanjyoti Goswami, Aromar Revi & Shriya Anandndia's, *Cultural and Creative Economy: New Imaginations and Emerging Practice*, 2013, UNDP at http://www.unesco.org/culture/pdf/creative-economy-report-2013.pd

beneficial to all. A trans-border community living has to be incubated for creating connected minds and hearts.

Further to social and economic activities getting traction, the possibility of developing a common school curriculum for children may be explored. Differences in language would have to be bridged through a deeper understanding of the mutual needs on both sides. There would be issues over language that need further detailing. Security concerns need to be addressed through issuance of biometric identity cards and a full mapping of the population, the development of border zones that become an interactive space rather than a dividing line will enable creation of an integrated economy and stable, friendly neighbourhood.

Distance education is well established within India. The Indian apparatus can be expanded to include greater geographical and subject bandwidth for imparting quality education far and wide. Transmission of distance education can be in a variety of languages as demanded by the member countries. Given Indian technological advancement, distance education can reach out to different audiences with different needs. India has initiated a specific platform to impart content for children between ninth and twelfth standard through the Swayam programme on television channels. Given the limited internet access reach (33 per cent in India) but much larger access to television, this programme can be expanded further.

Common certifications are another area that other regional groups have successfully implemented. Integration of IT would be imperative for promoting such initiatives.[35]

---

35 NEC, *Vision 2020, May 2008 NEC, at* http://necouncil.gov.in/sites/default/files/about-us/Vision_2020.pdf Accessed 15 April 2018

This is most effective for vocational courses, including common areas like tourism, culinary, yoga, etc. In India many fraudulent practices abound, duping unsuspecting students. If formally implemented, this would address the gaps. An entrepreneurial culture can thus be encouraged through concerted efforts by both state and civil society organisations. While such schemes are available for NER, these could be introduced for cross-border development programmes too.

Cross-Border Skill Development

The Ministry of Skill Development and Entrepreneurship through National Skill Development Corporation, is implementing Capacity Building scheme for skilling of unemployed youth of NER in various sectors.[36] The proposed scheme would encourage entrepreneurship amongst those under-represented. Their mandate would include large parts of eastern and NE India. Special efforts will also be made to enroll incubators and mentors catering to these groups within the national entrepreneurial ecosystem. This also includes hospitality, housekeeping and the food and beverages sector.

Similarly, the sector of beauty and wellness would be of interest to Sylhet and can be a collaborative venture between two neighbours. The partners in this programme would find scope in the Northeast. This can be also introduced through the common initiatives already underway between India and Bangladesh, contributing to employment opportunities at various levels. Youth from the Northeast have already established themselves

36 Lok Sabha Unstarred question 3012, 31 Dec 2018 at http://loksabhaph.nic.in/Questions/QResult15.aspx?qref=76481&lsno=16 Accessed 15 April 2020

in such industries across India. Due to lack of any opportunity, many have moved away to other parts of India. Developing this sector will help to retain local talent too.

An interesting case study is that of the cross-border shopping that occurs at Akhuara-Agartala border crossing. This border has witnessed a constant stream of people enjoying the markets and shops available on the Indian side. But the excellent border facilities remain underutilised. There has not emerged any scope for large trade, except for the building materials that are traded at this border. Nor has there been much initiative to tap the newly emerging markets.

The trade at this recently modified facility seems almost negligible. The limited list of traded goods needs review to examine possibilities. As is well-known, border trade is at the Benapole-Petrapole border is often choked. Truck movement becomes sluggish due to congestion. Given the new infrastructure that is being developed through railways and ports, hopefully the hesitancy in Bangladesh to use the Akhaura land port more extensively will be removed. To facilitate trade at specific local points, the list needs re-examination and review. Bureaucratic procedures need some creative re-adjustments. The permitted list for border trade needs to be expanded with revisions at regular intervals.

The evening joint ceremony of border security forces is attracting many on both sides and improving the facilities (as planned) on the Indian side, include having an exhibition along with other recreational facilities. It will increase the presence of people on both sides.[37] Thus Agartala, which has close linkages

37 Interview with Director ICP, Agartala, Tripura , 20 May 2018

in trade including energy trade, can be a cultural and economic hub to create more people mobility and contribute to the growth and development of both sides.

People Mobility and Movement

Borders are the place through which migration occurs and this continues to be an issue of concern for India. This region has a thriving informal labour movement, given the porosity of the borders. While governments are reluctant to admit and resolve the issue of informal labour mobility given the associated issues of human security, state intervention alongside civil society support can address this issue. Search for equitable solutions which will benefit both the demand and supply side will move the states towards the creation of a non-securitised atmosphere. As has been pointed out in a UNESCAP report, 'Existing national governance structures do not have well-defined spaces that delineate the relationship between government responsibilities and the rights and obligations of public citizenship.'[38]

People's lives and their welfare are an integral element of any migration and population movement and cognition of that will remain the core to the welfare of the populace. While all the three states under review have some mechanism in place for movement of professionals, limited institutional arrangement exists for the likes of blue-collar workers. To be effective, regional cooperation needs to establish common standards to protect the rights of migrant population. This has

38 UNESCAP Report, 'Regional Connectivity for Shared Prosperity,' May 2014, p64 at www.unescap.org/resources/regional-connectivity-shared-prosperity. Accessed 15 April 2017

been possible in developed and mature nation-state systems, where the identification of a cross-border region is based upon a functional approach to spatial integration, particularly the flows of cross-border workers.

Similarly, the US-Mexico border is understood as a specific product of globalisation, where cross-border labour flows and 'twin plants' industrialisation generate social, economic and environmental interdependencies which are part and parcel of the integration process.[39] While this may be ahead of time in the Indian context, the fact that unilateral mechanisms have not been effective to deal with this outstanding problem is rather well known. Although economic factors have been cited as overriding cause of migratory trends, political and security issues often cloud the issue and this problem needs a regional solution.

Suggestions of a free mobility zone in Tamabil-Sylhet to address a common mobility needs and common services needs for the people of Bangladesh and Meghalaya has much potential through small entrepreneurship programmes (details heed to be worked out). Taking a cue from the existing facility that exists at the Indo-Myanmar border, it is possible to create a common interest zone to tap local resources and develop common activities. A very nascent introduction to this can be understood through the successful attempts at re-opening of the border *haats* at the Indo-Bangladesh borders.

India shares a border with Myanmar at Manipur, Mizoram, Nagaland and Arunachal Pradesh too. Some have formal structures in place such as the market at Moreh-Tamu on the

39 Christophe Sohna, 'Modelling Cross-Border Integration: The Role of Borders as a Resource', *Geopolitics,* a Department of Urban Development and Mobility, CEPS/ INSTEAD, Esch-sur-Alzette, Luxembourg Published online: 26 Aug 2014, p590

Indo-Myanmar border which has limited exchange of local produce. The Northeast and Myanmar are yet to have a full-scale exchange of goods and services through the land border. In sharp contrast, formal trade at the land border between the Northeast and Myanmar has been conducted for limited items on a positive list basis, which are limited.[40]

Conclusion

To paraphrase, borderlands are a ways of conceptualising social space and local identity, and the roles these have played in promoting the development of modern states.[41] While the larger initiatives and projects take time to evolve and be fully implemented, the possibilities of creating a border economy that engages with the local population to tap the unexplored potential is waiting to be discovered. The economic momentum in the NER has to begin small. The geography and the environment, cannot support overnight transformation. NER's way of life moves at a different pace and ethos and to expect that the entire traditional ecosystem will harmonise with the large-scale growth spurt possible elsewhere in India is unrealistic. The transformation at the borders will support and complement the larger initiatives that are being planned. But to wait for the transformation to take place without factoring in local conditions is unlikely to yield rich dividends. In the short or immediate terms, NER can be stakeholders through increasing cross-border linkages. The border zones have ethnic

40 Prabir De, 'India's Emerging Connectivity with Southeast Asia: Progress and Prospects', *ADBI Working Paper Series, No. 507 December 2014*

41 Michiel Baud & Willem van Schendel, 'Toward a Comparative History…' op cit

and geographical similarity which is conducive for convergence of similar economic and social activities. The cross-border ecosystem will also complement the economic corridors that may eventually develop in the region. While this was asserted way back in 2007, it still remains pertinent, for the future on India's NER lies in 'emotional and political integration with the rest of India and economic integration with the rest of Asia'.[42] The economic integration however needs to start small at the borders that can then further expand across the lands.

Beyond the Development Matrix

The AEP has led to NER receiving increased attention by both New Delhi as well as internationally. The Centre's intentions are clear. The next decade will be known as the decade of the Northeast and the Act East Policy given by the Prime Minister will go down as one of the most illustrious achievements of the present government.[43] Such a belief has been premised on two primary considerations. First, the assets of NER need to be exploited and utilised and second, the region can be better explored if it is integrated with mainstream India and with the countries to its east. Perhaps so, but not before the region has grappled with many of its residual issues. This includes how it reacts to many of the undergoing projects. While at one level, NER with its vast resources and endowments should be willing to partner the large projects planned and implemented by the Centre, the region's uneven relationship with the Centre tends

42 G Srinivasan, 'India's Look-East policy must first look at North-East', *BusinessLine*, 13 July 2007

43 PIB, Northeast key to 'Act East': Dr Jitendra Singh 8 Nov, 2016 at https://pib.gov.in/newsite/PrintRelease.aspx?relid=153384

to cast a shadow over their full implementation. The region has a substantial presence of the large number of indigenous tribes and their traditional societies and economies are organised differently. Many belong to the realm of the unorganised sector. It contributes to the complexities that are inherent to the region and continue to influence many of the social and economic factors.

Going Beyond Sheer Numbers

The previous chapters have examined some of the core factors that would make the NE a core component of the Act East Policy but also point to many gaps that exist in the schemes, policies and projects. While the region holds great promise for making way to higher levels of growth, there is a need to go beyond just NER's economic statistics. Importantly, the prism to examine success and development in the region is not necessarily the conventional one. For NER, the calculations and indicators need to assimilate beyond what sheer statistics reveal and needs to be understood beyond the number of trucks and cargo movement. Unlike how prosperity is understood in modern India, NER has an ethos that cherishes old world values and ethos. The region's growth cannot be understood only through monetary transactions, there are several other factors that provide terms of reference for guiding their growth and development. The fragile ecological environment, an integral factor in the region, the close-knit societal framework, individual faiths and beliefs play a significant role not only for livelihood patterns but also interaction with the state. As political scientist Chatterjee argues, India's Look East Policy at its imaginative best most likely 'vacillated between the conventional spatial idioms of geopolitics and a form of liberalism co-existent with the cartographic certainties of our times. It is not fundamentally opposed to the market conception of space espoused by the liberals, but it puts the claims of community prior to those of the market'.[44]

Essentially, markers based on market revenue methods do not have a great fit in NER. Resistance to drastic change is instructive for policies to be successfully planned and implemented in this region. Cultural ethos, traditional value system continue to influence the people's choices.

It has been argued that given the low base of industry and commercial activities as many of the infrastructure projects are in various stages of completion, their ability to fuel greater momentum or draw in investments will take time to unravel. Given that NE shares borders with the neighbours, the expectations for NE to be a critical stakeholder in the Centre's foreign policy in the neighbourhood does not bear out. The rush to bring out the region and push it in the forefront of cross-border relations may not necessarily bring about the most optimum results. The ground conditions of the region are difficult to ignore or bypass. The transformational changes which are planned may not be necessarily welcomed across the region. Indeed, they often refresh the fissures that already exists. Importantly, is the region prepared to accept the changes brought in through big projects and infrastructure developments? As pointed out by Deka, the NE is 'a geopolitical and geocultural unit that requires micro-adjustments to India's macro-projections.'[45]

44 Shibashis Chatterjee, 'Conceptions of Space in India's Look East Policy: Order Cooperation or Community?' *South Asian Survey*, 2007, 14; 65, p80

45 Kaustubh Deka, 'Debates around NRC show the common thread of trauma that binds the people of Assam', *Scroll.in* 3 Sep. 2019 at https://scroll.in/article/936017/debates-around-nrc-show-the-common-thread-of-trauma-that-binds-the-people-of-assam

This, in fact, has been the bane of NER. Given the diversity, it is not surprising to find that no single voice speaks for all. While Assam with its geographic location, and its other its advantages, is predominant in the region, it cannot represent all the other seven states. But the other states, in their varied levels of development, have options and opportunities that are often not similar. Their expectations also do not necessarily converge with the plans the Centre has designed for them. Inevitably, the Centre's planning and imagining for the region is not surprising, nor unexpected. With the continued financial support that each state requires, this has become a double-edged sword. The region that for a longish time has been in a state of flux, now once again has to undergo some major re-adjustment with the large projects that the Centre has planned. As pointed out by political scientist Rajni Kothari, there must be simultaneous goals, not goals that are in conflict.[46]

Essentially, the Centre has to dovetail with the needs and aspirations of the region and not the other way around. The NER needs to determine their journey and goals, only then will there be a meaningful experience – the bottoms up approach as compared to the top down processes will ensure sustainable growth.

46 Rajni Kothari, *Politics in India,* Little Brown & Co, Boston, 1970, pp334-39

POSTSCRIPT

Conventionally, it is accepted, improvement in physical infrastructure will usher in development. However, often analysis of facts and figures tends to miss the big picture. In some instances, numbers have been misleading and not reflective of realities on the ground. Indeed, at times, many changes that occur are often not planned and some do not necessarily materialise as per plans.

To premise NER's role as a gateway to the AEP on its geographical location is well understood but given the region's inherent capacity and limitations, its ability to go beyond providing a transit point or the bridge between South Asia and South East Asia has little clarity now. In the short term, development of infrastructure will bring the region closer to other parts of India. NER will be able to access and develop markets for local and outside needs and increase consumption, hopefully ushering in more employment and higher purchasing capacity.

While NER as the gateway to Act East Policy is a great peg to give a boost to the growth and development momentum, the region's capacity to contribute to the fulfilment of India's core foreign policies for the neighbourhood looks limited at present. Immediate drastic transformation is not how the NER unfolds, instead incremental measures that the region can absorb allowing the energy and momentum to develop from the ground and preparing the region for a greater role to play in the longer term. The Act East Policy will substantially contribute to the region's connectivity with the rest of India while ushering in all the consequent developments of being connected with the mainland, thereby addressing the locational disadvantage the region faced for long.

Growth of Industry

As discussed, the plan for creating a network of transportation corridors is underway, leading to greater economic momentum. But despite the potential that exists, the problems on the ground are several—least of all incomplete planning; lack of synchronisation of the hardware and software linkages continue to impede actualisation of the promise. Many of the border structures are underutilised due to this. Arguably, specific measures are required for greater link to public capital and economic performance.

The NER economy needs to focus on small units that could multiply effectively. A big-ticket economy boost is not workable as neither the environment nor the logistics nor the capacities support larger transformational initiatives.

At the domestic level, to expect realisation of increased industrial activity and greater production levels is unlikely within the next decade. Although several policies and schemes have been put in place because of various other factors at play, (which as discussed earlier have often been ignored) the scope to develop a high level of economic growth in the region has inherent limitations. As is evident, the region will witness a slow incremental growth that is supported by the ecosystem and the prevailing physical, social and political environment.

Given the low level of cross-border trade facilitation, any substantial economic boost to the region is unlikely to emerge from cross-border trade or commerce. In fact, the 'ease of doing business' factor continues to be a roadblock. The paperwork and logistical support for MSMEs seems only on paper and has not translated into substantial progress on the ground. The new policies and schemes to give a thrust to indigenous industry and creation of supporting infrastructure is the initial step but there are several measures required at various levels to tap the fuller economic and commercial possibilities. The cross-border multimodal transportation system that is slowly falling into place with Bangladesh and Myanmar will allow for greater commerce with the region but that does not address the existing weak capacity-building within the region.

The textile industry is a case in point. Unless private players are introduced and issues of design, material, fashion of the times and—more importantly—access to markets is improved and local issues are sorted out, the potential will never be fully realised. Indigenous weaves and traditional patterns will soon vanish in the face of other competitive clothing. The exclusivity of Northeast's textiles and designs can be preserved and nurtured through investment and marketability that will not happen in isolation but only through implementation of necessary policies and development of both hard and soft infrastructure.

Thus, while there are several initiatives for development of industries in NER and policies and schemes directed towards development of infrastructure, entrepreneurship skills, markets and flow of credit to entrepreneurs, exportable goods will remain confined to tea, bamboo and pharma, medicinal plants and few other agro-based industry, turmeric, ginger and food processing, livestock and poultry development, tourism, software development, handloom and handicrafts.

Minor Forest Produce, that includes all non-timber forest produce of plant origin including bamboo, brush wood, stumps, cane, *tussar*, cocoons, honey, wax, lac, *tendu* leaves, medicinal plants and herbs, roots and tubers can find markets with improved transportation systems and provide a major source of livelihood for tribals living in the forest areas. The improved railway system will enable this commerce. The lack of resources and capacity has stymied the region's growth and development. In the post-Covid phase, there will be greater focus on developing cross-border value chains in agro and horticultural goods but as yet the economies of scale do not offer larger supply nor demand within the region.

The region is still a long way off from becoming a source of exportable commodities for the South East Asian economies. The tourism sector that targets certain specific groups has greater potential than large manufacturing unit.

Development and focus on service industry and capacity building in medical, hospitality, IT and education will give better dividends within this region. Human capital will remain the most critical resource to focus on and capacity building for developing specific industry-related skills will provide greater employability. The region earlier was well known for boarding schools, that attracted many students from the neighbourhood. This can be revived as the basic structure remains, provided political stability is returned to the region.

Transport Systems

The new developing transport systems will bring NER closer to the rest of India and the wide network of roads will facilitate people-to-people movement and play a greater role in tourism if the other necessary local conditions improve. However, road maintenance has been a perennial problem in the region, and this has to change if commerce has to improve.

While many airports have been built, it will be difficult to operate all of them due to erratic weather and climatic conditions. Unused facilities that often become white elephants can be turned around for providing other facilities to the public if an effort is made to recover costs and make them a viable alternative. Cutting losses needs a proper estimation without any political agenda.

The Railways, a recent addition to the region, have shown potential for both passenger and cargo movement at far more competitive rates. As trends elsewhere have shown, investment in railway systems has greater ability to bring down costs and reduce inter-regional price gaps, thereby increasing increased trade flows and providing local goods greater access to markets. The accrued economic dividends far outweigh the investment and eventually bring in greater capital and public spending. As the transportation network continues to grow over time, the roads should be kept free for passenger movement. That would facilitate tourism and replicate the momentum and robust traffic that would have spinoffs for the larger hospitality industry as well as medical services, music and sports industries.

Undoubtedly, with accessibility through development of wide network of quality road and rail network, NER's economy will respond with greater opportunities. The internal and cross-border transport infrastructure development is the first step of the Act East Policy, moving the region to South Asian and pan-Asian regional integration. The work pace has certainly increased but given the magnitude of these projects, the transport corridors continue to be a work in progress. For them to be fully functional and dovetail into each other will take time. Not only that, corresponding efforts to synchronise software issues and introduce ground reforms alongside are necessary. While many projects are being implemented, it is critical to optimise their potential. Last mile connectivity becomes critical for fully effective implementation of the route. Seamlessness remains a challenge as of now. Hopefully, Centre-state coordination will be improved and there is equal energy to ensure that the roads, railways, airports all prove beneficial to the people of the region and others too. Once the cobweb of transport network falls in place it will certainly get the region closer to other parts of India and vice versa.

For now, the transportation network will encourage cross-border tourist movements and also medical tourism that the region offers and ought to develop further. But cargo movements within India will be competitive through the usage of the Railways, and international trade will continue to have greater impact through the ports.

Energy

Many of the initiatives for greater generation of energy have stemmed out of available resources, ideas and methods relevant for the region. The attainment of energy self-reliance remains a major goal. While there are several Government schemes and projects to augment the energy capacity in NER, it is increasingly becoming, clear despite the potential that exists, it will take time to be actualised. Questions have already been raised about the cost effectiveness of these projects. There is little clarity, more opaqueness. For now, a few projects that are already underway, like the one in Tripura, may be augmented to slightly greater capacities. But whether these projects will be able to deliver to the mainland or even the neighbouring states seems doubtful. Indeed, for now, NER needs to increase its capacity to provide for its own population. And towards this end, many of the schemes that are underway need to increase and find greater implementation and higher efficacy. Under the present circumstances, NER being a substantial contributor to the neighbourhood's energy cooperation remains confined to the domain of ideas but far from actionable plans.

The energy component is limited to a certain geography and is not all-encompassing to the entire region. Hopefully, with the full implementation of the new reforms and new regulations, each state's capacity for energy development will be greater and their usage will be greater as the economy broadens its base. It has taken long, but hopefully a beginning has been made.

Cross-border Economies

Cross-border transportation has greater likelihood of enabling robust cross-border economies with Bangladesh as well as Myanmar. Although in the past, despite the huge investments on the Indo-Myanmar side, a number of factors have stymied the potential on that border, but that is likely to change with the transformation taking place with Manipur and Mizoram border facilities. Seamless India-Myanmar-Thailand travel is a real possibility but local political conflicts within Myanmar have a tendency to flare up and be used as negotiating tool with the government. This issue will need resolution before India can establish seamless movement with Myanmar. India, Bangladesh and Myanmar will enjoy movement, trade and commerce through this region once some of the ground issues are resolved.

To prepare the ground better for the changes to be ushered in, it has been suggested that cross-border activities more at the level of low hanging fruits that do not require huge investments nor long-term gestation period can bring about a significant change to the local population on all sides, especially the borders. The existing border haats and the proposal to open more, can indeed provide the minimum and immediate physical space to allow and enable greater cross border activities and encourage greater economic development at the same time. Along with bottoms up development that the local population is capable of managing, larger changes that are taking place side by side will bring about greater change in NER.

The ability to create jobs and provide employment will be most important for the successful implementation of the projects. Many projects will need relevant skill and knowledge systems that will need to create greater capacity among local youths. Tapping the local and rural economy for such development poses greater possibilities but expecting overnight success will always remain a challenge in the region. The large number of youth in the region, both skilled and unskilled, would need to be accommodated in the system. There seems to be increasing evidence that small-size units that grow into medium-scale enterprises provides greater job creation. That being so, the potential in this region is remarkably high. Policies specific to the local condition needs greater identification and schemes formulated to support and encourage such growth. The broader objective of attaining sustainable socio-economic development that is equitable and inclusive needs to be implemented—and not just on paper. The people need to feel the benefits of the policies being decided.

Often for the sake of academia and the state's point of view, the perspective on borderlands is kept distinct and separate. In this region, the distinction should be kept at the minimum for enabling local and ground comprehensive growth, keeping in mind the permeable nature of the states. Borrowing words from PM Modi, we need to examine how the Frontier becomes mainland, where the vision and development initiatives can lead to integration of the Northeast with the rest of the country. As seen elsewhere, border regions have contributed to manufacturing industries providing greater employment and job creation and enable capacity building. The development could allow for the border population to be made a strategic use of and support the local administration for ensuring profitable economic activity.

Many studies point to greater growth and development in various sectors once the physical and infrastructure projects have been implemented in the region. Investment especially Foreign Direct Investment (FDI) would have to be invited to allow commerce to develop albet slowly. The connectivity infrastructure will facilitate commercial openings, NER will be in a stronger position to trade with mainland India, but this would still not be fully understood in the short or immediate term. The severe lack of an effective transport system for decades is being addressed but the surrounding economic activity that ought to grow around the transport corridor will take a while to finally develop, given the ground difficulties and the unpreparedness of the region.

In the meantime, border trade should be further facilitated. A border knowledge system should be spread that would penetrate the population living on the marginals and allow them to also experience the progress that is taking place in mainland and more urban zones. Focus on the undeveloped pockets of NER would allow for greater assimilation of the population with the developments that are taking place at present, increase capacity building and ensure more comprehensive development.

The growth in the region to be robust and all encompassing will need to close the gap between urban, rural and borderland pockets.

For long, rapid urbanisation has dominated the Indian landscape, leaving behind a huge marginal population unable to enjoy or contribute to the Indian growth story. This is true for NER too. The stark difference between the urban and rural economy and borderland is vivid. It is just not the physical infrastructure but making available services in education and health that will allow the overall development pattern to change from the eschewed trend that exists at present. Making Northeast a stakeholder in the Act East Policy is a work in progress, which will see its maximum success only if ground energies can match the pace of projects and schemes brought in from the top. The thrust on infrastructure, however, will bring the region closer to India and enable a momentum hitherto unknown in the region. But not at the cost of ignoring the ground realities and the people that make up the region.

People are the real stakeholders in the success of not only the Act East Policy but all the other regional and bilateral cross-border developments that are underway and in various stages of implementations. Top-down governmental policies need to be complemented by bottom-up people's involvement with processes. Their involvement in the planning as well as execution will ensure effective policies and the equitable distribution of the benefits accrued. A people-friendly environment-cognisant developmental process can lead the Northeast region to prosperity and growth. An effective Act East Policy has much to contribute to the development of the Northeast region.

The physical transformation of NER has to find resonance with the people's expectations. Making them invested stakeholders in the developmental policies will usher in the real change and will enable the region to enjoy the dividends of the processes underway. The convergence of the NER with rest of India has to be at political, social and economic levels. Anything short of that will continue to fester fears and apprehensions. It is imperative the people of NER understand, trust and engage in the discourse being offered. It is certainly a work in progress but it is hoped that a fresh start can be made for the region and its people.

ABBREVIATIONS

A

AAI	Airport Authority of India
ADB	Asian Development Bank
AEP	Act East Policy
AEZ	Agriculture Export Zones
AH	Asian Highway
ASEAN	Association of South East Asian Nations

B

BBIM MVA	Bhutan- Bangladesh-India-Myanmar -Motor Vehicle Agreement
BCIM EC	Bangladesh-China-India-Myanmar Economic Corridor
BCS	Border Community Zone
BIMSTEC	Bay of Bengal Initiative for Multi-Sectoral Technical and Economic Cooperation
BJP	Bharatiya Janata Party
BMP	Bharatmala Pariyojana
BNP	Bangladesh Nationalist Party
BPC	Bangladesh Corporation Limited
BPDB	Bangladesh Power Development Board
BRO	Border Roads Organisation

C

CLMV	Cambodia-Laos-Myanmar-Vietnam
CSST&DS	Comprehensive Scheme for Strengthening of Transmission and Distribution System
CTDP	Comprehensive Telecom Development Project

D

DoNER	(Ministry of) Development of North Eastern Region
DPG	Delhi Policy Group
DPIIT	Department for Promotion of Industry and Internal Trade

E

EDF	Export Development Fund
EDI	Electronic Data Interchange
EPW	Economic and Political Weekly
EXIM	Export Import

F

FDI	Foreign Direct Investment

G

GDP	Gross Domestic Product
GSDP	Gross State Domestic Product

H

HPCL	Hindustan Petroleum Corporation Limited

I

IBP	Indo-Bangladesh Protocol
ICP	Integrated Check Point
ICC PWC	Indian Chamber of Commerce Price Waterhouse Coopers
ICT	Information and Communication Technology

IGGL	Indradhanush Gas Grid Ltd
IMT	Inter-Modal Terminal
IOCL	Indian Oil Corporation Limited
IRADE	Integrated Research and Action for Development
IWAI	Inland Waterways Authority of India
IWT	Inland Waterways Transport
IWTT	Inland Waterway Trade and Transit

J

JICA	Japan International Cooperation Agency
JNPT	Jawaharlal Nehru Port

L

LCS	Land Custom Stations
LEP	Look East Policy
LNG	Liquefied natural gas
LPG	Liquefied Petroleum Gas
LoC	Letter of Credit

M

MIDH	Mission for Integrated Development of Horticulture
MNRE	Ministry of Non-Renewable Energy
MoPNG	Ministry of Petroleum and Natural Gas
MoU	Memorandum of Understanding
MEA	Ministry of External Affairs
MMT	Multi-Modal Terminal
MMTPA	Million Metric Tonnes Per Annum
MoU	Memorandum of Understanding
MP	Member of Parliament
MSMEs	Micro, Small and Medium Enterprises
MT	Million Tonnes

N

NDA	National Democratic Alliance
NE	North East

NEC	North Eastern Council
NEEPCO	North Eastern Electric Power Corporation Limited
NEFA	North East Frontier Agency
NER	North-East Region
NERPSIP	North Eastern Region Power System Improvement Project
NERSDS	North East Road Sector Development Scheme
NER-BPMC	North Eastern Region Biotechnology Programme Management Cell
NESIDS	North East Special Infrastructure Development Scheme
NH	National Highway
NHAI	National Highway Authority of India
NHIDC	National Highway and Infrastructure Development Corporation Limited
NHM	National Horticulture Mission
NHPC	National Hydro-Electric Power Corporation Limited
NLCPR	Non-Lapsable Central Pool of Resources
NRL	Numaligarh Refinery Limited
NSCN	Nationalist Socialist Council of Nagaland
NSU	National Sports Unit
NW	National Waterways

O

ODC	Over Dimensional Cargo
OVL	ONGC Videsh Limited

P

PIB	Press Information Bureau
PGCI	Power Grid Corporation of India Limited
PIWTT	Protocol Routes for Trade and Transit
PMKSY	Pradhan Mantri Kisan Sampada Yojana
PSU	Public Sector Unit

R

RCE	Revised Cost Estimates
ROW	Right of Way

S

SAARC	South Asian Association for Regional Cooperation
SARDP	Special Accelerated Road Development Programme
SAZ	Special Administrative Zone
SDG	Sustainable Development Goals
SHM	State Horticulture Missions

T

TARN	Trans-Asian Railway Network

U

UNESCAP	United Nations Economic and Social Commission for Asia and the Pacific
UPA	United Progressive Alliance
US	United States

V

VGF	Viability Gap Funding

Z

ZIDCO	Zoram Industrial Development Corporation

BIBLIOGRAPHY

Primary sources

'ADB President Proposes $10 Billion Support for India's Low-Income States and East Coast Economic Corridor.' *Asian Development Bank*, 16 Feb. 2018.

'ASEAN 2030: Toward a Borderless Economic Community.' Asian Development Bank, 22 July 2014, www.adb.org/publications/asean-2030-toward-borderless-economic-community.

'Supporting Internationalization of Small and Medium-Sized Enterprises: Linking India and the Greater Mekong Subregion: Technical Assistance Report.' *Asian Development Bank*, ADB, Dec. 2019, ADB;

News release. 'ADB, India Sign $375 Million Assistance for First Phase of East Coast Economic Corridor.' *Asian Development Bank*, 23 Feb. 2011.

ASEAN-India, Association of Southeast Asian Nations, Overview ASEAN-India Dialogue Relations, 2015, www.adb.org/sites/default/files/publication/156320/adbi-wp465.

'ASEAN-India, Association of Southeast Asian Nations, Overview ASEAN-India Dialogue Relations. 2015, https://asean.org/wp-content/uploads/images/2015/November/asean-india/Overview%20ASEAN-India%20Dialogue%20Relations%20-%20November%202015.pdf.

Asian Development Bank Institute. 'A Joint Study of the Asian Development Bank and the Asian Development Bank Institute.' Asian Development Bank, 2014, www.adb.org/sites/default/files/publication/159310/adbi-asean-prc-india-transformation.pdf.

Government and Non-government Publications

'India-Myanmar Joint Statement During the State Visit of the President of Myanmar to India.' Ministry of External Affairs, Government of India, Feb 2020, www.mea.gov.in/bilateral-documents.htm?dtl/32435.

Speech by Foreign Secretary at National Maritime Foundation on 'India as a Consensual Stakeholder in the Indian Ocean: Policy Contours', 19 Nov 2010, Lecture.

Chand, Manish. *Act East: India's ASEAN Journey*, 2014. www.mea.gov.in/in-focus-article.htm?24216/Act+East+Indias+ASEAN+Journey.

Government of India, Ministry of Commerce and Industry, Department of Commerce Foreign Trade Policy statement 2017, dgft.gov.in.

'India and ASEAN to Work Together to Realise Potential in Agri and Food Sector', 2015, www.mea.gov.in/aseanindia/press-releases.htm?dtl/22575/India+and+ASEAN+to+work+together+to+realize+potentials+in+Agri+and+Food+Sector.

Joint Statement on 60th Anniversary of India-Malaysia Diplomatic Relations. www.mea.gov.in/bilateral-documents.htm?dtl/28297/Joint_Statement_on_60th_Anniversary_of_IndiaMalaysia_Diplomatic_Relations.

Joint Statement on a Strategic Partnership Between India and Singapore- 'Renewed Spirit, New Energy', November 24, 2015. www.mea.gov.in/bilateral-documents.htm?dtl/26060 Lok Sabha; Government of India. Question No 3846. MEA, 2019, www.mea.gov.in/lok-sabha.htm?dtl/32189/question+no3846+phd+fellowship+to+asean+students.

Ministry of Defence, Government of India Annual Report 2018-19, 2019, www.mod.gov.in/sites/default/files/MoDAR2018.pdf.

Ministry of Development of North-East Region and Dr Jitendra Singh *Look East Agenda*, PIB, July 2019. pib.gov.in/Press Release Page.aspx? PRID=1579067.

Ministry of Development of North-East Region; Government of India. *India-ASEAN to play a lead role in Post-COVID World Economic Recovery*: Dr Jitendra Singh. PIB 2020, pib.gov.in/Press Relese Detailm.aspx?PRID=1640937.

Ministry of External Affairs, Government of India, Amb (Retd) Sajjanhar Ashok, 'From Look East to Act East: Semantics or Substance.' 11 Feb. 2017, Central University of Kerala, Kasaragod, Lecture.

Ministry of External Affairs, Government of India. *India-Japan Relations*. www.mea.gov.in/Portal/ForeignRelation/Japan_2015_07_23.pdf>.

Ministry of External Affairs, Press Release, 'Celebrating 25 Years of the ASEAN-India Dialogue Partnership.' Ministry of External

Affairs, Government of India, 28 Jan 2017, www.mea.gov.in/aseanindia/press-releases.htm?dtl/22614/Celebrating+25+years+of+the+ASEANIndia+Dialogue+Partnership.

Ministry of External Affairs, *Responding First as a Leading Power.* :www.mea.gov.in/Portal/IndiaArticleAll/636548962666860480_Responding_First_Leading_Power.pdf.

Prime Minister's Office, *ASEAN-India: Shared Values, Common Destiny: Narendra Modi.* Press Information Bureau, 2018, pib.gov.in/PressReleaseIframePage.aspx?PRID=1517931.

Rajya Sabha, Minister of State in the Ministry of External Affairs (MJ Akbar), Unstarred Question No. 26 Act East Policy, 2017, www.mea.gov.in/rajya-sabha.htm?dtl/27982/question+no26+act+east+policy.

Speech by MoS, Ministry of External Affairs, Government of India. 'ASEAN-India Youth Dialogue.' Valedictory Session of ASEAN-India Youth Dialogue, June 2020, India Foundation. https://www.mea.gov.in/Speeches-Statements.htm?dtl/32753/speech+by+mos+at+the+valedictory+session+of+aseanindia+youth+dialogue+june+10+2020. Speech.

Raja Mohan, C, *From Looking East to Acting East.* 2015, www.mea.gov.in/in-focus-article.htm?24714/From+Looking+East+to+Acting+East.

Kathuria, Sanjay. 'Bangladesh Corridor Vital to India's 'Act East' Policy.' *World Bank*, 27 Sept. 2017.

Khanna, Sushil. 'Economic Opportunities or Continuing Stagnation.' *Seminar* magazine, New Delhi, www.india-seminar.com/2005/550/550%20sushil%20khanna.htm.

'South Asia Economic Update 2010: Moving Up, Looking East', World Bank, 7 June 2010, www.worldbank.org/en/news/feature/2010/06/07/south-asia-economic-update-2010-moving-up-looking-east.

Kaul, Mandakini. 'Encouraging More Women to Take Part in Regional Trade.' *World Bank Blogs*, 29 Mar. 2018, https://blogs.worldbank.org/endpovertyinsouthasia/encouraging-more-women-take-part-regional-trade.

Korwatanasakul, Upalat. 'Time to Look East: Lessons from Revisiting Asian Economic Integration,' Asian Development Bank, ADB, 20 Apr. 2020 https://www.adb.org/sites/default/files/publication/579741/adbi-wp1110.pdf.

Mathur, Priya. 'India's North Eastern Region is Poised to Capitalize on Its Core Strengths.' *World Bank Blogs*, World Bank, 14 Dec. 2019, https://blogs.worldbank.org/endpovertyinsouthasia/indias-north-eastern-region-poised-capitalize-its-core-strengths.

Ramesh, Jairam. 'Northeast India in a New Asia.' *Seminar* magazine, New Delhi, 2014, www.india-seminar.com/2005/550/550%20jairam%20ramesh.htm.

Yun Jeong, Hoe. 'India's First Coastal Corridor to Drive Manufacturing, Growth.' *Asian Development Blog*, 12 May 2017, https://blogs.adb.org/blog/indias-first-coastal-corridor-drive-manufacturing-growth.

Wignaraja, Ganeshan. 'Assessing the Experience of South Asia-East Asia Integration and India's Role' Asian Development Bank, Feb. 2014, www.adb.org/sites/default/files/publication/156320/adbi-wp465.pdf.

'South Asia Economic Update 2010: Moving Up, Looking

East.' World Bank, 7 June 2010, www.worldbank.org/en/news/feature/2010/06/07/south-asia-economic-update-2010-moving-up-looking-east.

Secondary sources

Books

Akkemik, Kucik A. *Industrial Development in East Asia: A Comparative Look at Japan, Korea, Taiwan, and Singapore*. World Scientific, 2009.

Baruah, Sanjib. *Durable Disorder: Understanding the Politics of Northeast India*. Oxford UP, USA, 2007.

Baruah, Sanjib. *Durable Disorder: Understanding the Politics of Northeast India*. Oxford UP, USA, 2007.

Gogoi, Dilip. *Making of India's Northeast: Geopolitics of Borderland and Transnational Interactions*. Taylor & Francis, 2019.

Haokip, Thongkholal. *India's Look East Policy and the Northeast*. Sage Publications India, 2015.

Henderson, Jeffrey. *East Asian Transformation: On the Political Economy of Dynamism, Governance and Crisis*. Routledge, 2011.

Muni, S.D., and Rahul Mishra. *India's Eastward Engagement: From Antiquity to Act East Policy*. SAGE Publications India, 2018.

Ram, Amar N. *Two Decades of India's Look East Policy: Partnership for Peace, Progress and Prosperity*. 2012.

Sarma, Atul, and Saswati Choudhury. *Mainstreaming the Northeast in India's Look and Act East Policy*. Springer, 2017.

Singh, M. A. *Northeast India and India's Act East Policy: Identifying the Priorities*. Routledge, 2019.

Singh, MA, *Northeast India and India's Act East Policy: Identifying the Priorities*. Routledge, 2019.

Singh, MA and Komol Singha. *Understanding Urbanisation in Northeast India: Issues and Challenges*. Taylor & Francis, 2020.

Swami, Anju, and Manisha Swami. Mekong-Ganga Co-Operation and India's ACT East Policy. 2019.

Articles in Journals

Bajpaee, Chietigj. 'Dephasing India's Look East/Act East Policy.' *Contemporary Southeast Asia*, Vol. 39, no. 2, 2017, pp. 348-372.

Chakraborty, D. and A. Chakraborty. 'India's Act East Policy: Walking the Talk,' 2018.

Chatterjee, Shibashis. 'Conceptions of Space in India's Look East Policy: Order, Cooperation or Community?' *South Asian Survey*, Vol. 14, no. 1, June 2007, pp. 65–81,

Dhawan, Ranjit K 'India's 'Act East' Policy Towards the Two Koreas: Issues and Challenges.' *Strategic Analysis*, Vol. 42, no. 5, 2018, pp. 490-502.

F Lynch III, Thomas, 'Balancing China & Transcending Pax-Americana: India and Japan As Emerging Strategic Bookends.' *The Asan Forum*, July 2020, www.theasanforum.org/balancing-china-transcending-pax-americana-india-and-japan-as-emerging-strategic-bookends/.

Haokip, Thongkholal. 'India's Look East Policy.' *South Asian Survey*, Vol. 18, No. 2, 2011, pp239-57.

GVC Naidu, 'Whither the Look East Policy: India and Southeast Asia.' Institute for Defence Studies and Analyses, *Strategic Analysis*, vol. 28, no. 2, Apr. 2004.

Jaffrelot, Christophe. 'India's Look East Policy: An Asianist strategy in Perspective.' *India Review*, Vol. 2, No. 2, 2003, pp35-68.

Kaur, Inderjit and Nirvikar Singh. 'Financial Integration and Financial Development in East Asia.' *Millennial Asia*, Vol. 5, No. 1, Apr 2014, pp1–22,

Kumar, Suneel. 'Reinvigoration of BIMSTEC and India's Economic, Strategic and Security Concerns.' *Millennial Asia*, Vol. 11, No. 2, Aug. 2020, pp. 187–210,

Ngaibiakching, and Amba Pande. 'India's Act East Policy and ASEAN: Building a Regional Order Through Partnership in the Indo-Pacific.' *International Studies*, Vol. 57, No. 1, 2019, pp67-78.

Panda, Jagannath. 'A View from India.' *The Asan Forum*, Jan 2020, www.theasanforum.org/a-view-from-india/.

Sharma, Rikeesh. 'India's Look East to Act East Policy: Tracking the Opportunities and Challenges in the Indo-Pacific,' Book review of Manmohini Kaul and Anushree Chakraborty (Eds), *International Studies*, vol. 55, no. 2, 2018, pp. 207-210.

Singh, Abhijit. 'The Nautical Dimension of India's 'Act East' Policy.' *South Asia Journal*, Apr. 2018.

Yasmin, Lailufar. 'India and China in South Asia: Bangladesh's Opportunities and Challenges.' Millennial Asia, Vol. 10, No. 3, Dec. 2019, pp322–36.

Ziipao, Raile R. 'Look/Act East Policy, Roads and Market

Infrastructure in North-East India.' *Strategic Analysis*, Vol. 42, No. 5, 2018, pp476-89.

Articles Online

'Can 'Act East' Address Northeast India's Isolation?' *East Asia Forum*, 27 Oct 2017, www.eastasiaforum.org/2017/10/27/can-act-east-address-northeast-indias-isolation/.

Bhanu Singh and Dr Udai Bhanu Singh. 'Five Years of India's Act East Policy and the way Ahead.' *Diplomatist*, Mar. 2020, diplomatist.com/2020/03/04/five-years-of-indias-act-east-policy-and-the-way-ahead/.

De, Prabir. 'Big ideas to shape BIMSTEC's future.' *East Asia Forum*, 15 Sept. 2017, www.eastasiaforum.org/2017/09/15/big-ideas-to-shape-bimstecs-future/.

Hussain, Nazia. 'Is BIMSTEC re-modelling for a bigger role?' *East Asia Forum*, 23 Nov. 2018, www.eastasiaforum.org/2018/11/23/is-bimstec-re-modelling-for-a-bigger-role/.

Kumara, Sarath. 'Burma Visit Highlights India's 'Look East' Strategy.' *World Socialist Web Site - Marxist Analysis, International Working Class Struggles & the Fight for Socialism*, 29 Nov. 2012, www.wsws.org/en/articles/2005/04/indi-a06.html.

Mukherjee, Rohan. 'East by Southeast: Three Challenges for India's 'Act East' Policy.' *Business News, Finance News, India News, BSE/NSE News, Stock Markets News, Sensex NIFTY, Latest Breaking News Headlines*, www.business-standard.com/article/economy-policy.

Neog, Ruhee. 'India's Northeast and the Look East Policy: Challenging Established Notions.' *IPCS*, Aug, 2014.

Ollapally, Deepa. 'Second Chance to Boost Ties in Tsai's Second Term.' *The Asan Forum*, Apr. 2020, www.theasanforum.org/second-chance-to-boost-ties-in-tsais-second-term/.

Shahin, Sultan. 'India's 'Look East' Policy Pays off,' *Global Policy Forum*, Oct. 2003, www.globalpolicy.org/component/content/article/162-general/27908.html.

Singh, Dr Rajkumar, 'India's Journey from Look East to Act East in Southeast Asia.' *South Asia Journal*, 2 Sept. 2020, southasiajournal.net/indias-journey-from-look-east-to-act-east-in-southeast-asia/.

Suryanarayana, PS 'India Acts East, Looks West.' *South Asia Journal*, 2 Dec. 2018, southasiajournal.net/india-acts-east-looks-west/.

Wignaraja, Ganeshan. 'Assessing the Experience of South Asia-East Asia Integration and India's Role.' Asian Development Bank, Feb. 2014,.pdf.

Yhome, K. 'Re-imagining Regions Through BIMSTEC.' *ORF*, 15 Oct. 2014, www.orfonline.org/research/re-imagining-regions-through-bimstec/.

Annexure 1

Citizenship (Amendment) Act, 2019
No. 47 of 2019

[Dated December 12, 2019]

An Act further to amend the Citizenship Act, 1955.

BE it enacted by Parliament in the Seventieth Year of the Republic of India as follows:

1. (1) This Act may be called the Citizenship (Amendment) Act, 2019.

(2) It shall come into force on such date as the Central Government may, by notification in the Official Gazette, appoint.

2. In the Citizenship Act, 1955 (hereinafter referred to as the principal Act), in section 2, in sub-section (1), in clause (b), the following proviso shall be inserted, namely:

"Provided that any person belonging to Hindu, Sikh, Buddhist, Jain, Parsi or Christian community from Afghanistan, Bangladesh or Pakistan, who entered into India on or before the 31st day of December, 2014 and who has been exempted by the Central Government by or under clause (c) of sub-section (2) of section 3 of the Passport (Entry into India) Act, 1920 or from the application of the provisions of the Foreigners Act, 1946 or any rule or order made thereunder, shall not be treated as illegal migrant for the purposes of this Act;

3. After section 6A of the principal Act, the following section shall be inserted, namely:
'6 B. (1) The Central Government or an authority specified by it in this behalf may, subject to such conditions, restrictions and manner as may be prescribed, on an application made in this behalf, grant a certificate of registration or certificate of naturalisation to a person referred to in the proviso to clause (b) of sub-section (1) of section 2.

(2) Subject to fulfilment of the conditions specified in section 5 or the qualifications for naturalisation under the provisions of the Third Schedule, a person granted the certificate of registration or certificate of naturalisation under sub-section (1) shall be deemed to be a citizen of India from the date of his entry into India.

(3) On and from the date of commencement of the Citizenship (Amendment) Act, 2019, any proceeding pending against a person under this section in respect of illegal migration or citizenship shall stand abated on conferment of citizenship to him:

Provided that such person shall not be disqualified for making application for citizenship under this section on the ground that the proceeding is pending against him and the Central Government or authority specified by it in this behalf shall not reject his application on that ground if he is otherwise found qualified for grant of citizenship under this section:

Provided further that the person who makes the application for citizenship under this section shall not be deprived of his rights and privileges to which he was entitled on the date of receipt of his application on the ground of making such application. (4) Nothing in this section shall apply to tribal area of Assam, Meghalaya, Mizoram or Tripura as included in the Sixth Schedule to the Constitution and the area covered under "The Inner Line" notified under the Bengal Eastern Frontier Regulation, 1873.'.

4. In section 7D of the principal Act,—(i) after clause (d), the following clause shall be inserted, namely:

"(da) the Overseas Citizen of India Cardholder has violated any of the provisions of this Act or provisions of any other law for time being in force as may be specified by the Central Government in the notification published in the Official Gazette; or";

(ii) after clause (f), the following proviso shall be inserted, namely:

"Provided that no order under this section shall be passed unless the Overseas Citizen of India Cardholder has been given a reasonable opportunity of being heard.".

5. In section 18 of the principal Act, in sub-section (2), after clause (ee), the following clause shall be inserted, namely:

"(eei) the conditions, restrictions and manner for granting certificate of registration or certificate of naturalisation under sub-section (1) of section 6B;".

6. In the Third Schedule to the principal Act, in clause (d), the following proviso shall be inserted, namely:

'Provided that for the person belonging to Hindu, Sikh, Buddhist, Jain, Parsi or Christian community in Afghanistan, Bangladesh or Pakistan, the aggregate period of residence or service of Government in India as required under this clause shall be read as "not less than five years" in place of "not less than eleven years".'.

Dr G Narayana Raju
Secy to the Government of India

Annexure 2

Memorandum of Understanding (MoU) Between the Government of the Republic of India And the Government of the People's Republic of Bangladesh Establishing border haats across the border between India and Bangladesh

The Government of the Republic of India and the Government of the People's Republic of Bangladesh

Recognizing that Border Haats aim at promoting well-being of the people dwelling in remote areas across the border of two countries, by establishing traditional system of marketing the local produce through local markets;

Recalling the decision of the Prime Ministers of Bangladesh and India during the visit of the Prime Minister of Bangladesh H.E. Sheikh Hasina to India from 10 to 13 January 2010 that Border Haats shall be established on a pilot basis at selected areas, including Meghalaya border to allow trade in specific products and produce and in accordance with the regulations agreed and notified by both Governments;

Welcoming the inauguration and running of activities in four border haats, namely Ballamari (Kungram District, Bangladesh)–Kalalchar (West Garo Hills, India), Lauwaghar (Dalora, Sunamganj District, Bangladesh)—Balat (East Khasi Hills, India), East Madugram and Middle Place of Sagaria (Feni District, Bangladesh)—

Srinagar (West Tripura, India) and Tarapur (Brahmabaria District, Bangladesh)—Kamalasagar (Sipahijala District, Tripura, India);

Expressing satisfaction for the fulfilment of long standing demand of the local people of the area;

Noting that the resulting economic activity would contribute to the economic upliftment of the people of the area surrounding the border haats; and

Recognizing the need for the opening of more border haats in the places along India-Bangladesh border as agreed by both the governments;

Have agreed as follows:

1. Opening of New Border Haats

1. Border Haats shall be established across the border
2. Locations for opening Border Haats may be selected jointly between India and Bangladesh based on, inter alia, historical location, difficulty in access, inter-dependence of the population on both sides of the border and availability of suitable location;
3. The Border Haats shall be operated as per Modalities to be agreed upon between the two countries

2. Joint Committee:

A Joint Committee for Border Haats at the level of Additional Secretary/Joint Secretary from both the countries shall review the Border Haats operations, suggest modifications in the operational modalities and propose new locations for Border Haats. The Joint Committee will also comprise officials from Border Haats of relevant departments from both countries. The meeting of the Joint Committee will be held every year, or earlier as would be mutually decided.

3. Validity:

This MoU shall be valid for 5 (five) years with effect from the 23rd day of October 2013. It shall automatically be extended for successive tenures of 5 (five) years unless either Government terminates the MoU by giving a written notice of its intention to terminate to the other Government at least six months before the end of such a term. In case of termination, it shall cease to operate on the expiry of the respective term. But termination shall not affect the actions taken or MoUs reached pursuant to this MoU.

4. **Suspension of MoU:**
Any party may suspend the operation of this MoU by giving 30 days advance notice in writing.

5. **Amendments:**
This MoU may be modified, reviewed or amended with the mutual consent by means of any implementing arrangements or additional protocols, which will be an integral part of this MoU.
Signed at New Delhi on this 8th day of April 2017, in English, in two originals, both being equally authentic.

For Ministry of Commerce and Industry Government of the Republic of India	For Ministry of Commerce Government of the People's Republic of Bangladesh
(signature) Commerce Secretary	(signature) Secretary-in-charge

INDEX

A

Adani Energy 131

Agartala 16, 17, 66, 71, 72, 73, 74, 80, 103, 118, 191, 194, 195, 198, 199, 200, 202, 203, 204, 205, 255, 258, 273

Agriculture 7, 15, 18, 19, 20, 23, 27, 32, 36, 40, 99, 126, 138, 150, 183, 260

Airport 72, 73, 74, 189, 223, 225

Aizawl 67, 72, 80, 118, 213

All Assam Students' Union (AASU) 151

Arunachal Pradesh xviii, xx, xxiii, xxiv, 1, 2, 12, 15, 21, 24, 28, 30, 32, 33, 35, 36, 37, 61, 62, 63, 64, 65, 68, 71, 72, 73, 74, 78, 79, 80, 84, 85, 86, 87, 90, 92, 95, 114, 115, 116, 118, 119, 120, 122, 123, 126, 178, 210, 275

Ashugunj 129, 206

Asian Development Bank 69, 101, 184, 185, 208, 212, 293, 299, 300, 303, 308

Asian Highway 67, 175, 224, 229, 231, 293

Asian Railway 224, 225, 228, 297

Assam xiii, xv, xviii, xix, xxiv, xxvi, 2, 3, 4, 6, 8, 11, 12, 14, 15, 16, 23, 24, 25, 26, 28, 30, 31, 32, 33, 34, 35, 36, 37, 42, 48, 52, 62, 64, 68, 71, 74, 77, 78, 79, 82, 84, 86, 87, 89, 90, 91, 93, 95, 96, 98, 100, 101, 102, 103, 104, 106, 107, 115, 117, 118, 119, 123, 130, 141, 149, 151, 152, 153, 154, 155, 156, 157, 158, 159, 160, 161, 163, 164, 167, 169, 173, 174, 175, 178, 192, 193, 195, 198, 209, 211, 214, 221, 229, 231, 253,

254, 255, 256, 263, 269, 279, 280, 310
Assam Energy Development Agency (AEDA) 118
Atal Bihari Vajpayee 161
Autonomous Councils 146

B

Bagerhat 131, 207, 209, 225
Baghabari 130
Bagrakote 67
Bangladesh xviii, xxi, xxii, xxiii, xxiv, xxv, xxvi, 3, 9, 16, 17, 20, 24, 42, 43, 47, 48, 49, 53, 54, 66, 86, 87, 88, 89, 91, 93, 105, 113, 114, 123, 126, 127, 128, 129, 130, 132, 133, 134, 135, 136, 139, 149, 157, 161, 162, 169, 178, 179, 180, 181, 185, 186, 188, 189, 190, 191, 192, 193, 194, 195, 196, 197, 198, 199, 200, 201, 202, 203, 204, 205, 206, 207, 208, 209, 219, 221, 222, 223, 224, 225, 226, 227, 228, 229, 230, 231, 232, 233, 234, 235, 237, 238, 241, 246, 247, 249, 250, 252, 253, 254, 255, 256, 257, 263, 264, 265, 266, 269, 272, 273, 275, 283, 287, 288, 293, 294, 302, 306, 309, 311, 312, 313, 314
Bangladesh Petroleum Corporation (BPC) 131, 207, 208
Bangladesh Power Development Board (BPDB) 129, 131, 207
Barak 12, 86, 87, 89, 94, 98, 126, 192, 255
Bay of Bengal xix, xxii, 91, 210, 224, 293
BBIM MVA 293
BCIM EC xxi, 293
Behrampur 132, 207, 208, 232
Bengali 149, 151, 157
Bharatmala Pariyojana (BMP) 46, 61, 98
Bheramara 132, 207, 208, 232
Bhutan xviii, xxi, xxii, xxiv, 25, 47, 54, 87, 113, 127, 128, 134, 135, 136, 178, 179, 180, 185, 190, 196, 201, 220, 221, 222, 224, 225, 227, 229, 230, 231, 232, 234, 238, 247, 252, 293
BIMSTEC xxii, xxiv, 187, 224, 228, 293, 306, 307, 308
Biodiversity 107, 108
Biogas 117
Bodoland 147
Border Roads Organisation 68, 293
Brahmaputra 7, 12, 79, 80, 86, 87, 88, 89, 90, 92, 94, 98, 120,

123, 190, 231
British xvii, 35, 146, 149, 201, 202, 246
Brunei 135

C
Census 2, 34, 149, 150, 152, 162
Central Electricity Authority (CEA) 120
Chattogram 53, 67, 131, 191, 195, 198, 199, 200, 201, 206, 208, 219, 222, 246
Chicken's neck 3, 219
China xviii, xxi, xxii, xxiii, xxiv, 24, 42, 52, 65, 67, 123, 149, 177, 178, 179, 230, 247, 252, 255, 259, 262, 293, 305, 306
Chinese xvii, 53, 246, 256
Citizenship Amendment Act (CAA) 143, 152, 160
CLMV 183, 185, 294
Coal 4, 25, 76, 90, 92, 115, 128, 132, 179, 209, 232, 254
Constituent Assembly 1, 145
Corridor xvii, xviii, 3, 7, 45, 88, 106, 109, 136, 137, 139, 178, 198, 212, 218, 220, 223, 225, 226, 229, 289, 303
Covid-19 xi, xiii, xv

D
Dhaka 132, 169, 191, 196, 198, 199, 201, 202, 203, 205, 206, 226, 229
Dhoklam 67
Dhubri 86, 87, 88, 90, 91, 95, 106, 130, 231, 257
Dibang 73, 122, 123
Dimapur xxiii, 42, 66, 71, 72, 73, 81, 103, 118, 247

E
Electricity 120, 212
Employment xiv, xv, xxv, 5, 16, 20, 28, 29, 36, 38, 40, 41, 42, 48, 110, 117, 135, 150, 176, 272, 281, 288, 289
Exim Bank 182, 209
Export 23, 182, 293, 294

F
Food processing 14, 17, 27, 30, 34, 138, 183, 284
Foreigners' tribunals 154

G
Gangtok 67, 73, 80, 103
Gas pipeline 134, 135, 136, 211
Gomati 195, 198

H

Handicrafts 26, 29, 34, 138, 223, 284
Handloom 29, 38, 138, 284
Hydrocarbon Vision 112, 114, 135, 211

I

Import 17, 47, 113, 128, 132, 133, 135, 139, 184, 196, 207, 210, 217, 223, 224, 233, 260
Indian Ocean xix, 300
Indian Oil Corporation Ltd (IOCL) 131
Indonesia 134, 184, 214
Indo-Pacific xix, 106, 306
Indradhanush Gas Grid Ltd (IGGL) 136
Inland Waterways Authority of India 87, 192, 295
Insurgency 5, 9, 10, 55, 66, 148, 152, 161, 186, 249
Integrated Check Post xxvi, 194
Itanagar 72, 73, 78, 79, 80, 103, 118

J

Japan International Cooperation Agency (JICA) 65, 100
Jorhat 71, 72, 74, 118

K

Kohima xxiii, 66, 80, 81, 103, 106, 118
Kolkata ix, 74, 89, 90, 91, 92, 191, 192, 193, 195, 196, 197, 199, 202, 203, 205, 215, 216, 221, 223, 225, 263

L

landlessness 55, 150
Lao PDR 183, 230
Lilabari 71, 72, 74
Look East Policy xx, 60, 172, 186, 187, 247, 264, 265, 278, 279, 295, 304, 305, 306, 307
LPG 131, 135, 136, 208, 211, 295

M

Malaysia 135, 214, 300
Manipur xviii, xx, xxiii, xxiv, 2, 12, 18, 19, 21, 23, 24, 25, 31, 32, 33, 34, 36, 37, 62, 64, 66, 68, 70, 71, 78, 80, 85, 87, 93, 101, 102, 106, 116, 118, 119, 120, 126, 147, 148, 174, 178, 193, 210, 217, 218, 228, 229, 234, 256, 258, 260, 269, 275, 287
Meghalaya xiii, xv, xviii, xix, xxiv, 2, 11, 12, 14, 15, 23, 25,

27, 28, 30, 31, 32, 33, 34, 35, 36, 37, 62, 64, 65, 68, 71, 73, 78, 80, 81, 84, 86, 91, 92, 96, 100, 101, 102, 103, 104, 105, 106, 114, 119, 120, 125, 126, 152, 158, 166, 174, 178, 253, 254, 255, 263, 265, 275, 310, 312

Meghna 192, 195, 201

Migrant xiv

Mizoram xviii, xx, 2, 3, 6, 11, 12, 20, 21, 23, 24, 25, 30, 34, 36, 37, 62, 63, 67, 68, 71, 74, 78, 80, 81, 85, 86, 87, 93, 96, 100, 101, 102, 103, 104, 105, 107, 118, 119, 120, 121, 126, 134, 147, 148, 158, 178, 193, 210, 213, 214, 215, 216, 217, 218, 228, 234, 253, 254, 255, 256, 263, 269, 275, 287, 310

Monarchak 130, 207, 208

Murshidabad 132

Myanmar xvii, xviii, xxi, xxii, xxv, 9, 20, 24, 42, 43, 47, 48, 49, 53, 54, 67, 113, 134, 135, 136, 178, 179, 180, 183, 184, 185, 186, 188, 210, 211, 212, 213, 214, 215, 216, 217, 218, 219, 220, 221, 224, 228, 229, 230, 234, 237, 238, 241, 246, 247, 249, 250, 252, 253, 254, 255, 256, 258, 259, 260, 261, 263, 264, 265, 269, 275, 276, 283, 287, 288, 293, 294, 300

N

Nagaland xviii, xx, xxiii, xxiv, 2, 11, 12, 19, 20, 23, 24, 30, 36, 37, 56, 62, 63, 66, 68, 71, 80, 81, 85, 86, 87, 93, 95, 105, 107, 108, 118, 119, 120, 142, 146, 147, 148, 158, 174, 178, 193, 210, 234, 256, 258, 262, 263, 269, 275, 296

Naga National Council (NNC) 148

Narendra Modi xx, xxi, 1, 21, 73, 77, 112, 115, 141, 161, 177, 237, 302

National Gas Grid 137

National Highway 63, 296

National Register of Citizens (NRC) 143, 152

National Waterway 88, 92, 95, 191, 192

Natural gas 15, 16, 34, 35, 115, 128, 134, 135, 210, 211, 295

Nepal xxi, xxii, xxiii, xxiv, 54, 91, 113, 127, 128, 132, 133,

134, 135, 136, 149, 179, 180, 185, 196, 197, 201, 220, 221, 222, 223, 224, 225, 227, 229, 230, 232, 233, 234, 238, 247
NHIDCL 62, 63, 64, 65, 67, 68
North East Council 59, 158
Northeast Vision 2020 59
NTPC 92, 193, 233
Numaligarh 65, 92, 103, 130, 207, 209, 211, 296

P

Pakyong 68, 72, 73
Paradip 136, 197
Partition xvii, xix, 3, 35, 53, 54, 86, 198, 240, 244, 246
Pasighat 71, 72, 74, 120
Pawan Hans Helicopters Ltd 73
Petrapole-Benapole 198
Petronet LNG Ltd (PLL) 211
PHD Chamber of Commerce and Industry 181
Philippines 184
Port 53, 67, 90, 129, 184, 190, 191, 194, 195, 196, 197, 198, 199, 200, 201, 215, 216, 219, 220, 221, 222, 223, 230, 231, 246, 273
Power Grid Corporation of India (PGCI) 207
PV Narasimha Rao 186

R

Railways 76, 80, 81, 82, 83, 84, 110, 198, 203, 204, 285, 286
Rampal 131, 207, 208, 209
Rangpo 67, 68, 82
Refugee 159
Reliance Group 131

S

Sabroom 66, 197, 198, 200, 204, 206
SARDP-NE 60, 61, 98
Sheikh Hasina 128, 129, 169, 189, 196, 209, 312
Shillong 28, 32, 65, 71, 72, 73, 75, 80, 82, 84, 103, 105, 125, 148, 206, 258
Sikkim xv, xviii, 1, 2, 3, 6, 12, 15, 21, 23, 25, 28, 30, 32, 35, 36, 37, 62, 63, 67, 68, 72, 73, 80, 82, 101, 102, 105, 107, 108, 114, 116, 119, 120, 121, 123, 126, 166, 178
Silchar 64, 66, 71, 72, 82, 87, 89, 95, 103, 161, 192, 257
Silghat 88, 130

Siliguri xviii, 88, 92, 191, 198, 201, 202, 204, 207, 209, 220, 221, 225, 227
Sivasagar 65
Sixth Schedule 1, 145, 158, 165, 310
software xxvii, 48, 49, 109, 138, 235, 282, 284, 286
Solar 118, 119
South East Asia xxviii, 3, 54, 142, 177, 179, 181, 186, 187, 219, 248, 252, 281
Subansiri 87, 122
Sylhet 126, 194, 206, 257, 258, 272, 275

T

Tezpur 71, 72, 74, 87, 88
Tibet xvii, 42, 53, 246, 247
Tinsukhia 16
Tipaimukh 126
Titas 201
Tourism xix, xxi, 17, 31, 34, 37, 56, 98, 100, 110, 122, 138, 168, 183, 194, 230, 248, 272, 284, 285, 286
Tripura xiii, xviii, xxiv, 2, 12, 14, 15, 16, 17, 23, 24, 25, 30, 32, 33, 35, 36, 37, 62, 63, 66, 68, 71, 73, 78, 80, 85, 87, 93, 101, 102, 105, 106, 107, 108, 116, 118, 119, 121, 129, 131, 132, 134, 138, 147, 152, 166, 174, 178, 191, 193, 194, 195, 196, 197, 198, 199, 200, 201, 204, 206, 207, 208, 209, 219, 228, 231, 233, 253, 254, 255, 258, 263, 265, 266, 269, 273, 287, 310, 313
Tuirial 72, 121

U

Upper Karnali 133, 233
Upper Marsyangdi 133, 233

V

Vayudoot 71

W

West Bengal xxvi, 2, 43, 63, 68, 82, 96, 123, 132, 158, 166, 190, 192, 194, 196, 198, 202, 220, 221, 225, 231, 255, 269
World Bank 12, 13, 14, 40, 41, 44, 47, 64, 67, 69, 70, 87, 92, 93, 100, 103, 104, 115, 178, 184, 185, 302, 303
W Synrem 116